SEEN YET UNSEEN

BOOKS BY BÄRÍ A. WILLIAMS

NONFICTION

Seen Yet Unseen: A Black Woman Crashes the Tech Fraternity

Diversity in the Workplace: Eye-Opening Interviews to Jumpstart Conversations about Identity, Privilege, and Bias

SEEN YET UNSEEN

A BLACK WOMAN CRASHES THE TECH FRATERNITY

BÄRÍ A. WILLIAMS

BLACK STONE PUBLISHING

Copyright © 2024 by Bärí A. Williams
Published in 2025 by Blackstone Publishing
Cover and book design by Alenka Vdovič Linaschke

All rights reserved. This book or any portion
thereof may not be reproduced or used in any manner
whatsoever without the express written permission
of the publisher except for the use of brief quotations
in a book review.

Some names and identifying details have been changed
to protect the privacy of individuals.

Printed in the United States of America
Originally published in hardcover by Blackstone Publishing in 2024

First paperback edition: 2025
ISBN 979-8-8748-1272-0
Business & Economics / Women in Business

Version 1

Blackstone Publishing
31 Mistletoe Rd.
Ashland, OR 97520

www.BlackstonePublishing.com

To my Black women in tech, who want to tell these stories and can't in the name of self-preservation. I see you, and I got you.

CONTENTS

Preface ix

Introduction 1

Chapter 1: Nobody Sees Me or Everyone Sees Me: When They Do, They Are Surprised I'm Here 11

Chapter 2: This Is How They *Actually* See Me: A Token . . . and a Threat 25

Chapter 3: The Myth of Meritocracy 44

Chapter 4: Paying Lip Service 62

Chapter 5: Black Three-for-Ones: Employee Resource Groups as Support Systems, Free Company Labor, and Public Relations 80

Chapter 6: This Is Why I Feel Like an Outsider: And Leave Once I've Worked Long Enough to Put You in My Résumé 95

Chapter 7: This Is What True Allyship Looks Like 114

Chapter 8: This Is What Happens When We Don't Have a Seat at the Table: Technology Gone Bad 130

Chapter 9: Blind Spots and Big Dollars: People and Profits 159

Chapter 10: This Is What Tech Is Doing to My Community: You Can Disrupt Without Gentrification 186

Chapter 11: This Is Why I (And Other Black Women) Leave 200

Chapter 12: We Would've Stayed Had You Done *THIS*: How Tech Companies Could Have Made Us Want to Stay 218

Conclusion 242

Acknowledgments 247

Notes 249

PREFACE
to the paperback edition

The more things change, the more they stay the same.

I was hopeful when this book was published in the spring of 2024 that this would be a time capsule of experiences that were soon being ushered out of the door. Fast-forward to July 2024, and we saw the ascension of the first Black woman, Kamala Harris, to head a major-party presidential ticket. The parallels were not lost on me—a Black woman from Oakland, a soror of Alpha Kappa Alpha Sorority, Inc., and a graduate of UC Hastings (UC College of the Law)—to see someone assume a leadership position after the unfortunate failure of a white man who had bit off more than he could chew. Because I've walked a similar road, albeit not in politics but in tech, I was cautiously optimistic. See, I've been the clean-up woman before, and it's a hard, thankless job. But I was hopeful for this new era.

How wrong I was. In the span of six months from July 2024 to January 2025, we saw not only Vice President Harris lose the presidential election but, along with it, the House and the Senate to a MAGA mandate hell-bent on ridding the nation, public and private, of DEI initiatives. First on the chopping block? My beloved Supplier Diversity Program at Facebook—something I put my soul into—was disbanded in the first week of January 2025 in a show of Mark Zuckerberg's real political leanings and his revelation of performative allyship with Meta. The Facebook I left is not the "Meta" I see today. It wasn't perfect, but it was better than this current iteration. The good news is at least we know who and what we're fighting. The bad news is we're going to have to work twice as hard, and there's no time to be tired now.

It has left me where I started—to remind those who can't speak out or won't: I see you, and I've got you. We're all we got! So, take a well-deserved rest, and reconvene when you're replenished. The work isn't over. Keep on keeping on!

INTRODUCTION
Welcome to Being a Black Woman in Tech

> Never be limited by other people's limited imaginations.
>
> —Dr. Mae Jemison,
> astronaut and physician

Imagine working your whole life to achieve a piece of the American dream, to finally join the industry that's changing the world right there in your own backyard . . . only for people to continuously dismiss or downplay your work and ask how you got there or if you deserved it—if they even acknowledge your presence at all. Over the years, I've been asked by one boss if I was accepted into UC Berkeley via affirmative action and if my husband, an engineer, went to Harvard on a basketball scholarship; another tried to touch my hair after wondering how it "does that"; and I've been mistaken for the secretary by opposing counsel more times than I can count. I've been told I sounded "angry" after asking why I hadn't been invited on a team excursion. I've been dismissed with a flippant "Well, sometimes life's just not fair" when I tried to ask why I was passed over for a promotion that was given to someone with fewer accomplishments. Welcome to being a Black woman in tech.

I have watched the tech industry transform not just my city of Oakland, California—a blue-collar, incredibly diverse metropolis known affectionately as "the Town"—but the entire region into a gentrified haven of oat milk lattes and vegan BBQ–purchasing tech transplants. And yet—while I was born next door to Silicon Valley and have worked for many years as a lawyer in some of its most storied companies and start-ups—I couldn't feel more like an outsider. Welcome to the glass cliff.

Silicon Valley has always made much ado about serving a noble and progressive cause: democratizing the world and giving everyone an equal voice. It promised an open marketplace of products, ideas, and conversations. But I, like the few other Black women and underrepresented minorities who work in tech, know this is bullshit. We are not often heard. We are overlooked when we accomplish something. People are all too eager to take credit for our work while believing we should just be happy to be in the room. We are hardly *seen*. Yet when we refuse to just accept that minimum standard and instead make note of it, we are often *too* seen.

When I relay the burdens, complaints, and observations of Black and brown employees about companies not having their back, I'm the messenger. And you know what they say about the messenger: *don't shoot them*. Being *too* seen is exactly that. If I'm bringing something to the company's attention, if I'm saying they live and work in a bubble (yes, Silicon Valley is a bubble) and are not adequately supporting their employees who do not look like them, then I'm the troublemaker. I have put a target on my back because I brought up something that made the company uncomfortable and they don't want to deal with it. Just because I spoke out about something somebody didn't like or didn't want to hear, just because I am not effusively praising them or kissing their asses, I'm a problem. I'm *too* seen.

Being both not seen and too seen is exhausting. I put up with daily microaggressions with a smile. My work is questioned and my contributions are overlooked. I have to show up to work and pretend everything is fine after yet another public shooting of an unarmed Black man, feeling like the world is burning and those around me don't care. I've had to abstain from sharing my outrage at groups organizing to overturn our election results on Facebook—the very social media platform I'd worked on for years—because I feared being labeled "too angry" and "reactive" by white colleagues who felt perfectly entitled to share *their* outrage, or indifference, without any consequences for how *they* are perceived.

This book is about what it is like to be a Black woman in tech today, what it's like to work among people who are surprised you are there at all, and why so many of us leave fed up. It zeroes in on my unique narrative of what it is like to be a two-for-one: both a woman *and* Black in tech. Who else will talk about the question I most often ask myself after suffering through yet another traumatic and shocking workplace experience: Did this happen because I'm Black, a woman, or both? And who else will discuss the societal implications of us not having a seat at the table in tech? This book is about what it means that so few of us are working in the industry—not just for Black women but for everyone globally. Because when Black women don't have a seat at the table, *everyone* loses. It's bad for tech. It's bad for business. And it's dangerous for society.

Inclusive products are not born in a vacuum but made thoughtfully and intentionally, and without the input of marginalized people, socially harmful products abound. I've looked bald on Zoom meetings because my hair didn't show up on the mandated background image. I was chastised both for having the wrong background and for not looking happy. But how could I be happy when the chosen background didn't present me in the most productive light? Why would I be happy when it's clear this company didn't care how its employees were being depicted? If my camera is off, I'm unprofessional. But if I turn it on and I'm not depicted in how I actually look or how I present myself in person, tell me how that's still doing me a service. That is a disservice. I would rather everyone just hear my voice. And I would definitely rather have a Zoom background that didn't stall and fail at the sight of my natural hair.

I live and breathe tech as much as anyone in Silicon Valley—I was born and raised in Oakland and have spent the majority of my life here. I've worked as lead counsel at Facebook, where I built the company's supplier diversity program. I was head of North American business operations at StubHub, where I was responsible for managing operations and overseeing product innovation, metrics, and partnerships. I've testified before Congress on the impact of bias in fintech and artificial intelligence (AI) on home lending, school loans, and interest rates. Not only am I embedded by using all these products, but growing up in their birthplace has offered me a unique chance to observe how the tech boom has changed my professional and personal life. It has given me a front-row seat to see how tech's massive blind spots—and growing confirmation bias—have continually hurt me and the many communities that have, until recently, called this place home.

The generational footprint left by communities like my own is being eradicated. Large pockets of Oakland and surrounding areas have essentially gone under the knife. We are being colonized, yet again, through the tendrils of technology. Tech companies are pillaging the resources and discarding whatever they don't believe is relevant to *them*—white, able-bodied, straight males. Many of these transplanted workers share the same vision: products tailored to the typical user, *not* products invested in understanding the widest range possible of use cases and users. They are not interested in products that reflect the generations of people who were here long before the seeds of technology were planted, only those who inhabit the area now. But for me, these products need to include everyone—most definitely those who came before. This ongoing narrative is why tech has struggled to hire and retain Black women. We know; now it's time for the world to know. I will explore how the treatment of Black women in tech impacts our everyday lives as global citizens, the cultural and societal repercussions of not having diverse perspectives when developing and launching products, and the negative impact tech companies have had and will continue to have on communities of color unless they change their approach. This book is my canary in a coal mine.

In tech, Black women are the canaries. We're always saying, "Here's some shit coming!" Right now the companies are sitting on the tracks, and that shit is the train. Even with their employees all but demanding they get off the tracks, they won't. These companies believe the train will stop for them. They will stand there and dare it to hit them. They will stare it in the eye and say, *I don't care if I get run over.* But what they're really saying is, *I don't care if others*—because it's the people underneath who get screwed over with these faulty products—*are run over. So go ahead. We'll fix it on the back end.* But the back end is after they've already circumvented democracy, engaged in perpetuating housing and employment discrimination, and created products that other people are now using to steal from people of color and gentrify whole communities. It's not just that these things are happening in front of us in real life; they're also happening online and through the technology being built.

There has to be conscious consideration to include Black women when technologies are being designed, developed, and marketed. Without inclusive input and testing, we end up with products that don't work the same way for everyone and are embedded with biases before we even download them or take them out of their shiny new boxes. Instead, with the lack of dissenting voices in the room or even just the acknowledgment of a different perspective, we end up with widespread disinformation campaigns that undermine American democracy and disenfranchise voters. A clear example is how the lie that the 2020 presidential election was stolen spread through social media like wildfire (even after the major platforms tried to stop it a day late and a dollar short), leading to the January 6, 2021, attack on the Capitol. We end up with technologies that can be weaponized against anyone. From digital advertising platforms that violate discrimination laws by allowing users to purposely exclude people of a certain gender, race, or age group to AI-powered financial programs that treat women and other underrepresented loan applicants as inferior to others—these products, intentionally or not, are designed and marketed by mostly white people with white users in mind.

Without the voices of Black women in tech, AI algorithms will continue to determine your creditworthiness based on stale redlining housing loan datasets from the 1970s. Without the voices of Black women in tech, those same stale AI algorithms determine policing in your neighborhood. Without the voices of Black women in tech, the ads shown to you on TV, as well as those that are excluded, are decided by others who don't look like you or understand the cultural nuances of your life. Facial recognition technology mistakenly tags you, your family, and even beloved members of the Congressional Black Caucus as convicted felons, as was the case with Amazon's facial recognition technology.[1] Your social media feeds are a treasure trove of digital segregation, where you are fed stories and threads that "should" appeal to you based on stereotypes and old behavioral patterns and not on your actual interests. When the tech industry ignores marginalized people's voices, decisions you should be making for yourself are made *for* you before you even realize you should have had a choice in the first place. When tech excludes these voices, it does so to its own economic and legal detriment, and we all lose. Tech has so much at stake when it comes to solving the often dangerous, biased blind spots in their products and policies, from missed use cases to policies promoting content that needs a trigger warning, such as videos of unarmed Black people being killed by police (or wannabe vigilante police). Black women and other underrepresented minorities can provide the missing perspectives.

We can't ignore the urgency of this issue as we recover from a pandemic that has led to massive tech layoffs. In March 2020, the online site Layoffs.fyi began tracking layoffs at tech start-ups. By the end of April 2020, just one month later, 269 start-ups had already laid off 26,651 employees.[2] The companies that published the names of the terminated employees and their affiliated departments and roles clearly indicated that *a huge number of them were women and people of color* and, oftentimes, women of color. A good majority of them were working in diversity departments. The pandemic emphasized the reality that, in tech, diversity is a "nice-to-have," not a "must-have." Tech companies didn't employ many of us before COVID-19 hit. How many of those who lost their jobs will be able to return in the aftermath of the pandemic? What will their absence cost us all?

Seen Yet Unseen answers that question. I'm going to take you through the hallowed halls of tech's biggest companies, where unconscious biases run rampant and unhindered in middle and upper management meetings, where diverse voices are marginalized and often shut out entirely. I will take you through the lived experiences of myself and other people of color as we struggle to work multiple jobs for the pay of one and are often pigeonholed into the "diversity stuff" because managers want to keep us quiet. I will take you into the heart of my home, where long-standing cultural corners and beloved mom-and-pop businesses are being run out because of tech's gentrification. The point of all this is to give a voice to tech's biggest blind spot: Black women. There is no "mystery" for our absence; companies just don't want to acknowledge the blatant reasons for comfort's sake.

Well, it's time to get uncomfortable. Surviving as a Black woman in tech requires impeccable credentials, tenacity, and a sort of deference to white men that never quite feels natural. This book unearths the hidden daily indignities that lurk within the trendy atmospheres of tech communities, from ideas stolen from Black women and presented to leadership with a different face attached to the realization that we are all collectively contributing to making products that not only aren't inclusive but also could be weaponized against our very own communities of color.

In the aftermath of George Floyd's murder and the civil unrest that followed, many corporations, especially Silicon Valley companies, scrambled to make loud and definitive statements in support of Black Lives Matter. Tech companies, large and small, made a big show of donating loads of money to social justice efforts and quickly ramped up (and publicized) their efforts to increase diversity in their ranks (which currently show appalling numbers). With all that has happened since then—the

2022 election, another COVID-19 surge, the January 6 insurrection, Joseph Biden's inauguration, Donald Trump's second impeachment, the vaccine rollout, states passing laws restricting voting—it's clear these companies' "woke" commitment to diversity won't truly inspire lasting action.[3] And they haven't lasted, particularly in a downturn, but back then, their panicked reaction didn't go unnoticed by us, not even my then ten-year-old son, Gabriel.

He asked me how we fix it.

I said that we start by telling the truth.

CHAPTER 1
Nobody Sees Me or Everyone Sees Me: When They Do, They Are Surprised I'm Here

> The fact that the adult American Negro female emerges a formidable character is often met with amazement, distaste and even belligerence. It is seldom accepted as an inevitable outcome of the struggle won by survivors and deserves respect if not enthusiastic acceptance.
>
> —Maya Angelou, author and civil rights activist

A few weeks before I went on maternity leave with my daughter, I was scheduled to handle a negotiation for licensing technology in one of the large conference rooms at Facebook. I was eight months pregnant and had decided to take full advantage of the company's "Come as you are" attitude and wore an outfit to match: jeans, flip-flops, huge curly hair, and blue nails.

The opposing counsel, an Asian woman, was already sitting with her client in the room, talking about their legal strategy, including what they would ask for and what they would reject on my side. She looked me up and down and gave a curt smile but no greeting. It was the type of smile you give someone you either aren't eager to socialize with or feel you don't *need* to socialize with. When my in-house client, an Asian male engineer, walked in, she turned to him and said, "When is your attorney going to get here?"

My client turned to me with a wry smile and gestured my way. I responded, "I've been here the whole time."

The woman turned bright red and apologized profusely. "It's okay," I told her. "I'm used to popping up in places people don't expect."

Black women are typically never expected to be in certain environments, like corporate leadership roles; science, tech, engineering, and math (STEM) classes; or playing tennis and lacrosse. We aren't expected to be in boardrooms or at negotiating tables. We are expected to be secretaries and scribes. I'm not expected to be the attorney in the room. When I was a kid, my mother, Linda, and my grandparents preached to me that I had to be twice as good as a white man just to get half as much. And this adage has been true at every stage of my life. I wasn't expected to skip a grade in school. My white peers stared at me when I walked into gifted and talented education classes in elementary school. I wasn't expected to be in honors classes, and I truly wasn't expected to show up on the campus of UC Berkeley as a seventeen-year-old in a class of only two hundred Black freshmen on a campus of thirty thousand students. And I really wasn't expected to graduate in three years with over a 3.0 GPA after having worked jobs and internships the entire time I was matriculated there. The majority of my classmates didn't have to work, and if they had internships, it was for fun, and they were easy to come by thanks to access through family and friends. I worked out of necessity so that I wouldn't have to take out more student loans, and my internships were to prepare me for a job. Other students had jobs lined up already, whether they were for a family business or from an in that allowed them to skip interviewing. They were on the club VIP list versus my having to wait and see if I could still get in for free before 11:00 p.m. Eventually, I got used to being unexpected, but it's never been comfortable. It's just something I expect to encounter, coming up with witty answers to the inevitable questions.

One of the more interesting things about working in tech is how I have to constantly straddle the dichotomy between being seen and unseen. Being ignored by a lawyer when I'm literally *right in front of them* is not the only story I have about being seemingly invisible to others. I've been unseen more times than I care to remember, whether it's people continuing to mispronounce my name as "Barry" when I've corrected them repeatedly without being too harsh (even if it is the *fifth* time I've adjusted their erroneous pronunciation), or literally calling me by another Black woman's name (who wasn't even in the same department), or completely excluding me. The thing is, when people do see me, they want me to explain *how* I got there and *why* I am there at all. I've been asked point-blank if I got into Berkeley via affirmative action (spoiler alert: no) or whether my husband got into Harvard on a basketball scholarship (no, again) or how I actually came to work at my company (like everyone else—I applied, I interviewed, I got hired). It never ends. I often see a look of surprise when I talk about having multiple degrees as well as parents and grandparents who are college educated, while also being the granddaughter of another set of grandparents who were sharecroppers on the land where their grandparents had been enslaved—that sort of duality isn't something most tech bros can conceptualize or accept. You have to be one or the other, either educated or disenfranchised, to fit into the tiny box they have reserved for Black women in their minds.

The flip side to this is being *too* seen. It's always a constant fear in the back of a Black woman's head that if you disclose too much about your background or hobbies or are too vocal in meetings or about social issues in the cafeteria, you'll put a target on your back. I vividly recall having a discussion with a dark-skinned Indian colleague—who, funnily enough, has a darker complexion than my child with two Black parents—about a contract after George Floyd's murder. He stopped in the middle of a sales call to discern how we would proceed with a deal, and because I wasn't telling him exactly what he wanted to hear, he proceeded to tell me, "You know, you're too Black and too loud." I was immediately taken aback and offended. Instead of focusing on the task at hand, going over which deal terms were acceptable and which I would have to reject, he was focused on my tone because I was telling him no. I thought, *As much as you say I can, I clearly can't bring my whole self to work here.* I gently reminded him that I don't go around quoting Tupac or W. E. B. Du Bois in meetings, so I didn't know what he could possibly be talking about, and that he is a person of color himself. He actually laughed and responded, "Well, I think I'm a white man in my own head." Which is a great example of why I don't love the term *people of color* in general because other people of color, particularly in the tech industry, are so busy assimilating into the white broski culture that they aren't always in solidarity and don't even always identify as "of color." I will never understand the level of personal cognitive dissonance it would take to feel this way, and furthermore, I wouldn't want to.

This same colleague seemed to take what I said to heart and decided to speak at an all-hands Zoom meeting a week after our conversation. I presumed he'd had some introspective come-to-Jesus moment and decided to speak. His speech started well with a proclamation that Black lives matter and then smoothly segued into, "And blue lives matter too." I immediately turned off my camera. I internalized his comments and felt blamed for reminding him he was a person of color. The sting of feeling like my humanity was negated was quickly eclipsed by having to answer questions thrown at me as the only Black person in leadership by the handful of Black employees we had. I was riddled with guilt. Perhaps if I hadn't asked him to question his place in the world as a person of color, he wouldn't have volunteered to speak and proceeded to unintentionally insult our few Black employees.

That guilt carried over into worrying about whether I've said enough or too little in similar workplace situations. There have been instances when I've made an observation about how diversity is talked about as an imperative from those in the C-suite but there's a lack of attention to it among middle management, where most hiring takes place. I've noted that companies want members of employee resource groups (ERGs) to essentially take on part-time jobs, but they aren't accounted for in reviews or with additional compensation. Sometimes those comments have been met with whisper campaigns, and in other instances, doing such diversity work has put a target on my back. It feels like you can't win for losing. Many times when I've told my mom about my day and something I said or pointed out to a colleague, or even the process of writing this book, the first thing she says is, "You made a good point." Then she feels compelled to follow it up with, "But are you going to get in trouble for saying that? Are people going to be mad at you or blacklist you?" The very irony of the turn of phrase isn't lost on me.

When I received a job offer from Facebook, I also received Facebook friend requests from my hiring manager and my new teammates. While I found the gesture welcoming, I also had a sense of panic, and when I left work that night, I went home and had an extensive conversation with my husband about what to do. It's seen as rude if you don't accept the requests or leave them in purgatory, neither accepting nor denying. My Facebook page felt like a very personal slice of my life, where I shared information about and pictures of my family, in-group cultural jokes, political views, and thoughts on Black Lives Matter and social justice. I feared exposing that would make me "too seen" and lead to judgment without questions, or questions I wasn't comfortable answering, all with possible career implications. My husband suggested that I create a "limited profile" and add my new coworkers to that instead. All of that felt like a part-time job and was exactly what I meant by trying to figure out how to be my authentic self . . . to a point. In the end, I decided to just add them to my regular Facebook page and not silence myself at the risk of being too visible. The thought that my white male colleagues probably never gave this a passing thought, let alone agonized over it in their personal time, struck me with how freeing that must feel.

My fear of visibility persisted with each call for social justice raised during the racial reckoning our country began to undergo in 2020. My colleagues' nonchalance and tone deafness toward these occurrences meant not only did they not see me, but they didn't see Black people collectively as a people. They were completely unaware of the very persistent air of privilege to have the luxury of not needing to think about any of this, nor having it damage their emotional psyche. It peaked for me during the pandemic amid the protests after the murder of George Floyd. My husband participated in two protests. Our team had a routinely scheduled thirty-minute coffee klatch every morning at nine as a check-in. Mostly people talked about what they had watched on Netflix the night before, what they had cooked, or what new hobby they were exploring. Frankly, I was preoccupied with explaining to my then ten-year-old son why people were protesting during a pandemic and how to conduct himself to stay safe—yes, even from law enforcement.

Finally, one day, when it was my turn to share, I simply said, "I totally appreciate the spirit of what this is supposed to be, but what I watched last night was the news. What I did was explain to my child how to conduct himself if the police ever approach him. Then I explained why people were protesting. When he asked me why police keep doing this, because there is a new name each year, and why do they get away with it, I called a friend who was a Ferguson protester, Netta Elzie, and let him talk to her. So, I'm sorry if I'm not engaged in what Tim cooked last night or what Jen watched on Netflix, because I'm dealing with real life over here." Everyone was quiet, and it was quite clear that my declaration that my Blackness and Black motherhood be seen and acknowledged had changed the tone of the entire conversation. But at least I was seen, even if they couldn't relate.

The toll of constantly feeling marginalized and othered at work, of not being able to be authentic on the job, to navigate or feign knowledge or interest in cultural reference points that aren't mine is hard to put into words. It's exhausting—and extremely challenging. It sets me, and other Black women, up to be on the defensive. It's hard to develop working relationships built on trust when one party constantly has to explain why they deserve even to be there—why their life experiences matter.

There is a sociological basis to this too. Several studies have shown that Black women in the workplace are seen neither as a "woman" nor simply as "Black," as that distinction is reserved for Black men. We aren't an either/or, or a both/and. We're just an anomaly. Two prominent studies from 2008 concluded that Black women were basically interchangeable and easily mistaken for one another by white colleagues. (Fun fact: this happened to me in high school with a girl I was four inches taller and three shades darker than, so it starts early.) In both studies, the notion of invisibility was tested with white observers by assessing if Black women go "unnoticed" (their faces being indistinguishable or unrecognizable) and their voices go "unheard" (their contributions incorrectly attributed) relative to Black men and both white women and men.[4]

First, the 2008 Stephanie Fryberg and Sarah Townsend study surmised that white participants were the least likely to accurately recognize Black women in comparison to the other groups, primarily Asian and white women.[5] So, they weren't able to tell a Black woman they'd seen or met before from a "new" Black woman they had never encountered.

Second, in the study by Valerie Purdie-Vaughns and Richard Eibach, Black women and their work tended to be implicated in every error type of the study. There were four error types researched: within-race/within-gender (meaning Black women being confused for a different Black woman), within-race/between-gender (a Black woman being mistaken for a Black man), between-race/within-gender (a Black woman being confused for a white woman), and between-race/between-gender (a Black woman being mistaken for a white man). This included having their contributions, ideas, and statements confused with those of the other groups in the study (Black men, white women, and white men).[6] The only conclusion that can be drawn is that, to many, Black women are all the same and generally unrecognizable and unremarkable, and proper credit for their work and statements is easily attributed to others. We count for diversity reporting purposes, but not really. We are there but not there.

Add to that, per the global management consulting firm McKinsey & Company's 2019 *Women in the Workplace* report, more than 40 percent of Black, Latina, and Afro-Latina women reported being interrupted and spoken over in a work setting, and a third also said that others had stolen and taken credit for their ideas.⁷ This is yet another problem of invisibility. There is this constant push-pull and internal dialogue of, *Should I say something? What happens if I do?* More often than not, we don't say anything because we don't want to fall into certain tropes of Black women at work. A simple, neutral statement or question can easily be misconstrued: it is no longer a query about being included and getting attribution for your work but becomes a narrative about being aggressive and accusatory, even greedy. The questions are always the same: *Why do you want to hog all the credit? Can't you just be happy that you were able to work on this project?* It creates a "victim as villain" dynamic, where our silence is taken as permission. Damned if you do, damned if you don't. You can't win.

Fortune has a conference called Brainstorm Tech with all the important C-suite who's who in tech. When I attended in 2018, one of the main-stage sessions was called "Tech Backlash," and there was a ten-minute update on the state of diversity in tech. That certainly piqued my interest, and I was eager to hear this talk. Out walked the chief executive officer of OpenTable at the time, Christa Quarles, a striking, tall blonde woman. She proceeded to do a ten-minute presentation on the state of diversity—but it was focused solely on white women. So, while the stats and information were good to know, I raised my hand when they asked for comments. I got up and noted how the focus on diversity in her presentation was primarily centered on white women's progress and ascension, as delivered by someone of that demographic. While the information was useful, if the focus was supposed to be about women, the plight of *all* women—particularly Black women—had been ignored in the presentation, the commentary, and the statistics. Further, if it was about all facets of diversity, nothing was said about LGBTQ+ people, disabled people, or even people of different ages, considering that tech is still viewed as a young *man's* game. All of that is exclusionary. I don't think Quarles had any ill will or bad intentions, but this was a very clear example of how we don't know what we don't know, and when you don't *have* to see the world through a colored lens, you don't.

The focus on "women in tech" for the past decade has been due to public attention on equal pay and gender parity. This makes sense on its face since women make up about half of the global population. However, when the media talk about gender parity in tech, the default subject is white women. Even some tech companies have expanded their use of the Rooney Rule—which I'll cover in depth later—a rule initially used in the National Football League with the goal of diversity hiring for coaches by promising that at least one minority candidate would be interviewed for the job. Tech companies moved to adopt this rule to include women, and we know who benefits most: white women. Studies such as Michele Goodwin's 2012 *Chronicle of Higher Education* study, "The Death of Affirmative Action, Part 1," noted that white women disproportionately benefit from affirmative action, even as the very term evokes images of underprivileged Black children to white adults of all social classes.[8]

Additionally, Tim Wise's 1998 study, "Is Sisterhood Conditional? White Women and the Rollback of Affirmative Action," noted that in 1995, six million women, the majority of them white, held jobs they otherwise wouldn't have had but for affirmative action.[9] It's very similar to Sheryl Sandberg's philosophy in *Lean In*, which bills itself as a playbook to corporate success by encouraging women to first adapt to their (often racist and sexist—so double the fun for Black women) environments, then change the environment with little shifts and great work. The book has been criticized for having blind spots in how it centers white women's experiences at work and how *they* can succeed. Upon reading the book, I agreed.

At my Facebook orientation, I was surprised to find a copy of *Lean In* in our new backpacks with our laptops and phones. I had already read it but figured I could give it to someone else.

When I got home on my third day, my mom came to visit, and the book was out on my coffee table. She picked it up and asked, "What's this about?"

"Oh, this is a woman's career book about how to succeed at work."

She flipped through the pages, smirked, then set it down. "What is 'lean in,' though? When have we ever had the option to *lean out*?! Uh-uh," she grunted. "This ain't for us," she said as she shook her head. Touché, Mom, touché.

I am certainly not the only one with experiences that even *Lean In* couldn't touch on. Many Black women I've commiserated with have similar stories of being called the wrong name, mistaken for someone else, or worse, asked to help on a project that is someone else's job in another department because part of being unseen means you should just be happy to be there and that you can't say no, lest you become too visible. So, if people can't even be bothered to remember you as a person, as a Black woman, you can't presume they will remember your work or the impact you've made on the business . . . unless they want to find a way to undercut you.

To say that all of this fosters an environment where I and other Black women feel unwelcome is an understatement. I've come to realize, with a mixture of horror and irony, that this may be the actual intent of some workplaces. If companies can keep you complacent with decent pay and promises of career growth and promotional opportunities (which may or may not come to fruition), you'll stay just long enough to be a good worker bee and pad diversity statistics reports. The flip side to this is that for individual employees, particularly middle management where most people toil, creating an unwelcome environment also ensures that Black women "know our place," won't ask for much, are likely to do more for less, and are less likely to flinch when credit for our work is given to someone else. It's a lose-lose situation.

But I also know that, intentionally or not, creating such an environment will end up doing the company no good. From lackluster retention numbers to whispers during recruitment events, the company will develop a reputation for being a hostile work environment. Internally, the signs of a hostile work environment may look subtle. Externally, the reputation around company culture and its treatment of Black women will be openly discussed. Public opinion of a company will suffer from just one whiff of a hostile work environment claim, usually covered in tech publications like *TechCrunch*, *Fast Company*, and *The Verge*. Depending upon the reach of the company and what it does, such coverage can lead to social media boycotts and loss of revenue.

Take, for example, two Black women employees from Pinterest, Aerica Shimizu Banks and Ifeoma Ozoma, who were subject to "glaringly unfair pay, intense discrimination, and terrifying retaliation," in the words of Banks, who spoke with me about their experience. This included death and rape threats, being questioned by private investigators when a presentation by Banks "embarrassed" an executive, and Ozoma being doxed on the internet. They decided to rip off the Band-Aid, quit publicly on Twitter (now X), and tell their story without caution. They've since cowritten and cosponsored the California Silenced

No More Act, put in effect January 1, 2022, allowing employees, formerly unseen and unheard, to openly discuss racism and other forms of workplace harassment and abuse even if they sign nondisclosure agreements.

This unwelcoming environment is behind the industry's embarrassingly low numbers of Black women. Prior to the pandemic, Black women made up roughly 65 percent of the women's workforce, including both white-collar and blue-collar positions, the largest of any subset of the women demographic, but they constituted just barely 3 percent of tech workers.[10] These numbers are not likely to grow anytime soon. With the emergence of the pandemic, according to a 2020 Lean In study, Black women were almost twice as likely to say they had been furloughed, laid off, or had their hours cut than white men— to the tune of 58 percent to 31 percent, respectively. The study notes that only 26 percent of Black women said they've had access to sponsorship, with 59 percent having never had an informal interaction with a member of senior leadership. Black women tech founders have found an even more hostile environment, comprising just 0.6 percent of *all* funding annually.[11]

Subjected to endless microaggressions, Black women are made to feel utterly unwelcome by the very industry that claims to want to solve all the social injustices of the world, where the leading companies are seemingly all "liberal" and "progressive"— let me tell you what that really means. Silicon Valley presents itself as a liberal playground, but there is a duality we must acknowledge: the oligarchs and the plebs. We've read the public criticisms of Jeff Bezos and Elon Musk and the well-known politics of Peter Thiel—there is no veil we're hiding behind pretending that these industry leaders are progressive. They're not, and they don't pretend to be. But their *companies* do, and this duality is the reason that perspective remains. The majority of those hired in this sector actually *are* open and eager to connect, they care about diversity and making inclusive products, and just their presence alone means the companies can project a progressive aura. Furthermore, the narrative of liberalism runs deep, which means that employees who *are* more conservative won't speak up for fear of being judged. They will make their feelings known anonymously, which I saw at Facebook with people writing "Trump" over "Black Lives Matter" on the chalkboards and others crying crocodile tears when he was elected. So, with all this hush-hush over the liberal stigma, it's little surprise that tech appears—to most on the outside—wholly devoted to progressiveness. But in actuality, all of this is lip service until the industry leaders need something from us.

Some of these stories are pretty funny if you're into dark humor. Sometimes you can only laugh to keep from crying. Others, however, are heartbreaking. All, I hope, will make you mad, like they make me mad. But sometimes, that anger is what fuels our fire.

CHAPTER 2
This Is How They *Actually* See Me: A Token...and a Threat

> What white folks don't understand, it's like, that is so telling of how white America views people who are not like them. You know we don't exist. And when we do exist, we exist as a threat. And that, that's exhausting.
> —Michelle Obama, former First Lady of the United States

When I was an attorney at Facebook, I noticed that the company didn't have a proactive program of partnering with minority-, LGBTQ+-, and women-owned businesses. The consultants, service providers, and hardware and infrastructure suppliers it engaged with reflected the demographic majority of the company itself: young, white, cisgender men between the ages of twenty-five and forty-five. From my diversity, equity, and inclusion (DEI) standpoint, these products weren't holistic. How could they be when Facebook both didn't have enough diverse employees and wasn't engaging with diverse suppliers? There was zero representation either internally or externally.

For me, diversity is a four-legged stool. You need to focus on employees, customers, suppliers, and board members. People, particularly C-suite executives in tech, always forget about the last two legs of that stool, so companies end up not having truly integrated and well-rounded DEI programs. Within new product meetings, these executives don't think about the need for diversity until somebody brings it to their attention. They do not understand the value of representational diversity, whether those are suppliers or board members. In fact, they love to push back and say, "Why are we giving these spots to women? Just because they're women?" No, you're giving those spots to women because we offer a different perspective, and if you actually used the data you purport to love, you would see that the populations you are actively ignoring have trillions of dollars in spending power. Women are more than half of the adult population in the US, and they, on average, make over half of household purchasing decisions.[12] Why would you *not* want them at your table? Selective bias. Confirmation bias. That's what was happening at Facebook, and I was no stranger to it.

My father owned a computer store in West Oakland in the 1980s, and I watched him work tirelessly, pitching to larger companies to be a supplier, only to be denied those lucrative contracts in favor of white-owned businesses. Those contracts could've changed both his business and our lives. With that impression seared in my mind, as well as an understanding that it would be difficult to hire more diverse candidates, I knew that it would be good for Facebook to have a strategic secondary DEI program to showcase. If they didn't have diverse employees, then they had to go with diverse suppliers. One was better than none, and chances were they would listen if they had someone external. When I asked specifically about supplier diversity, the now chief diversity officer, another Black woman, said while she liked the idea, it was not a priority because they were focused on employees. But she told me to have at it if I wanted to give it a go. Seeing that need and the taxed resources of the then two-person diversity team and taking a cue from my favorite Black woman proverb, "Fuck it, I'll do it," I decided to start. I pitched the idea of working on this internally to a vice president, and she thought it was a great idea but warned me that someone had tried it four years prior and wasn't successful. I simply said, "That person wasn't me."

I did a good deal of due diligence into the classic definitions of supplier diversity, how we could tailor it to apply to Facebook's business, and which departments could easily switch to diverse suppliers. I then took all this data, packed it into a five-slide deck, and had a thirty-minute meeting to pitch it to the chief finance officer for funding. He understood the value of the program within fifteen minutes, and I walked out with funding for additional research and a consultant. The goal was to have the company seek out and do business with Black and brown people, women, disabled people, and LGBTQ+ folks. In June 2020, Facebook pledged to do $1 billion of business "annually with 'diverse suppliers,' including $100 million with Black-owned businesses, starting in 2021."[13] This is my lasting legacy there.

I wanted every marginalized employee to feel that Facebook valued their unique perspectives and experiences. It is one thing to pay lip service to diversity and appreciate the contributions of a marginalized community. It's quite another to offer access to large contracts, economic opportunities, and the chance to employ more members of these communities. What better way to do that than by partnering with a minority-owned small business to, say, produce all the hoodies the company hands out? Or by supporting the Black employee community by having a daylong event featuring speakers like Jada Pinkett Smith and Common and ensuring that every piece of swag, every bite of food, every photo taken, and every beverage served came from Black-owned businesses? I had a vision, and I worked hard to make it happen.

I didn't realize that I'd basically signed up for a second full-time job without additional pay and with little recognition of the value of that work from my direct manager. I worked nights and weekends for two years. I had one person, Lynette, for support, but on the back end, the same woman who'd told me she didn't have time to build a diverse supplier chain was actively trying to take credit for my work. She told people in the diversity and comms department that I needed her permission to do interviews at any speaking engagements regarding the supplier diversity program. This became a double block and tackle because I already needed permission from my own legal team. And I didn't need her permission; I didn't work in her department. Why would I need to ask her for anything? It was her way to find out if somebody had asked me to do these things so she could reallocate them, usually to herself. For two years. She didn't want to do the work, but she wanted the credit and the attention. She was laying the groundwork to become the official face of the supplier diversity program without doing any heavy lifting. Saying, "Look what *we* did." There was a *we*, but it didn't include her. It was a nightmare and a half and couldn't have come at a worse time. I was due to go on maternity leave in a matter of weeks. What would happen to the program in the interim?

It would stall. No one—save Lynette, who had her own job to worry about—would work on it. Definitely not this woman, nor my boss, who referred to it as "that diversity stuff." I knew that if I dropped the project for those four months, no one would pick it up and it would lose steam. I surmised that this was the company's way to placate me because they knew it was a passion project and it kept me busier and quiet (to a point). I was always the person beating the diversity drum in legal, and having been the first (vocal and visibly) Black employee in the department, I knew there is nothing worse than being a token, except being a token who is always talking about being a token or the need to increase diversity. For my manager, the diversity project was a win-win: it could keep me occupied and less vocal, or so he hoped, and the company got a new program they could point to for diversity metrics and marketing narratives. All of this *would* have been well and good had Facebook not rushed to hire two people to run the diversity initiative after I had finished the launch and declined their offer to head the department—a move that confirmed I was actually doing three jobs for two years and was only paid for one.

That isn't an anomaly, as Black women are used to doing more for less. Per the US Department of Labor, as of 2021, Black women get paid, on average, sixty-three cents for every dollar their white male counterparts make.[14] According to a 2021 survey by Hired, in tech, men were offered higher salaries than women for the same job title at the same company 59 percent of the time, and on average, women were offered salaries 2.5 percent less than the ones men were given for the same roles.[15] This surely happened to me. I found out after leaving Facebook that a white male colleague with only one more year of experience than me made almost $80,000 more for the same role. Additionally, I was told that promotions were only given to those with at least fourteen months in a role. So explain to me why a colleague was promoted just shy of a year, while I was both exceeding expectations in my role *and* building supplier diversity? Sure, be a workhorse, but don't expect to be rewarded for it. Facebook was happy to overwork me, underpay me, and reward someone doing less impactful work and *then* make sure I wasn't aware of those facts while someone else reaped the benefits. Oh, did I mention I was doing this while pregnant?

Black women in tech are rare—like unicorn rare. So rare that I made a T-shirt for me and my friends with different shades of Black unicorns sitting on a cloud, making it rain money. We are a two-for-one when it comes to diversity statistics, being both women and Black, and as a result, quickly become bona fide "mascots." I have been featured on branding collateral and companies' career and diversity web pages and have been asked to speak on behalf of companies I worked for on diversity or race-related issues as long as I didn't go off script. My favorite personal instance of this was doing a short interview with human resources at the company Retirement 101 because they were updating the website. It was a thirty-five-minute call about the substantive process and issues around my work in legal and compliance and how I enjoyed particular aspects of it. When prompted by a question about work-life balance, I also noted how my work helped me explain financial services and proper saving to my kids for their future well-being, which is something that isn't taught in schools and isn't typically taught to women and Black folks, and I also can log back on after school pickups. Guess what quote they clipped and used? If you guessed the blurb about how working there helped me teach my kids better financial literacy and allowed me to make it to school pickups, you'd be correct. And you'd be correct in thinking I was *highly* irritated when I heard about it. They discarded over half an hour of dialogue, in which I discussed the actual substance of my job, in favor of hammering home that I'm a double minority with a side of motherhood. As if that's my entire essence. Well, let me say it out loud so there's no mistake: I do not solely identify as someone's wife or mother or center my proximity to others as the basis of my identity. My identity is not intrinsically tied to either. And for that entire conversation to be whittled down to presenting me as a wife and mom who just *happened* to work was infuriating. The other Black employees felt for me but, in a show to hide their own frustrations, made light of it. *You're the only Black person on the leadership team, and you have to get home to your kids. They just had to have you because of how "realistic" you are.* It was ironic because it wasn't an accurate portrayal of either me or the company, whose culture was all about clock watching. Many times I had to sneak out the stairwell near the bathrooms and catch the elevator on a different floor—just to pick up my kids on time. That whole call and website revamp was a bastardization.

While it may seem flattering to some to be featured on the company website and in collateral, it can often come off as disingenuous. If you have few Black employees, particularly in leadership, then deciding to showcase them on marketing collateral—especially for recruitment purposes—feels like you are being dishonest. Oftentimes, that is exactly what it is: performative one-offs giving a false sense of caring and inclusion. These cosmetic efforts aren't results. That's a form of token puffery, and I don't want to be the face of it. Most people of color (POC) don't, but often they don't have a choice.

This mascot marketing behavior is so ingrained in the day-to-day tech living that it's difficult to speak up against it. From company TikToks featuring women and people of color as stealth recruiting tools (been there) to even how POC "joke" about dodging photographers at company events (done that) so as to avoid becoming collateral, these cosmetic efforts have a sinister systemic nature. It goes against *my* nature. If you ask anyone who knows me or has heard me speak at an event or on a podcast, I always start by saying, "I'm a girl from East Oakland, California." Period. Most of what you need to know about me should be inherent in knowing East Oakland and the "code" there, which is more or less "I can show you better than I can tell you." It is truly a place where efforts are not results, and we also don't do "fake," let alone let ourselves be the face of something that is the antithesis of what we stand for. So, to be used as a catalyst for duping other people into joining a company that will only chew them up and spit them out is never what I'm about. But tech doesn't care. How do you say "No, thank you" to that *and* keep your job? There is always that dance you have to do along those fine lines as a Black woman. When Retirement 101 "voluntold" me—telling me in the form of a request—for that call, I walked that line. It didn't work, but that doesn't mean it wasn't worth the effort. I still want to make sure me and mine eat, but not at the expense of selling my people a false dream akin to selling them oceanfront property in Montana.

These deceptive marketing ploys come down to "being a team player." If you're not willing to do these performative exercises and engage in marketing that may or may not be accurate, then you're not being a team player and your life cycle at the company may not last much longer. I saw this at Facebook—everyone had to get permission from comms anytime they were asked to speak at an event, and a lot of prep went into the talking points. *Talk about this; don't bring that up. If the conversation turns to this, deflect.* So, how much of what you see is actually a real day in the life versus the *version* of the day in the life that these companies want to portray? Take Maddie Macho, for example.16

Macho joined Facebook in 2021 as a recruiter, and buoyed by the excitement of having landed a "dream job," as it goes, she posted a TikTok similar to a day in the life. In her video she talked about the great benefits Facebook offered, the perks, and what it was like to work there, and it went viral. Facebook *loved* it. They put it everywhere. Free marketing, right? A year later, Macho was fired for posting videos that were a "conflict of interest," meaning they weren't as Facebook-positive as her initial ones. Facebook got upset by her TikToks, in which she discussed backroom things that were happening at the company, how her manager didn't know what she was doing nor effectively managing, and how her team never really worked because there wasn't enough to do, and made her take them down. The irony is staggering. So, the company gets to pick and choose what content they post when they don't allow their employees to do the same on their personal social media accounts? They forced a one-way street where there was none. Taking what Macho did voluntarily, on her own time, and using it as organic marketing gave them no legs to get mad when she talked about something the company did poorly.

So then the question becomes how to solve for not being a token and help a company determine how to attract and retain diverse candidates appropriately. The rub lies in how you define *diverse*. I am an attorney, and we live and die by diction and definitions. Knowing how an organization defines diversity, equity, and inclusion is key to properly assessing how they live it.

First, let's define what *tokenism* is. Per Merriam-Webster, it is "the policy or practice of making only a symbolic effort (as to desegregate)."[17] It's essentially performative and doesn't go further than that.

The bigger problem lies in defining what *diversity* is. Now, I can tell you, from a historical perspective and on a legal basis, diversity was initially meant to solve for representation for Black, brown, Indigenous, and Asian American people in certain schools and jobs. But today? Ask someone what diversity looks like in a tech company. Ask them how they define it, and you won't get any two answers that are the same. What's key here, according to a 2021 study by Built In, is that prior to the summer of 2020 and the death of George Floyd, only 11 percent of tech companies had dedicated staff for diversity and inclusion initiatives. Post-summer 2020, at that time, there were more programs (although there has been a shift downward after the Supreme Court's affirmative action ruling in June 2023), with dedicated staffing then projected to increase to 35 percent, which is a substantial gain.[18] So, why is this a problem?

Because while there might be more diversity programs, there are *also* more definitions of diversity. Each company defines it differently, yielding fifty-eleven different definitions. What's *fifty-eleven*? It's African American Vernacular English (AAVE) for "a lot." Furthermore, individual employees may define diversity however they want and in a way that suits what they currently have going on on their team. When that happens, it usually does not fit the corporate definition of diversity. Corporations define it as—and the order is important for a matter of relevance—women, people of color, LGBTQ+, and veterans. Now, due diligence tells us that nationwide the bulk of veterans are non-Hispanic white, which further changes the definition of diversity so that representational diversity encompasses a demographic we aren't trying to solve for. Meanwhile, the military population is aligned with the US Black population, though some branches overindex with higher percentages.[19] So, with these expanding and shape-shifting definitions of diversity, it can also modify who, or what, is "Black." If I want to be specific about the term we usually use for ourselves, it's *Black* because we aren't first- or second-generation Americans. We are not African immigrants, most of whom comprise the statistic of "Blacks in tech."

It's easy for a company to claim diversity when they can jump between definitions and choose them based on their current team. Throwing diversity into a category is great for numbers but not much else. Companies can say, "We have representation from fifteen different countries," but they're all in Africa. And what's worse is when they throw those numbers into the "Blacks in tech" statistic *without* distinguishing African immigrants from Black Americans or recognizing the cultural nuances that come with those identities. Black Americans have a different experience and different worldview than actual first- or second-generation African Americans, and those differences, counterintuitively perhaps, make it harder for us to adapt and fit in. First- or second-generation Africans comprise 21 percent of the Black population in the US and make up the bulk of "Black students" in Ivy League and elite colleges, often attributed as the primary African American beneficiaries of affirmative action,[20] which was intended to improve the educational and economic opportunity of Black American descendants of enslaved people, and yet we are not the primary beneficiaries. With the recent Supreme Court rejection of affirmative action in college admissions in June 2023, it is yet to be seen if that statistical admissions representation will continue—for *any* Black students. That goes to white women and first- and second-generation African immigrants. As reported by the American Enterprise Institute, in 2004 "black Harvard law professor Lani Guinier and Henry Louis Gates Jr., chairman of Harvard's African-American studies department, said that somewhere between one-half and two-thirds of the black Harvard students were 'West Indian and African immigrants or their children, or to a lesser extent, children of biracial couples.'"[21] In 2007 Jeffrey Cord reported the following for the *Baltimore Sun*: "[F]irst- and second-generation black immigrants comprise 41 percent of all black students at Ivy League schools." He summarily continued:

> The large numbers of African immigrants on American college campuses, coupled with the remarkably

small numbers of native blacks on those same campuses, calls into question the effectiveness of America's affirmative action programs. While affirmative action started as a system to right the wrongs of slavery and institutional anti-black racism, helping wealthy immigrants who weren't here for those struggles doesn't serve any of the program's original intentions.[22]

Where we are similar is around the racial wealth gap, due to income. According to a 2022 Pew Research Center study on educational and economic attainment, researchers noted that Black immigrants are more likely to earn more than US-born Black households, particularly sub-Saharan African immigrants, with the former having a median income of $57,200 in 2019, while the latter's was $42,000. Black immigrants, however, still fall behind other immigrant racial groups, with a median of $63,000 for all households in 2019.[23] No surprise here, as it also corroborates the Pew study in 2016 in which researchers found what we all already know about workplace disparities for people of color: they get paid less money for the same jobs or don't get hired for the position at all.[24]

So, that affirmative action law? It did not fulfill the mission it set out to achieve. This is key because those colleges and universities are the gateway to meeting classmates who may become cofounders for your own company; funders through syndicate funds, venture capital, or private equity; founders you eventually work for; or employers, because recruiters haven't seen a Black Ivy League graduate they (mostly) didn't like. Bless Lyndon B. Johnson because he tried but just didn't hit the mark. On the rare occasion affirmative action appears to work, it always seems to happen to the detriment of Black American women. So, what is the appropriate answer?

This scenario plays out as wanted and warranted inside the walls of big tech. Going to work for a company that wants you just to do as you're told and not question the strategy, marketing, or method to achieving the bottom line is what is desired. There is an inherent demand that you just be quiet and happy to be there. I wasn't raised that way, so it was always going to be an intense push and pull for me. It also goes against the message I was given at my Black graduation from UC Berkeley—yes, there is a "Black graduation" for all the students who identify as Black—when Dr. Michael Eric Dyson told us to be Trojan horses. So, sitting on the sidelines is not only something I was raised *not* to do but something to actively work against in my professional life. The other issue with this? Other Black colleagues, who were not raised to question authority, to ask who is in charge, why, how, and what else can be done to change their minds (if the products are harmful, exclusive, or can be perceived as intentionally leaving certain communities out). It's hard to change minds that are made up, and often you are screaming into the void and speaking into the wind. It creates a huge juxtaposition between someone who is raising issues and will be seen as complaining versus an employee who is going along to get along.

So, if you have a healthy number of employees who are in agreement with what you are doing or the path you're charting for the company, everything seems good, right? No. Dig deeper. That is usually an issue of confirmation bias. You (the company or its leadership) are seeking to be validated in your opinion. So, you aren't going to ask someone like me. You're going to ask someone who will tell you that you can do no wrong—so ignore those stats, the internal rabble-rousers (hi!), or anyone who questions not only your vision but also your authority.

That is tokenism at its best, and worst. Black tech employees don't have the numbers to stick up for ourselves as we only comprise an average of 7.4 percent of the tech workforce in total, per an Equal Employment Opportunity Commission report, but make up 13 percent of the US population.[25] Per a 2021 study by AnitaB.org, Black women specifically make up only 1.7 percent of Black tech workers.[26] It only got worse during the pandemic as we typically occupy positions that serve as overhead: legal, human resources, diversity, marketing, etc. So, it's truly last in, first out. We also don't have authority because we haven't risen through the ranks—our efforts be damned. Never mind that the stats say that Black women want to ascend the corporate ladder. These are not just anecdotal stories, including my own; the data supports us. McKinsey & Company's *Women in the Workplace* 2019 report confirmed this, citing statistics that tell us what we already know. Just as many Black women (41 percent) as white men share the desire to ascend to a leadership role. One of the reasons why we want to be in leadership is the importance of improving company culture and being a role model, as more than half of the Black women surveyed noted.[27] I know that was, and still is, my motivation.

For those of us who made it through the pandemic with our jobs intact—despite increased stress with homeschooling our children and the racial reckoning protests after the killing of George Floyd—we were now singled out and looked to as the de facto authorities and spokespeople for all Black people. I know because it happened to me. Helping launch a Black ERG at the company where I served as head of legal—and being the only Black person on the leadership team, again—I was now tasked with doing something outside my scope of work. But you are damned if you do, damned if you don't. I lost count of the number of questions I fielded that would start with "Can you teach me . . ." or "How can I be a better ally?" and I was exhausted. Every day I would find a reason I didn't want to have my camera on for Zoom because I could hear my mother's words as we used to sit in church: "Fix your face!" It grew incredibly tiring to listen in earnest to people who were all hat and no cattle, but if I said that, I'm sure it would have been grounds for termination for not being a team player or helping a coworker. Being asked to curate a reading list and documentaries to watch was draining, especially after watching the news, balancing my actual work, and homeschooling. No one realized that or seemed to care.

The problem is that the people asking usually have good intentions and genuinely mean well (sometimes it's performative), but there's a complete lack of respect and acknowledgment for the emotional labor and time it takes to engage in these discussions. Like everyone else, I just want to go to work, do my job to the best of my ability, and not have to explain my humanity every day or justify my thoughts. I want to go to work and make great products. It's enough that I already have to code switch constantly.

Code switching is a tiring necessary evil and a lasting vestige of W. E. B. Du Bois's theory of double consciousness, introduced in his book *The Souls of Black Folk*. Double consciousness refers to the experience of feeling as if you have two identities, one that is shaped by your sense of self and another that is imposed upon you by society's perceptions and stereotypes of your identity group. Du Bois believed that Black Americans, as a result of living in a society dominated by white people and white culture, have a unique experience of double consciousness. He deemed it "this sense of always looking at one's self through the eyes of others, of measuring one's soul by the tape of a world that looks on in amused contempt and pity. One ever feels his two-ness,—an American, a Negro; two souls, two thoughts, two unreconciled strivings; two warring ideals in one dark body, whose dogged strength alone keeps it from being torn asunder."[28] In other words, Black folks must see ourselves both as we really are and how we are perceived by white society.

It is something we are taught as children: there is one way to speak in private and another way to speak in public. I had it constantly drilled into my head, and I still fight it as a grown woman. There was an edict that my grandmother had on a constant loop for me: *"You represent not only yourself, but the totality of the family and our people when you step outside of this house. So, look and act your best."* There is an embedded sense of honor and duty, but it comes with a large side of immense, suffocating weight on the shoulders of an eight-year-old who doesn't yet understand what you're talking about in order to navigate the world and just knows she needs to impress it. Show them I'm "one of the good ones" and be a Trojan horse for the others. If you want to get ahead, you play their game. But at what personal cost? It's certainly a mindfuck—and that's the easiest and most eloquent way I can put it. You lose many things when you sacrifice elements of your personal authenticity as a trade-off for workplace and monetary gain and someone else's comfort.

What are the many costs of being a shape-shifter when it comes to your appearance, behavior, communication style, and topics of discussion? I'm so glad you asked. While it is a necessary skill for Black women to navigate in tech workplaces—most workplaces, if I'm being honest—it can also come with significant costs, mainly of the mental health variety. These include the following:

1. Mental exhaustion: Constantly switching between different communication styles, topics of conversation, and even styles of dress or how you wear your hair can be mentally taxing and lead to exhaustion.

2. Limited authenticity: Code switching can also lead to individuals feeling unable to express themselves

fully or authentically in the workplace, which can be demoralizing.

3. Increased stress: The pressure to code switch can lead to increased stress levels, negatively impacting an individual's mental and physical health.

4. Reduced productivity: Code switching can take up mental energy and time, which can reduce an individual's productivity.

5. Reinforcement of oppressive systems: When individuals are expected to code switch to fit in with dominant workplace cultures, it can reinforce oppressive systems and limit diversity and inclusion.

6. Impostor syndrome: Code switching can foster feelings of inadequacy or impostor syndrome, where individuals feel like they don't truly belong or are not valued for their true selves.

7. Unequal burden: Marginalized individuals may bear a disproportionate burden of code switching compared to their privileged counterparts, leading to a sense of unfairness or frustration.

This emotional labor, and the toll it takes, is a silent killer. It's an invisible set of additional expectations to meet. I recall going on several interviews and choosing my hairstyle very carefully. In law school and while working at a law firm, I kept my hair straight because that is deemed "professional." For Black women, our hair is often considered a distraction just based on how it naturally grows out of our heads. It's something to be tamed, not allowed to be in its true state. Well, I flipped that on its head when I decided to work as an in-house attorney in tech. I learned the hard way as a summer associate at a large law firm that if I showed up to work as my "authentic self," including my naturally curly hair, I'd be subjected to people whispering, asking questions, and full-on touching my hair without asking or provocation. A firm recruiter running her fingers through my curls actually caused me to break character. The code switching stopped, and the AAVE jumped out. I exclaimed, "Girl! Jessica, ma'am, what are you doing?! If you don't get yo' hands out of my hair . . . !" I nervously laughed so she would feel at ease while I simultaneously asserted my bodily autonomy. Even worse, she'd done this in front of others, including a Black associate, who I could tell sympathized and was equally horrified. Jessica, completely lacking awareness of her error, turned bright red and said, "Oh, I'm so sorry! I just thought I could touch it to see what it feels like." *I'm not an animal and this isn't a petting zoo*, I thought while I accepted an apology that was both embarrassing and dehumanizing.

Determined not to have this experience again when I interviewed at Facebook, I straightened my long hair so it was past the middle of my back. When I got the job, I showed up on my first day with my naturally curly hair, which was the reason for my exuberant smile in my badge picture. *Surprise!* I thought. *You thought you were getting one thing, but you're getting another.* Showing up authentically was going to help me do my best work, and it did . . . until microaggressions reared their ugly heads so often that they became intolerable and made it difficult to enjoy the work I loved with clients I adored.

Tech work is about creating something fulfilling with a clear purpose and mission while producing a product or service that resonates with the widest audience possible. However, if you have very little representation of the Black community, how can you truly make products and services that bear them in mind? The short answer is you can't, and probably don't care, to your detriment and society's.

CHAPTER 3

The Myth of Meritocracy

I've had to work twice as hard for half as much.
—Eboni K. Williams,
lawyer and television host

"So, did you get into UC Berkeley on affirmative action?" my manager casually asked me in the loud company cafeteria.

We had gone to lunch because my manager had made a big production about how I hadn't made an effort to get to know him personally; we hadn't had any meals together and never spoke outside of work. And truth is I didn't care to because I didn't particularly vibe with him. He had said one too many questionable things for my liking—"How does your hair curl like that? What do you do to it?"—and this was just the latest insulting query. People milled around us, so it was hard to hear, and at first, I wasn't sure if I'd heard what I thought I heard. But he repeated it with no shame in his game.

While I tried to hide my abject horror at being asked such an offensive question by none other than the person in charge of my livelihood, my Filipino colleague, who was sitting with us and who had also gone to Berkeley, sensed the imminent danger in the air, grabbed his tray, and said, "Oh, I just realized

I have a meeting." I found him later that afternoon in a conference room, eating alone. I asked, "You didn't have a meeting, did you?" He chuckled and told me he didn't have a meeting at all but didn't want to witness that conversation for his own sanity. What I gleaned from that? He would've been a witness to something that may later be investigated, and he wanted no part of that. Can't say I blame him, but more people standing up for or bearing witness to others would go a long way.

My heart was racing. It was enough that I'd even gone to eat with my manager, and I was happy my colleague was there as a buffer after my being hounded about not getting to know my manager personally or wanting to talk to him about my personal life—but then to be subjected to a string of belittling, assumptive, and nosy queries was exhausting. My teammate was like my security blanket in that scenario, so seeing him get up and walk off was both understandable and anxiety inducing. I get it. He also had anxiety around the interrogation I was getting and wanted to protect his peace. Deservedly, he really didn't want to be in any mess. I totally get that. He could also sense that the discounting of my deserving to be there, within one of big tech's biggest names, because I got a perceived "handout" made me want to take off my earrings and get out some Vaseline.

"No," I told him as calmly as I could. I could hear and see my mom in my mind while we sat in McGee Avenue Baptist Church, saying, *"Fix your face!"* as she pinched me. "Affirmative action was actually voted down by California Proposition 209 before I graduated from high school and applied to Berkeley for my undergraduate degree. So, no, I didn't. But what if I had?"

What he didn't know is that my father *did* attend Berkeley by admission via affirmative action in 1968. The thing that people don't seem to grasp about affirmative action is that it may get you in, but it will not keep you there. You still have to do the work and get the grades. And we both did the work and proved to be phenomenal students: he graduated a year and a half early—just as I would thirty years later. So, one affirmative action recipient begat a kid who didn't need it.

Undeterred, my manager continued. "Oh, okay. Did you play a sport? Were you on an athletic scholarship?"

While seething on the inside and trying to stifle the laughter I emit before telling someone about themselves, I replied, "No. I lettered in tennis in high school but definitely was not good enough to play on the collegiate level. I had a partial academic scholarship my freshman year, though."

Nevertheless, he persisted. "Well, did your husband go to Harvard on a basketball scholarship?" he asked. *So, because you can't find fault with me, now you turn to my husband?* The unmitigated gall. He tried to act casual about it, but I could feel his utter amazement at the prospect of our meritocracy mounting. The audacity of two Black kids from Oakland with good grades, extracurricular activities, and stellar SAT scores. How could that happen? Meanwhile, in my mind: *You're just going to keep going down this prejudice rabbit hole, huh?*

I was utterly appalled that he would presume a Black man could only attend a good college if he were on a sports scholarship. "No," I told him. And I reminded him that while my husband is six feet six, he is an engineer.

Unsatisfied with my previous answers, my manager pressed on, more culturally tone-deaf and getting on my nerves by the minute. "Was he on a scholarship of any kind? Otherwise, how else could he afford Harvard?" I stared at him blankly. The man literally couldn't fathom the idea that not all Black people are in dire straits financially. When I told him that his parents wrote a check and that's how he afforded it, he looked completely confused. "Wow," he said emphatically. He simply couldn't believe there were actually smart Black people from Oakland, California, who could attend an elite school without being on sports scholarships or affirmative action beneficiaries, and with parents who could pay for their education. I found great joy in seeing his head almost explode when I told him my husband was a third-generation legacy, and his younger brother and uncle had also graduated from Harvard. He just kept staring at the ceiling after I said that, and it almost felt like he was examining where he went wrong in life after hearing all of this. It was delicious.

When it comes to diversity, tech companies express all the right sentiments through their progressive value manifestos and glossy photos of diverse employees on campus. During the summer of 2020, the racial reckoning brought on by the murder of George Floyd catalyzed a number of solidarity pledges. A few years later, we've heard nothing but crickets on the results. Corporations' often well-intentioned leaders launch ambitious initiatives to increase the number of women and people of color among their ranks when the spotlight is on them, but they almost always fail. Why? Because middle managers fail to integrate their newly hired minorities into their everyday interactions, with only 26 percent of Black women thinking their coworkers are fair to everyone and only 36 percent thinking they are treated with respect, according to a poll by the Gallup Center on Black Voices released in March 2021.[29] Those who disagree are assumed by the people interviewing them not to be a "culture fit" or belong there due to the myth of meritocracy.

The myth of meritocracy is built on the Western thought process of rugged individualism, the belief that "everyone gets what they deserve," that one's accomplishments are due to sheer grit, willpower, and intellect and without any help from anyone. This, of course, ignores the factors of parental investment and privilege along the way in the form of funding expensive private schools, tutors, lessons for "country club sports" (think tennis, fencing, lacrosse, sailing, and water polo), and private music lessons. All these integral factors are ignored for that person to be able to say they simply excelled on their own merit, making their privileged access to these additional forms of culture and education null and void in their eyes because they *earned* their success. Meanwhile, this myth of meritocracy perpetuates inequality and racism, helping believers deem that they've won the race solely due to their hard work, while leaving behind already marginalized people who often don't have access to the same modes of cultural, educational, and networking accelerants.

Per Michael Kinsley's 1990 *Washington Post* opinion piece "The Myth of Meritocracy," climbing the social ladder and moving seamlessly from one socioeconomic group to the next, solely through one's own merits, is not widely achievable in capitalist structures.[30] It is even worse for Black women because of the contradictions that haunt us: *isms*. Sexism, racism, elitism, colorism, classism—take your pick. It's even more fun when they all collide, as they often do for Black women. To fully buy into the American dream, you must believe "anything is possible," which means you ignore all the *isms* and what they beget: discrimination based on immutable traits, income disparity, wealth disparity, inferior educational options, and status. Limited class mobility continues to be widespread, regardless of work ethic, particularly as many Black women have more than one job or source of income.[31] Throw a rock into a crowd, and I guarantee you will hit at least five Black women with a side hustle. I'm included in that number. I believe that the wealth disparity has even increased because the myth of meritocracy has been so effectively promoted and defended by those who have "made it" and hold themselves up as examples or allow others to do that for them. Tech magazines have lauded the entrepreneurial spirit and success of "wunderkinds" like Bill Gates, Mark Zuckerberg, and Jeff Bezos while also leaving out that these male dropouts came from well-to-do families. Portraying them as scrappy, self-made men is far from the truth. Gates's father, William H. Gates Sr., was the Gates in the international law firm K&L Gates.[32] Zuckerberg had the help of a software developer as a computer tutor who helped him create video games at eleven years old, a Phillips Exeter education prior to a short-lived Harvard attendance, and then the financial support of his parents when he created Facebook.[33] Bezos's origin story revolves around Amazon being started in his garage in 1994, which leaves out the part where his parents invested almost $250,000 a year later to keep the company afloat. If his parents had kept their investment, it would be worth over $30 billion now.[34] But it must be nice to have a spare $250,000 lying around, let alone to give it to your child to help their business. I know if I asked my mother for $250,000, she would laugh in my face and think I was joking. And I would be because I know she doesn't have it, never did, isn't good for it, and won't be.

We can't choose the family we are born into, and discounting the luck of the draw is easy when you're in the winner's circle. It's easy to pull yourself up by the bootstraps when you have not only boots but two spare pairs with extra laces. It doesn't apply when you don't even have boots to begin the race with. Yet white people in tech feel like they not only made or found their boots and laced and tied them on their own, as the narrative of choice that they made it all by themselves, but that *they* are products of meritocracy. That means that everyone who isn't in their position isn't there because they aren't worthy or because they lack the work ethic, intellect, or ideas. If you want a quick and easy way to dispute this narrative, remind yourself that Jared Kushner's father donated $2.5 million just prior to

Kushner curiously being accepted to Harvard,[35] even though, as per the book *The Price of Admission*, his high school teachers said he wasn't a stellar student.[36] Or recall the Operation Varsity Blues scandal. Celebrities, wealthy hedge fund managers, investors, hoteliers, and vineyard owners not only paid someone to take their mediocre children's SATs but also photoshopped pictures of them in sports they didn't play, while also bribing school officials. Meritocracy, though, right?

Meritocracy is the story tech bros tell themselves to feel like they hit a home run, whether or not they realize they were born on third base. It is the narrative of choice for those who got into college as legacies or whose parents paid an obscene amount to the school of their choice (bonus: it's tax deductible), whose parents' and grandparents' wealth funded their start-ups and subsidized their livelihoods while they were just starting out, and who can do a "friends-and-family" initial funding round because they have friends and family members with disposable income to invest. Meritocracy is also the tale tech bros tell themselves when they don't hire (or promote) people of color: *Of course bias had nothing to do with it; they just didn't cut it. Oh sure, they might have gotten into the same schools, but they probably got there through affirmative action (the same way they must've gotten their last job). Yes, they might have hit the last few projects out of the park, but they don't have a "leadership presence."* Meritocracy opens the door for the worst kind of bias. This narrative is the root of why efforts to increase diversity in the tech industry are often seen as "lowering the bar." It doesn't matter how much unconscious bias training your company provides; if you let the myth of meritocracy run wild, then you end up with people being left out, often unintentionally. That's how unconscious bias works. We're often passed over for promotions for our white counterparts—like I have been twice—not based on merit, credentials, or performance but on the comfort of our middle managers and those up top not being close enough to the ground to care. Karen and Karter get promoted because they look, sound, and act like our predominately white management, all while they ask us to be patient.

The real problem with this is that Black women are subject to double the scrutiny and the demand to prove themselves. It starts before you're even *in* the company. I distinctly remember being told how articulate I was during an interview, and my first thought was, *Well, how did you think I would sound based on the résumé you read?* Later on, I recall being in a hiring position and discussing a Black woman's qualifications, and the other people on the panel were amazed that her presentation was so thorough. She and I are not alone. Per the National Center for Education Statistics, even though Black women enroll in college at a higher rate than all men, including white men, we continue to be held to the highest standards while being subjected to low expectations.[37] According to the McKinsey & Company's *Women in the Workplace 2019* study, 26 percent of Black women hear people express surprise when they demonstrate strong abilities, including being well spoken.[38]

Once you get inside the company, it doesn't stop. There is the constant need to drone on about credentials, how you got there, why you are there, and who you know. Imagine nonstop and consistent explanation and justification that you're where you need to be because you earned it. Again, I'm not alone in this. The McKinsey study also noted that 40 percent of Black women said they must provide more evidence of their competence, compared to 28 percent of white women and 14 percent of white men, while also being doubted about their area of expertise with similar statistics.[39] So, having the credentials and being an expert in your field will still yield you being underestimated and having to do more for less to prove you're worthy of being there. The big tech version of affirmative action is usually based on the understanding of the Rooney Rule. The Rooney Rule is a National Football League (NFL) policy that requires every team to interview at least one ethnic minority candidate for a head coach or senior leadership vacancy. This checks a box but doesn't actually effect real change. It merely allows a team to show internal policy compliance without regulating or mandating follow-through. The same is true for tech companies employing this method. It is basically a cop-out to allow companies to say, "Well, we tried." Tried what? And how hard did you actually try?

The Rooney Rule was created in 2003 and is "named after former Pittsburgh Steelers owner Dan Rooney, who was also chairman of the league's diversity committee" at the time.[40] By 2006 the percentage of Black coaches in the NFL rose to 22 percent.[41] Upon learning this, the civil rights activist Reverend Jesse Jackson pleaded for tech companies to use this tactic, claiming it's a "first step, not the final step."[42] However well-intentioned the rule is, it is riddled with faults. For starters, it only ensures that one candidate of a diverse background, whether a person of color or a woman, is slotted for an interview. That's all it takes. Just one. The problem here for Black women is that if there's an opportunity to interview a diverse candidate, it will usually be a white woman. Second, there is no guarantee that every opening is participating in the Rooney Rule. This means select roles, particularly midlevel and leadership roles, can pick and choose when to use the rule. Third, beyond that one person chosen for an interview slot—which could include just the initial phone screening with a recruiter—there is no guarantee that any records are being kept.

Metrics are magic. They are also essential. If you aren't measuring something, you have nothing from which to form a baseline, and you aren't interested in true progress but rather in saving face. There are five key questions that should have metrics and tracking behind them:

1. Who is being interviewed? Check the diversity of the candidates selected for initial screening. Track how many are from marginalized communities. If there aren't any, you need to widen your sourcing pool or look at candidates holistically, as opposed to just prior companies or schools.

2. Who is advancing in the process? Tracking this will inform you as to where diverse candidates fall out of the hiring cycle and can also point to indicators as to why. This offers an opportunity to audit the interview process. Who is involved? Is there a set order of questions asked of every candidate? If the majority of Black women drop out at the hiring manager interview stage, look into why that is and juxtapose it with who advances via the feedback given. Pattern matching is key here. If this is amplified, companies need to understand why and proactively work to change the practice. Researcher Ian Cook says, "If diverse candidates are rejecting offers of employment, recruiters need to understand why and make a change."[43] A drop in diversity at different stages requires a different response at each stage.

3. Who is on the interview panel? Typically, "there is reduced bias when the diversity of a job interviewer is matched to the candidate,"[44] or at least when a diverse interviewer is part of the slate of interviewers.

4. What are the interview questions? Are they consistent, or do they veer off topic to personal questions? Are they standardized? Without standardization, there isn't a one-to-one match with answers, making it hard to gauge one's candidacy and compare candidates fairly. Each candidate should answer the same set of questions to ensure a fair judgment of ability and competency.

5. Who is getting hired? It's important to understand who receives an offer after making it through the gauntlet, and why.

The irony isn't lost on me that tech and football have the same problem. For a league that is 69 percent Black,[45] there are few Black folks in decision-making roles in the front offices. The same is true of tech. Black people are avid first adopters and users, but the sting comes in knowing that the product is neither made for us nor keeps us in mind for potential ramifications. To that end, to make a meaningful impact, companies need to aim to interview a slate of candidates that are 30 to 35 percent diverse for *every* available role. "Companies could also set a standard of having their executive ranks mirror the gender and race breakdown of the usually much-more-diverse entry-level workforce" and use the same diversity standards applied to new hires for employees up for promotion.[46] The culprit can usually be traced back to the amorphous "culture fit" narrative.

Yes, "culture fit" goes together with what George W. Bush called "the soft bigotry of low expectations."[47] The low expectations paired with surprise at your presence in certain places extend to social graces too. One summer when I was in law school, I worked at a big firm as a summer associate. I was the only Black woman out of four women chosen as summer associates. On Tuesday, the managing partner told all four of us that he was going to take us to lunch at his country club on Friday. So, I came prepared, wearing khakis and a nice blouse, as did two other women. I knocked on the office door of the fourth woman and found her sitting in jeans, which is country club contraband.

"You can't go there in jeans. It's part of the dress code," I told her.

"Well, how was I supposed to know that?" she asked, panicking even before all the words left my mouth. "What do I do?"

Pointing out the window to the department store across the street, I suggested she go buy a pair of khakis quickly, and she did. Once we all arrived at the club, a waiter took a round of drink orders. I asked for an Arnold Palmer, half lemonade and half iced tea, named after the famous golfer.

The partner looked puzzled and said, "How did you know to order that?" I felt my back stiffen. *If you only knew the white woman in the new pants sitting next to me didn't even know what to wear here, but of course I'm not supposed to know proper etiquette, proper attire for a country club, or how to order.*

"Well, my father-in-law belongs to this country club," I answered.

Now he had a furrowed brow. "What does he look like?" he asked.

I knew what he was really getting at: *Was I married to a white man?* Having played this game before, I deflected my annoyance with humor and responded, "Well, he's about six-seven, three hundred pounds, and browner than I am. He sort of looks like a Black Santa Claus. You'd know if you met him. He is definitely distinctive and has a big personality." The conversation immediately changed to another topic.

In the corporate world, there are unwritten rules for achieving success, and one crucial aspect is to "look the part." This means wearing tailored suits and a certain unspoken range of approved coifs, as well as displaying other signs of prosperity, from jewelry to cars. And in terms of appearance, there are rules that apply to Black women that may not apply to other women, generally because we are perceived as "aggressive." Aggressive in body language, facial expressions, and even demeanor. Being *too* seen when asking for what we want. So, it's important for us to try to counterbalance that by looking as professional yet feminine as possible. Softening our looks within the realms of professionalism is, currently, how we can make ourselves "more palatable" to our peers and "acceptable," at least appearance-wise, to our companies that love to throw their "culture fit" narrative in our faces. And that is pretty much every company out there, especially in the legal profession.

Unfortunately, in my line of work, Black women often hear the refrain, "You don't look like a lawyer," implying that success, capability, and expertise are linked to conforming to a certain appearance, usually white and male. One of my girlfriends, an in-house attorney, experienced this on a regular basis. How could she fit into their perceived culture fit? She "softened" her workplace look by doing one thing consistently: never wearing her natural hair. She always had a straight sew-in weave. Always. And she made sure to dress up, have her nails done, makeup on, the works—then go in and be her badass self, which no one was expecting because how could she be pretty *and* smart? Impossible. The "culture fit" narrative forces Black women to combat the fact that if we show up as our natural selves, we're not considered feminine or professional, *but* on the other hand, if we show up looking put together, we're not capable. And when we open our mouths, we're angry and aggressive. It's a lose-lose situation, and it's the reason why many of us play along until we don't have to. However, the numbers aren't encouraging on this front. Per the 2019 National Association for Law Placement report and the Vault and Minority Corporate Counsel Association survey, Black women specifically continue to be significantly underrepresented, comprising 1.73 percent of all attorneys, and the long and short of it is because of "culture fit."[48] The problem is that people wonder what this all means, and no one—no company—can give us a straight answer, by design.

The noncommittal definition of what constitutes "culture fit" is what keeps most organizations white. Ever-elusive notions of "fit," mandating appearance norms born out of white standards of beauty, and expecting Black employees to code switch are seemingly subtle but blatant disadvantages for Black women. In addition, "fit" can refer to literally anything, from appearance to demeanor to education—all meant to keep others out. I've seen how these silent expectations can sink a candidate. We were interviewing interns one summer for Facebook, and I was one of three employees, and the only person of color, tasked with going through résumés to select those for an interview. As we did, I noticed my two colleagues were x-ing out applicants of color. When I looked closer, it appeared their choice to do so was based on the schools the candidates had attended. Never mind anything else. It was just the school.

When we got down to making the last choice, I presented my pick: a Black woman from Stanford Law. Unsurprisingly, both of them had crossed her out.

"Why did you x her out?" I asked. "She was a Gates Millennium Scholar and had almost a 4.0 GPA. She goes to Stanford."

"Yeah, but I've never heard of her undergrad," retorted my

colleague. "I've never heard of Spelman. I just don't know if she'd be a good culture fit. Is it any good?"

Google is free, I thought. And Spelman isn't exactly unknown, but that was neither here nor there. They were focusing on the wrong thing.

"Does it matter that you don't know her college? We're not looking for a college student, we're looking for a legal intern. And she goes to Stanford Law."

We went around in circles for another ten minutes, both of them reiterating they didn't know the college. Well, so what? Just because you don't know something exists doesn't mean it isn't worthwhile. It just means you didn't know it existed. Yet their stubbornness to stick to the "culture fit" point, as if one's ability to be successful at work hinges entirely on where they attended undergrad (spoiler alert: it does not), made me want to rip my hair out. But eventually, after more lobbying, we chose the woman from Stanford Law. It was a win that shouldn't have been so hard to bring about.

Examples such as this are just one of the reasons why the numbers for people of color are so low in tech. *I don't think they were a culture fit.* There is no phrase in the tech world I hate to hear more, and the more I hear it, the more I resent both it and the person uttering it. *What, exactly, is a "culture fit," and based on whose culture?* No one ever wants to answer that question. Yet middle management and recruiters will continue to automatically deem someone unfit or irrelevant just because they're not coming from the "right" place or because of some other arbitrary standard when it suits them. They are making these decisions based on associations rather than on the candidate as a person. But these associations can be anything. *Oh, can I associate you with this school? No? You're out. Well, this person went to Michigan, so we should talk to them.* Yeah, because *you* went to Michigan. What about their *actual, relevant* qualifications for this job? I would argue those are far more important to fit in with a company culture than seeing if they attended the same undergrad as me.

Another aspect of culture fit often not discussed as much is back-channeling. Back-channeling is a shorthand way of asking others about you by asking who you know and who knows you. Black folks have our own version of this, but it's typically friendly and done directly with the person of interest, not asking someone else who may know of the person of interest. Tech back-channeling is definitely not as stealthy but has many far-reaching effects. The way to engage in that process is to essentially ask someone about someone else—whether you worked with them or invested in their company, gathering intel on what you know about that person. The person you are asking about should never know that you inquired about them, though the Valley isn't known for discretion. These companies are incestuous enough that everybody knows everybody to a certain extent. Most of them are fewer than six degrees away from finding out who you are and what your experience was at a different company or school. It is also important to note that back-channeling is *not* the same as checking references—it's an informal way of getting dirt on someone, of allowing others to go off the record and say if this person was trash or not. Back-channeling allows people to tell their experiences about somebody without being liable, and it also lets employers blackball potential candidates. Based on the answers, the person may or may not hire you, invest in your company, ask you to be on their advisory board, or a host of other professional advantages. I experienced this myself.

One day, I received a Twitter (now X) direct message. Curious. It was from a name I didn't know.

"Hey, we're doing a beta test for a new social product. Would you like to get coffee in SF or South Bay?" the new friendly gentleman asked.

I agreed, and a few weeks later, we were having breakfast on the patio of a restaurant in Palo Alto.

"You know, I asked around about you," he declared.

"Oh, you did? Who did you ask?" I queried.

"I asked your old general counsel [GC]. He had great things to say about you, so I felt good asking you to meet up."

Wow. Why not get to know me for myself? I thought. *But good for C for saying nice things, though true anyway, about me.* We proceeded to have a great breakfast. We talked shop, and by the end of the meal, he asked me to test his product and be on his advisory board.

Despite this gentleman letting me know that my former GC had said nice things about me, I was still wary based on how those answers came about. The reason I was nervous about this process is because it most often plays out in hiring through recommendations and referrals. An overwhelming percentage of tech employees are referrals—almost 40 percent of new hires at big tech companies.[49] Referrals are so important there is now a market for them with a platform enabling people to bid on a *stranger* to recommend you for a company they work for, should you have a spare fifty dollars to bribe someone.[50] It's basically Operation Varsity Blues: Tech Edition.

This further exacerbates the myth of meritocracy and hinders the ability to get a seat at the table because you likely won't be invited to the party. New hires via referrals typically look just like those referring them: same schools, social circles, ideas, beliefs, and ethnicity. No wonder no real headway has been made in diversifying the workforce. While many tech bros laud the meritocracy of tech, they are confusing *potential* for reality—what could be with what is. The fallacy is that everyone has the same resources and chances, which is patently false. The tech sector's mistake is not inviting different perspectives to sit at the table or listening to them once there. That will also beget the "cognitive diversity" tech bros love so much and create better products that have more use cases and speak to a larger audience. To do that, you first must have Black women at the table so we can ensure the products are helpful not harmful, and multipurpose instead of exclusive.

But if you don't give us a seat at the table, we'll be like Shirley Chisholm and bring our own . . . that is, if we don't go make our own table first.

CHAPTER 4
Paying Lip Service

> Recognize and embrace your uniqueness. . . . Being a Black woman, being a woman in general, on a team of all men, means that you're going to have a unique voice. It's important to embrace that.
> —Erin Teague, director of product management at YouTube

Close your eyes and imagine a young tech founder with the right academic and social pedigree, a quirky personality, a curiously deep voice, and a "game-changing" product no one's ever seen and that's never been proven to work. Someone with an air of mystery and eccentricity who's able to fundraise with ease and stack a board with political and business icons. A founder who becomes a media darling and then loses it all in disgrace after the government declares the company a sham. They are then convicted and sentenced to eleven years in prison for fraud and conspiracy. *Quelle surprise!* What kind of person do you envision? I know who I *don't* see. A Black woman. We could never. There is an old Black proverb I love and live by: "Fuck around and find out." It means, "Do something without forethought, and let's see how that works out for you." Yet in tech, Black women don't have the luxury to fuck around and find out. We'll find out before we fuck around. It's that simple. Period.

Over the years, tech has found another way to pay lip service to diversity while doing little to increase the number of underrepresented minorities, especially Black women, by broadening the definition of diversity so it's not just about representational diversity but "cognitive diversity" as well. Cognitive diversity is all about the different ways people think or work or learn—how they approach a problem or solution. Sometimes it even refers to different personality types. On the surface, there is nothing wrong with the notion or even practice of cognitive diversity—but when you elevate it to the same level as racial, ethnic, gender, and socioeconomic diversity, the very concept of diversity is watered down. It also means diversity is reinterpreted to include what Silicon Valley has never had a shortage of: white men with quirky personalities. The problem is there is never enough room for women. Elizabeth Holmes may be the exception, though I postulate that her meteoric rise had more to do with her emulating the quirks of white men, namely Steve Jobs, by dressing in all black, obsessing over security, never taking vacations, and speaking in a masculine tone. Here's the thing: she *had* advantages that many other women, particularly women of color, will never have. She's pretty in a white standard sense of beauty, comes from an upper-middle-class family, went to Stanford, and had certain connections that made it easier for her to assimilate. Even if she's not a man, she *reminds* those men of someone they know, whether it's their mom, sister, daughter, or aunt. But Black women? We don't have any of that. If Holmes came in with three home runs, we come in with the same number of strikes. If we don't look traditionally pretty or feminine according to white standards, strike one. If we're from a lower-middle-class family, strike two. And if we went to the "wrong" school, strike three. We're already out. This is why I continue to surprise people whenever I walk into a space that wasn't designed to have room for me.

I should have never been an option. To have women of color from a middle- to working-class socioeconomic group who are *also* college educated? It's like we're a zoo attraction. Either we're shoved in the back to do the work, or we're pranced around like a show pony as a glittering example of how diverse and accepting the company is. It's situational, but the options don't change. And we grin and bear it because what's the other choice? We get labeled as combative, unsupportive, hostile. Either we're there to validate someone else's virtue of being open-minded and diverse, or we're not there at all. We're not accepted as people, only as what we symbolize to others. And that is tiring; it takes an emotional and physical toll. The people who are left in charge have to decide what is pertinent in the present but also what is relevant in the future. If you haven't been subjected to this ire, you definitely won't know what is relevant about this. It is an issue to navigate. The rub is you can't just rub against it. At all.

Cognitive diversity is now a catchall that allows managers to continue to hire white men and chalk it up to diversity as long as the new hires think, work, or learn "differently." To be sure, having diverse viewpoints in an organization is important, but only focusing on cognitive diversity won't address the well-documented dearth of Black and Latinx employees that plagues tech companies and represents a major shortcoming. Whether intentionally or not, tech companies can redefine diversity so that, conveniently, they've already achieved it simply by hiring those with personality quirks. There are examples of white men in leadership positions actively advocating for this, and that attitude trickles down to employees who have also begun to beat that drum. Loudly. In October 2017 I remember having a conversation with my husband about this phenomenon after reading articles quoting remarks attributed to Apple's former chief diversity officer (CDO) Denise Young Smith at a conference. Incensed, I read her comments out loud.

"Jaime, she literally said this: 'There can be twelve white, blue-eyed, blond men in a room and they're going to be diverse too because they're going to bring a different life experience and life perspective to the conversation.'[51] What does this even mean?!"

He chuckled. "Yeah, it sounds like diversity has worked out, if that's the point."

"This is actually the antithesis of what we're trying to solve in the industry, though. We're looking for representational diversity. Also, one begets the other. If you are from a marginalized community, that inherently begets cognitive diversity because groups aren't monoliths. All Black folks didn't grow up the same way. You're exhibit A."

"Wait . . . whaaaa? But, sure, I would think so too, based on what she said," he replied.

"Also, if twelve white men are considered diverse, then why does she have a job? If that's the standard, why do any CDOs have a job? Apparently, it's solved!" I stayed up for another hour stewing over this, sitting straight up in bed thinking, *There needs to be a rebuttal to this. This can't stand alone.*

The next morning I drafted a pitch for an op-ed and sent it to my friend, Jenee, who, at the time, was a *New York Times* editor and had also edited some other pieces for me. It was published a week after Smith's comments were made public, arguably a scathing rebuke of her assertions.[52] Three days later, she resigned.

"Bärí, you got that lady fired!" Jaime said when he read the subsequent article about her leaving Apple.

I was horrified and silent for a beat. I would never want to be what I'm working against. Not another log on the fire. "That was definitely not my intention, and I highly doubt I was the reason. Someone reporting to Tim Cook doesn't just up and quit. She clearly was already planning to leave. But, yeah, the timing is curious."

The proliferation of cognitive diversity being the answer to solve diversity in tech led to a backlash against diversity programs, even amid the resurgence of commitment to said programs after—yes, you guessed it—the summer of George Floyd and the racial reckoning. In the past six years, there have been several examples of individual white men at tech companies asking why these programs are necessary and where the equitable program or employee resource group for them is. The most prominent example of this was the August 2017 memo "Google's Ideological Echo Chamber," written by James Damore, a software engineer, who alleged that diversity at Google was "like a cult."[53] He attended a mandatory diversity training—which Google started in 2013—and he disagreed with much of what he heard, which he alludes to being a class on what *not* to do. The crux of his argument was that disparities between men and women aren't due to bias and oppression, but that women tend to focus on softer skills that show more interest in people instead of things, and women are more artistic and social. His solution was to focus on making women more comfortable in the office but not undo perceived wrongs with "reverse discrimination." He was eventually fired for his comments in an internally published memo, in which he had espoused hiring fewer women, which the National Labor Relations Board deemed encouraging employment discrimination. Damore's memo focused on technical fields, where few women occupy roles at tech companies. So, I can only imagine his thoughts on what Black women bring to a tech company, if he feels we bring anything at all.

While Damore was fired for his memo, he likely would've applauded what happened to a Black woman ex-Google colleague, the brilliant Dr. Timnit Gebru. She is an artificial intelligence computer scientist who coheaded Google's ethical artificial intelligence team, which focused on assessing the technology's fairness and risks. That came to an end the week after Thanksgiving 2020 when she was fired for sending two internal emails asking why a research paper she submitted was being squashed and her work being silenced. The initial response was cryptic but noted that it was due to problems with her conclusions that what Google was seeking to build didn't solve the problems she noted. Finally, she accused the company of "silencing marginalized voices"[54] and proclaimed the company's diversity programs pointless. The awful irony? Gebru's work focuses on fairness and the social and ethical ramifications of artificial intelligence. By pushing her out for advocating for the type of work that could keep more Black women safe, Google essentially demonstrated that this wasn't a priority. There is a wide gulf between advocating for race and sex discrimination in hiring versus advocating for more equitable technology to reduce harm, but it seems dissent of any kind will be silenced, even if for the good of product creation and use and how it will affect society—all in the name of not prioritizing diversity concerns. The way this is going is not how I would want it to go.

In some ways, tech has already played the "expanding the definition of diversity" card in order to water it down. In recent years, the industry has focused mostly on increasing gender diversity and not racial diversity. While many in tech have long advocated for increasing the representation of women in the industry, the changes they've been able to secure often benefit white women but not necessarily women of color. For example, Black women only make up 18 percent of entry-level positions in tech, as opposed to 30 percent for white women—and when women are recruited to a company, the majority are white women (and referrals).[55] The leadership ranks of the larger tech companies are not diverse. But while it's true that there are not enough women in leadership in tech companies generally, white women have made significant strides compared to Black and Latinx women. Take, as an example, Facebook. In 2019 it only had five Black women in leadership positions (director level and above).[56]

To see the prominence and advancement of white women in tech, look no further than Holmes, the disgraced founder of Theranos. For a while, she was the darling of the tech world and a poster child of gender diversity, seen as a sign that the tide had changed for women in the Valley, that they, too, could reach the pinnacle of the start-up world: founding a unicorn. She fit the narrative favored by the myth of meritocracy to a T: she was a "girl-wonder genius" and a Stanford dropout with all the right connections. Much like the men she was often compared to, Zuckerberg and her idol, Jobs, she didn't have to develop a minimum viable product in order to fund her medical company; her education and family connections afforded her access to elite professors and other influential people. She was able to raise more than $1 billion[57] while trading on an air of eccentricity she built around her Jobs-esque look and giving vague answers in interviews. Then she lost it all in disgrace after a 2015 *Wall Street Journal* article.[58] A year later, the government declared her company a sham, and only then did she face consequences. Was she the kind of person you envisioned when you closed your eyes and heard her story earlier? When you can imagine that founder is a Black woman—when Black women are allowed to fail as spectacularly and expensively as Holmes did—I'll know there has been real progress in the effort to fully diversify the tech industry.

Until then, let's take a look at what's *actually* happening. As white women have been the primary beneficiaries of affirmative action policies at the collegiate level, this is also true for tech company diversity initiatives.[59] The typical face of a "woman in tech" is white, and the diversity initiatives dedicated to *all* women tend to center *white* women. It makes sense. It's partially a numbers game, as white women comprise the majority of women in tech as new hires. At the beginning of 2022, white women made up 10.9 percent of new hires, while "Black, multiracial, Indigenous, Pacific Islander, and Latin women make up the bottom 6% of all tech industry new hires" collectively.[60] This is easily explainable through unconscious bias. The leaders in the company look at white women and see their mothers, sisters, daughters, aunts, cousins, and wives. Our brains are wired for certain types of bias for the familiar. It's just like my grandmother used to tell me, "Water seeks its own level."

Smaller tech companies, with a thousand employees or less, are often the better and faster way to ascend the ladder for marginalized people. According to *Finances Online*, those companies hire approximately 30 percent of women in tech.[61] Which begs the question of what the demographics of these women in those smaller tech companies are. Unlike big tech companies, smaller ones tend not to release their diversity data. Another rub is networking and back-channeling. Getting jobs at those tech companies with more women often depends on who you know. Roles are created for you or openings are only communicated through word of mouth. But the effect remains the same. These companies lack racial diversity, and having more women but *not* more women of color is the same as bigger companies just having white men. There is no ability for women of color to provide input on products.

The pandemic also did a number on Black women in the workforce. According to a December 2021 survey by Deloitte, the analysis of twenty major tech companies noted that while women disproportionately left the workforce during the pandemic, many of them women of color, those companies still managed to increase the total representation of women.[62] The Deloitte study also noted that while big tech companies prioritized hiring in general, there was a gap between big tech and start-ups. Only 43 percent of start-ups had made diverse hiring a company goal.

Whether it's big tech or a rising unicorn, the crux of the issue is that the door slamming shut for Black women because "cognitive diversity" centers white men with different thoughts and because the category "women" is predetermined to be white women can lead to disastrous results. Both groups make up the larger demographics in tech companies and therefore may be favored by a company that entertains their concerns to the detriment of everyone else. The problem is centering white women as speaking for all women or white men for thinking differently (as if we don't) negates the fact that we don't all share the same problems. When those problems get ignored, bad products are made.

Take, for example, Instagram's facial verification feature. Just last month I tried to verify myself using my driver's license, but the platform could not match it with the picture on my account even though between Instagram and Facebook, there are thousands of photos of me it could scour. The photo was clearly the same person—same face, different hair. We've seen how technology struggles with hair, particularly Black women's hair. Changing its color, style, or texture means the picture often won't be read, but *why* does the face have to include the hair at all? Just compare the face. Another well-documented issue is the lighting of people with darker complexions: the pictures aren't always consistent. So, if you're using something based on faulty data sets, you're using bad photography and bad technical requirements. Of course my photos won't match up. But again, this is predominantly an issue with Black women, so having the standard be a white man, or even a white woman, bars these complaints from surfacing during product testing.

Acknowledging these problems has taken on the term of being "woke," which initially was a positive thing but has now been weaponized to criticize anyone who dares to pay attention to the experiences and stories of marginalized people. It's now the equivalent of a four-letter word in some circles. "Woke culture" and companies' embrace of it dominated a lot of the talk around diversity in 2020 and 2021 until 2022, when a full-on backlash took hold everywhere, from schools to workplaces to amusement parks. For the uninitiated, woke culture, from a corporate perspective, is companies taking a public stance on social justice and policy issues. It is the expansion of corporate social responsibility initiatives, which tend to focus on environmental, philanthropic, and ethical issues, to now include social justice and contentious policy concerns. For all the talk about companies taking up the mantle of woke culture, some companies are now deciding to say . . . *nothing*. Some even went a step further and disavowed woke culture, saying they don't want any social activism or political talk in the company. These messages were disseminated both internally and externally. After two summers of companies rushing to outdo one another by making pledges, donations, and public statements, there is a slow but steady movement of companies now taking the opposite approach, feeling particularly emboldened and supported by seeing a wave of anti–critical race theory policies, including book bans and literal "anti-woke" laws from Virginia to Florida. Two companies took a scorched-earth approach to this by not only saying, "We won't be having these conversations, public facing or internally, here, and if you don't like it, you can leave," but also offering severance packages for those who didn't agree and wouldn't abide by the rules. The most egregious company doing this? Coinbase.

The CEO of crypto exchange Coinbase, Brian Armstrong, came out of the gate swinging on October 8, 2020. He made a very clear statement in a public post on his company's website, declaring, "Coinbase is a mission-focused company."[63] Not part of that mission? Social and political issues. He doubled down by taking his stance to Fox News to spread it far and wide: "We don't engage here when issues are unrelated to our core mission, because we believe impact only comes with focus." He elaborated,

> While I think these efforts are well intentioned, they have the potential to destroy a lot of value at most companies, both by being a distraction, and by creating internal division. We've seen what internal strife at companies like Google and Facebook can do to productivity, and there are many smaller companies who have had their own challenges here. I believe most employees don't want to work in these divisive environments.[64]

One, it's incredibly rich to point the finger at big tech as the reason you're adopting this policy, as if you wouldn't have done it otherwise. Own it. Second, the problem with these sentiments is that they come from a place of extreme privilege, where just because *you* can leave your personal identity and struggles at the door, everyone else not only should be able to but is *expected* to. That is a lot to ask of people who have to worry about their basic humanity and survival on a day-to-day basis while commuting to and from an office you demanded they return to. Willfully ignoring that is naive. To mandate it is tone-deaf and insensitive. Armstrong made sure employees knew he was serious by telling people to get on board or get out, with one week to decide to take severance or basically do the crypto corporate equivalent of Laura Ingraham's awful take: "Shut up and dribble."[65] Be quiet. Be happy to be there. Be profusely grateful. More than anything, keep quiet about anything untoward you experience or observe.

However, there is one thing I can respect about Armstrong's stance. Before he died, my grandfather always told me that one thing he appreciated more about his era than mine was "at least I knew when people didn't like me or didn't like Black people. It was blatant. You all have to guess now." He is correct. With statements like Armstrong's, I don't have to wonder. I can assess him and his values and decide if I want to partake. How I interpret his message is, "If you want to work here, leave your Black womanhood and all of that at the door. Just do the work and don't discuss anything but work with your coworkers." My answer is a resounding "No." Some may like a sterile environment. Good for them, but it definitely isn't for me.

Statements like Coinbase's may also create a sea change in an industry that for so long espoused free speech, liberalism, and support for causes and activism and undo the (minimal) gains diversity work has afforded marginalized groups. Silicon Valley is a big game of "you first," and companies like Coinbase being "brave" enough to step out there with an unpopular stance may spur others to follow suit. The more dangerous part is it isn't just about what you say publicly but how those values play out internally with hiring, promotion, retention, and inclusion. If you say diversity doesn't matter or one's identity doesn't matter, then you are saying your employees don't matter as people. They are merely cogs in a wheel, and this is especially felt among your employees who can't simply leave their identity at the door. Declarations such as Coinbase's also foster a state of fear and confusion among the workforce, which is only going to encourage Black women and other marginalized groups to leave. Hearing that "Black Lives Matter" is a political statement, as opposed to a moral one, makes it clear that Black women aren't wanted. This remix of company culture, and its enforcement by demanding people agree or get out, feels personal. While it is totally understandable to put the onus on product creation, if you negate my value as a whole person, then you don't value the contributions I can make to the products.

I know how it feels to have someone negate my lived experience by actively avoiding acknowledging it. When Mike Brown was shot in August 2014, no one at Facebook knew how to address it, so they just *didn't*. They talked about the Ice Bucket Challenge instead. I was sick of hearing platitudes—all week it was a mix of people saying empty hellos and some saying empty "how are yous" while they briskly walked past and didn't wait for an answer. There were two exceptions. Let's start with the bad. I had a colleague who liked to have casual conversations with me every day, analogous to the coffee chats at Retirement 101. And I understood bringing up Mike Brown made people uncomfortable or perhaps fearful that it would make me uncomfortable. But they didn't realize that by *not* bringing it up, they were acting, and wanting me to act, like everything was okay.

So, one day that week, when I'd reached my limit, I turned to my colleague and said, "You know, I don't really want to entertain this. I don't want to have these fluffy conversations."

"Oh, well, why not?" he asked. "What's wrong?"

I took a deep, measured breath. "You haven't seen the news?"

"No, what's going on?"

Liar, I wanted to shout. *You knew all about the damn Ice Bucket Challenges on Facebook. You've seen my posts about Mike Brown. But now you don't know anything about this man being shot?* I could hear my mom's voice in my head, but this wasn't on Zoom—I couldn't just turn my camera off. So, I walked away and found the nearest conference room to hide in.

No one was acknowledging the huge elephant in the room. I understood, to a point, that segregation doesn't just happen in real life but online too. People go to their corners and stay there. But I also knew that this particular colleague was privy to my posts and had *seen* what I'd been posting about Mike Brown. So how could he see those and ask me the next day why I didn't want to shoot the shit with him about something completely inconsequential? How does that work?

It works because he and the majority of my coworkers had the luxury of *not* caring. They could turn off the news and go about their daily lives because they were unaffected. They were not in danger of a cop randomly stopping or harassing them. So, of course they wouldn't be worried. Of course, they'd just change the channel to the game and move on. But what *shouldn't* have happened is expecting me to react the same way. I understand it may have been an issue of self-preservation, but that doesn't make it right. Unfortunately, that's what all of them did, except for one fantastic coworker: Mark Rodgers.

After excusing myself from the frivolous chat, I sat in the conference room, alternating between refreshing my feeds and silently weeping. Half of my Facebook feed was about Mike Brown and the other half was Ice Bucket Challenges. I, too, had participated in one on campus and immediately felt guilty.

Like, how dare I try to have a bit of levity during such a hard time? No matter. While thinking about that, I felt someone's presence. You know that weird, tingling sixth sense when someone is behind you? I had that, and I knew exactly who it was because it was a rare feeling of reassurance. Mark has that presence. He never commands fear, only attention and respect out of his kindness. He and I have always connected, and I could feel him standing outside the door the same way I could feel that he was still there during meetings when our teams faced away from each other and still available for me to swivel my chair around toward and bug. So, I turned, and he peered at me through the glass, knocked softly, and gave me a faint grin.

"Come in, sir."

"Bärí. How are you? Are you okay?" he asked. He grabbed a chair and made eye contact when he asked.

All week long, no one had genuinely asked if I was okay, and no one knew the shorthand he did to ask a simple question and impart so much inherent understanding.

"No, I'm not, Mark. But thank you for asking," I replied.

"Do you want some company?" he offered.

"I appreciate it, but not right now. But thank you."

"Well, let me know if I can do anything. I'm so sorry," he said. He walked out of the room and shut the door behind him so quietly it was like a whisper.

It felt like a therapy session's worth of conversation in about thirty words. To this day, that man is one of my favorite people on earth and also one of the best colleagues I've ever had. He walks it like he talks it, when most people don't even bother to talk it. Kindness and empathy cost nothing. He could've chosen to err toward his own comfort or not face any feelings of residual guilt or confusion, particularly because his dad is an Irish immigrant and has no ties to the historical issues of Blackness in the United States, but he didn't. Thank you for doing something different, Mr. Rodgers. I'm forever grateful for that.

So, what does this have to do with product creation? Well, the omission of the lived experiences of people, both inside and outside of these companies, meant that they were an afterthought as these products were designed for "users," not real people. Forgetting that your users are also people is a huge mistake. It also confirms that diversity is a buzzword, a mere public relations move, a press release, and a box to check, not something the company truly values. The inherent message in that action, or inaction, is that you don't really care about the experiences of marginalized people in your organization. That's what happened with Mike Brown. The behavior and attitudes of Facebook's employees after the fact were extremely telling of Facebook as a product. No one talked about it; it was all fluff instead. In 2014 the platform had a more insular purpose. It was used to connect with people you already knew; it distilled your worldview. If something wasn't in your personal feed from people you followed, then you didn't see it. Ergo, it didn't happen. And just the fact that my colleague was talking to me as if he knew nothing about it showed how our product was being utilized for nothing beyond Ice Bucket Challenges (which, at least, *was* for an important fundraising cause: the disease ALS). Facebook did not have the infrastructure to be used in a different way that could have helped Black people with this awful event, but another platform did: Twitter (now X).

In a tale of two platforms, X wins. It was the product of record for mobilization and activists. It had the means to allow people to get the word out. Everything was documented in real time, and because X feeds are vast, you're seeing tweets from people you don't know, so your worldview is instantly expanded. With that understanding of how X could be used to mobilize and spread awareness and activism, communities were able to reach millions of users, which then forced mainstream media's hand. They had staunchly refused to acknowledge it until then, but thanks to people with their boots on the ground and X's infrastructure, the case for Black lives eventually made it under the nation's scrutiny. I can't say with assuredness that the people behind X knew when they were building it that it would be used for such a purpose, but the bigger point is that the infrastructure *was* there at all. Facebook didn't have it. And they also never asked anybody, even after Brown's case went viral.

To distill the lived experiences of marginalized groups down to monetization and engagement doesn't fit our narrative for how we truly live, and it won't help your product, the same way it didn't help Facebook. In fact, it's quite telling. It's akin to saying, "Tell me you know nothing about Black people without telling me you know nothing about Black people." *Exclusion overhead* is a term created by computer scientist Joy Buolamwini describing the ramifications of systems that negate or don't consider the diversity of humanity, just like Facebook in 2014. Buolamwini asks, "How much does a person have to change themselves to function with technological systems that increasingly govern our lives?"[66] That's a question not only for how to survive within these tech companies but for how to survive when we use their products, sometimes against our will. Many of us *have* to use these products, especially those of us who work with them, and in some ways we can feel trapped and forced into confines that don't work for us. The way these products are structured limits our availability and ability to actively engage, so a lot of the time, it isn't possible to go any further or do a work-around. Facebook was good for sharing news with friends but not for spreading it beyond one's personal network. I should know: even though I was posting about Mike Brown daily during the week it happened, my posts were only seen by my friends and family. I was essentially preaching to the choir. I couldn't enact any real change because I had no mobility to reach a wider audience. X was the opposite. However, while we could mobilize there, it also opened us up to all forms of attacks and trolling. So, how do we game the system and work around a platform's limitations in order to fit our needs? And the bigger question I find myself and other people of color asking is, *Is it even worth it?*

Lip service around diversity isn't just something that applies inside a company, but it also determines that company's external impact. It controls how you view who you are making products for, how they will be used, how inclusive they are, how they can be weaponized, and how to neutralize that harm. An example of this is how Coinbase views their responsibility to consumers. As a financial services company, it is imperative they understand the history of systemic financial discrimination among some groups, particularly around creditworthiness, access to capital, business and personal loans, and housing issues. You can't be a company that espouses building an open financial system and economic freedom if you are willfully obtuse about the hardships of Black people trying to access that system. While the initial purpose of the internet was to democratize access to traditional systems, if the same attitudes and applications are in place, then nothing has been democratized. Choosing to ignore the identity and humanity of your employees is a huge red flag, not just for company culture but also for which products you will build and who you are building them for, which demonstrates a clear nonchalance in regard to who is collateral damage in the process.

CHAPTER 5

Black Three-for-Ones: Employee Resource Groups as Support Systems, Free Company Labor, and Public Relations

> We will all, at some point, encounter hurdles to gaining access and entry, moving up and conquering self-doubt; but on the other side is the capacity to own opportunity and tell our own story.
>
> —Stacey Abrams, former Georgia state representative

Tech companies have been good about working a hustle to make themselves look good *while* getting their employees to do additional free labor in the form of employee resource groups (ERGs). The phenomenon of tech companies starting ERGs, such as Twitter's Blackbirds, Facebook's Black@Facebook, and Slack's Mahogany, in the wake of the George Floyd protests in the summer of 2020 was supposed to have a twofold purpose: a demonstration of caring from the C-suite and a place for

Black employees (and those who deemed themselves allies) to congregate and find support and help navigating not just the company's work but also their emotions in the midst of such social and racial turmoil.

However, the problem is this isn't the typical impetus for why an ERG is created. Though the creation of Black@Facebook predated me, the motivation was the same: being lonely and often the "only" on your core team, your larger team, or department, compounded by not feeling seen or heard at the highest levels of the company. The collective thought is that if we organize, we have an opportunity to influence business decisions. Of course, all the while, you abide by the Black proverb "Lift as you climb," with the endgame being to influence the tech industry in totality. What begins as an innate need for Black people to congregate for support, learn to navigate the company ropes, and advocate for company change is then co-opted by the company for its own benefit. This results in the company's dependence on Black ERG labor to bolster the staid results of the recruiting or diversity teams while bastardizing the initial reasons for the ERG's existence, doing little to effect real change, and often weaponizing the ERG against employees deemed "too active" in these groups.

ERGs became the vessel to relay all the fears and both subtle and blatant injustices that Black employees deal with in silence while also serving as a source of inside information for executives and the de facto second arm of a company's diversity department. But diversity problems, particularly on an ERG level, can't be solved without executive buy-in and enforcement. This would be demonstrated by having

- an actively involved executive sponsor who supports events, champions the leaders, and advocates for their concerns to their executive peers;
- financial resources and an adequate budget to support the programming the ERG wants to host;
- money to work with diverse suppliers and to hire and retain internal resources to maintain the structures and programs put in place;
- the ability to provide bias training and workshops for proper interviewing skills, especially for middle management, where the majority of the hiring is done, with particular attention to how to interview Black candidates; and
- the support of the communities that participate in these ERGs and whom they serve, particularly for majority-minority cities and neighborhoods.

ERGs were not originally intended for these additional internal roles, let alone to become the public face of external marketing. The first ERG, the National Black Employees Caucus, was started at Xerox in 1970 with the support of the then chief executive officer (CEO), Joseph Wilson. The initial focus of the ERG was internal networking and support. It was a way to cultivate community in a space that may have felt foreign to Black employees. Ten years later, Xerox started the Black Women's Leadership Caucus, choosing to focus on the unique issues Black women face in the workplace and how to appropriately help them ascend the corporate ladder. Over time, ERGs evolved from networking- and support-oriented groups to strategically created ways to provide business value, from ensuring culturally sensitive product development and cultural competency in marketing campaigns to supplier diversity and customer service. Today's big tech companies have turned this idea into something monstrously self-serving and often counterproductive.

When I joined a small fintech company in 2020 as the first legal hire and a member of the executive team, there was a small contingent of Black employees who were a bit fractured. Some would speak to the others, and some distanced themselves, likely out of self-preservation. I'm generally an extrovert at work. I know that's unusual for attorneys, so I made sure to introduce myself to each one of them. It was important for me to let them know that I'm not like the usual executive team members; I'm approachable and down with and for my people. While there wasn't a formal ERG—there were no ERGs at all—we were starting to connect organically: casual meetups in the cafeteria area, going to pick up lunch together. But there wasn't anything formal for the eight of us. So, after the events with George Floyd, we decided to do something about it.

The ERG, initially known as Lift Ev'ry Voice, an abridged name of the Black national anthem, "Lift Ev'ry Voice and Sing," ended up landing the CEO as its executive sponsor. But before that happened, we had to tell him what the title even meant. Just picture a Black woman in leadership and about six (yes, "about" is needed) Black men trying to explain the necessity of a Black national anthem and what it meant to us to a privileged white male CEO in his forties. The confusion and blank stare were expected but still puzzling. The president of the ERG was happy to have the CEO as the executive sponsor because we had a direct line to the decision-maker. *BOOM!* It doesn't get any higher than that. While I could advocate as a member of the leadership team, nothing can trump the CEO hearing your ideas for the company. We were soon proven wrong. "Watch people's feet," my grandmother would say, and she was right.

We had to look at what he was doing, not what he was saying, and once we did, it became all too clear: he was all talk and no show. The ability to commiserate on a group chat and phone calls was the salve we all needed. To talk about how people didn't really want to *do* anything but wanted to *look* like they were doing something, while we *actually* did it, was ripe for analogies of slavery, sharecropping, Jim Crow voting, and servitude. We'd all heard it before from other Black employees. Except, we were tired of it.

Lift Ev'ry Voice had a variety of goals at the time, which were all the more urgent to us because of the momentum of the racial reckoning. We focused on internal support and cultural competency, donations to organizations, and ways to help the Black community outside of the company, especially since most of us were Bay Area natives and had observed the gentrification of our hometowns.

Throughout my time there, I came to realize that while ERG work was supposed to be part of the opportunities the company gave its employees to explore work outside of their day-to-day roles, it functioned more as extra work. It was not positioned as altruistic or an opportunity to grow. It was work they wanted you to do to also serve a purpose for them, and once those needs weren't met, it was seen as a detriment to your core work goals. And once we got into this ERG work, the company looked to us for guidance on everything from allyship workshops to assistance with writing press releases and giving a masterclass on what it's like to be Black in America. Expending this level of emotional labor made me consider if I really wanted to be involved in the ERG. It isn't something you decide on the fly because it could be a catch-22 where the company loves an ERG but then will later argue it's a distraction from the company's real mission and your job. Involvement must be a conscious decision.

I asked myself, *Who wants to do this and why?* It's always a valid question. What do I get out of this arrangement, other than a good conscience?

I can tell you what we don't get out of it: extra compensation via bonuses, equity, or any additional recognition for the work. Only a pat on the back. Well, where I come from, pats on the back don't pay the mortgage. If those extra opportunities were only supposed to take up 20 percent of my time, it soon became clear that 20 percent equated to 120 percent. I was doing 100 percent of my legal work, and then anything else I did would be in addition to my forty-plus work hours a week. This applied to the rest of the ERG members as well. ERG work had a caveat for me, though, since the company saw my participation and leadership of it, being on the leadership team, as a positive because it was a way to quell the other Black workers . . . or so they thought. We weren't getting paid for the work, nor was there a budget for events; they were passion projects and were treated as such. Though this work was encouraged because it made the company look good, managers made it explicitly clear that "promotions and bonuses are not tied to the ERG work." But you better believe the company was quick to promote said work when it benefited them.

One of my colleagues drafted a five-page report on how our policy issues and lack of financial literacy were why our product wasn't understood by Black business owners. He argued for a system change so that we could work with those business owners and presented it to the head of marketing and the CEO. Surprise: they didn't want to use it.

He voiced his exasperation to a few of us. "That was the most frustrating part," he said. "They were willing to tout these things and go to lobbyists and talk about policy and all these projects we were doing, but no one was getting paid to do that work."

Then I went in with the numbers and said I thought this was valuable because we were in the middle of a racial reckoning and the number of small and medium-sized businesses owned by people of color were growing, particularly ones owned by Black women. We'd been leading the charge on that for the last ten years, so this report would be a great way to break into that market and show the company's support, how we valued these businesses, and what we could offer them. That semiswayed them, and I say that because while they saw the importance of what we were saying, they *also* put my colleague who wrote the report on a performance improvement plan. In order to get off it, he was required to revise the report four times according to their parameters or he would be fired.

Well, guess what? He started revising, and in the middle of it, they fired him anyway. Then they still used his report and asked me to sign on at the end. *No, absolutely not. Why do you need me to sign it at all?* This was coming from the CEO, who could sign it himself. And why go to the head of legal? It would make far more sense to go to the head of revenue or the head of marketing assignments, but of course he didn't because neither of those people were Black. His move was utterly transparent, so I made my refusal just as plain. *I see why you're asking me, and I want you to see that. You don't need a Black friend to give you the okay.* I was not going to give my stamp of approval, the corporate version of someone rebutting the accusation of being racist with, "I can't be racist, I have a Black friend." I am *not* that friend.

After that, I went straight to my phone. Thank God for group chats! While at work, we kept our frustrations to ourselves because we didn't want the ERG to lose support or be seen either as disposable or as just a group full of gripes. But we had our own secret text underground railroad where we could voice our irritation with management and the frustration we felt doing work that was wanted for optics but undervalued for the effort we put in. I distinctly remember one exchange where we were able to express how we felt about sentiments shared at an all-hands company meeting. We wouldn't dare try that on the company ERG channel because HR and "allies" had access to it. "Wow. The tone deafness I just heard is astounding. So, because someone may not agree with Black Lives Matter, we shouldn't take a public stance because we don't want to alienate customers or potential customers?" one ERG member texted. "Yeah, well, the message is pretty clear. We don't really care how you feel or about your issues. Just do the work and leave the rest at the door. Pick it up on your way out," said another in response. I opted to respond with what a former colleague from a previous company, Cathy, had said to me: "Don't lose your sanity over these raggedy-ass jobs in 2020. There's enough going on to do that. We know where they stand. Collect your check, go home, and we'll mobilize from there." We all agreed. To this day, that text thread is still active.

Our main objection was that our company was, as my grandfather would say, "writing checks your ass can't cash." Basically, you are saying one thing, but you can't back it up. Now it would be called cosplay. Essentially, our company was allowed to pretend to be supportive of the Black community "when they're not actually supportive," my former colleague said. "It's about managing your image and brand. If I heard the word *brand* one more time . . ." He wasn't alone. We were all tired of hearing it, and the more we heard it, the more we understood that the real value of our presence and our ERG was branding and reputation management.

We weren't alone in our ERG experience at our company. Truth is this has always been the case with most tech ERGs, but since the summer of 2020, ERGs at Verizon and Electronic Arts, which a Yahoo writer led, were repeatedly asked to do the work of others, namely those in positions of power in the C-suite. It became the purview of Black ERGs at many tech companies to host panels on race. Electronic Arts's Black ERG, SoulFi, hosted an entire day of forums, panels, and virtual events for Juneteenth in 2020. The CEO asked the employees to listen to members of SoulFi, putting Black employees on the spot by asking them to share their own personal feelings in a public forum, which can be both intimidating and uncomfortable—not to mention later used against you. But while it had some rocky parts, the event wasn't taken in a bad direction. It wasn't co-opted. But curiously enough, after it concluded, the page announcing the event was erased from the internet, never to be found again. It was like, *We held it once, now we don't ever have to speak of it again.* To that point, there wasn't an announcement of one in 2021 or 2022.

ERGs were also charged with finding tangible actions the company could engage in, whether volunteerism or otherwise, and organizations the company should donate to. Lift Ev'ry Voice made a list of local and national organizations that are doing real work: organizing, registering voters, lobbying Congress. We were later told that the company would not make a donation but match employee donations to those organizations. It felt like a bait and switch and an ill-timed effort to create new diversity initiatives for the brand at large off our backs.

This is where the brand will be made or be dragged. Tech companies can garner earned media and publicity if there is an outward demonstration of engaged employees, especially Black employees, due to the overall dearth of them in the industry. There is a sort of currency and value add in being able to lord that over your competition. It is the corporate equivalent of papering over the cracks in a wall. The problem is companies can't have it both ways, so decision-makers need to choose wisely in terms of what to prioritize. Basically, do you want earned media and to actually do the work inside the company, or do you want paid media and to just put on a show?

While many of us are eager to do the ERG work of rallying around our colleagues and ensuring they have a place to practice advocating for themselves, it can also feel as if you are being voluntold or expected to do the work, especially if you bring it up in any capacity. I've experienced both—the former at Retirement 101 for their website revamp when my identity was boiled down to a minority mom balancing the work-life struggle, and the latter at Facebook and elsewhere. At Retirement 101, the voluntold issue was volatile.

Don't you think that we should have a follow-up to this event next month?

No. But do you?

Well, yeah. I think people will want something.

Okay, then start.

That was every discussion around the ERG: us asking and them voluntelling us to do it. That is something every person in a marginalized group should understand at smaller companies. If you give an idea even tangentially related to ERG work, that company is going to *love* the idea and then *expect* you to be the person to work on it.

At Facebook, it was less voluntelling and more filling in the gaps because no one else would do it. In June 2016, we realized there was nothing for Black Music Month. These events kept happening throughout the year: educational events, fun events like First Fridays, and roundtables where we could just sit and discuss ideas. We were filling in the blanks because we knew no one else would—they would remain empty slots on a calendar if it weren't for the ERG. And it evolved throughout that first year to become a *reliance* on the ERG rather than the company itself to identify what was missing, figure out what to do, plan it to be a success, and keep that success rolling.

The problem here is that ERG work gives the company a pass on doing anything meaningful from a leadership level and doesn't force a company's hand to institute positive change in the diversity of the leadership team. The deeper you dig into ERGs in big tech, the more you see they're being used as a manipulative and exploitative practice. Big tech's dependence on ERGs gives a false impression of progress, with no accountability for leadership. If anything, ERGs discourage these companies from hiring a chief diversity officer, if they don't already have one, by relying on the emotional and unpaid labor of what's likely a small workforce with little to no budget or additional resources. One such company was Slack.

Erica Joy Baker Astrella, an engineer at Beyoncé's Parkwood Entertainment, first made headlines in 2015 while working for Google. Baker Astrella began talking with coworkers on a lazy Sunday about equal pay and asked if they would be open to putting their roles, levels, and salaries in a spreadsheet. It made its way around Google with new contributions resulting in over 1,500 entries initially, and by the time she left, about 5 percent of Googlers had entered their information.[67] What did Baker Astrella get in return? Her manager denying every spot bonus her peers gave to her. A spot bonus is an internal bonus at Google; it's monetary recognition from your peers for a job well done, *but* it has to be approved by a manager. Now, I don't specialize in employment law, but that sounds like blatant retaliation to me. When she moved on to Slack, Baker Astrella's job was 75 percent engineering manager and 25 percent diversity, which she is passionate about, but they should've hired a dedicated diversity director. Baker Astrella and I have talked about the consequences of speaking up and what it's potentially cost us. I remember her sharing with me one day, "When people see me coming, they automatically think the worst [because they think I'm going to talk about some diversity issue], and it usually is. Also, it's exhausting to be the one to shoulder and relay all of this." Baker Astrella eventually moved on to Patreon.

If these companies were smart, they'd realize they should actively partner with Black women, who typically lead these tech ERGs, rather than just tap them as their diversity mascots to act as the "diversity help." They need to support the work of Black ERGs, providing the internal support, financial resources, and external resources needed for them to fulfill their missions. Being a diversity mascot and the only conduit in the face of diversity issues isn't what we all want to do, but it may be the best way to handle things, even if I disagree. The personal toll it took on people such as me and Baker Astrella, whether from dealing with other people's emotions all day or just knowing that when colleagues saw us coming, it was as if we were waving a giant diversity banner over our heads, was exhausting. Often I just wanted to say, "Fuck it, I'm tired."

Some people would point to the fact that the burden of change shouldn't fall on us. I can tell you from personal experience there are many days when I just want to do my job. I want to redline these contracts, take meetings, have light conversation with colleagues, and log off, but that's not where it ends. That's not all that is expected of me or any other ERG leader, especially because we love this work because it is of, from, and for us. While we all generally agree with that sentiment, we also don't have much of a choice since no one else is willing to do the work to advocate for Black employee issues in the workplace, fight for transparency in compensation and work assignments, push equitable promotion processes, etc. My ERG at Retirement 101, for example, worked with recruiting to discuss new schools to look for talent. My grandmother always told me, "To get something you don't have, you have to do something you haven't done." Intentionally recruiting from historically Black colleges and universities (HBCUs) with engineering programs is step one. That said, I don't have a cape on and there's no *S* on my chest. There's only so much I, or any ERG, can do. A company must decide if it wants to invest in ERGs and provide the necessary resources.

When I was on the leadership team for the Black ERG at Facebook, I vehemently lobbied to have a private communication channel on the company network. In its current iteration, the channel was open to anyone, including nonmembers of the ERG, non-Black employees, and managers. This meant certain topics begging to be discussed—from being passed over for a promotion to how to write a more compelling review to microaggressions from team members—were not discussions held out in the open. I went to the rest of the ERG leadership team and asked if they'd support me asking for a private channel. The other channel could still exist, but it would be for more general discussions and event publicity.

"So, what do you guys think? No one is going to have real conversations when they know their boss and teammates can read them," I said to the group. A chorus of "I agree" went around the conference room table to enthusiastically support the message that, according to the head of diversity, "the [private] channel should be created for Black employees, but the original Black@ channel should remain and be open to all." However, the head of diversity continued, "Pitching it to the diversity team, it was met with the response that, 'We should not have separate channels, because it's fostering segregation, and allies wouldn't want to be excluded, and they can't be proper allies if they aren't allowed to participate.'" Thus, this perspective forced us to allow non-Black employees into the conversation on the needs of Black people, which was hard enough for me to reconcile with allowing the ever-looming possibility of such non-Black "allies" co-opting a space that should have been private in the first place. You can see how this would be counterproductive.

During the 2016 presidential race, we hosted both conservatives and liberals at Facebook, but any topic concerning either of the candidates could easily be misconstrued. It was a polarizing time. After one event focused on Hillary Clinton, some people came out of the woodwork, claiming we were spending too much time on her and were not giving equal time or access to the other side. So, Facebook hosted a group of conservative politicians and activists. No harm, no foul. After that event and after Mike Brown was murdered, we welcomed Black Lives Matter activists on campus, who wrote the saying on a chalkboard at the entrance of one of the buildings. It was later crossed out and "Trump" was written next to it. People were horrified, and Mark Zuckerberg sent out an internal memo. I asked the diversity team about having a town hall because there was clearly some friction about why we were even hosting the activists and why they were welcomed. That request was denied. We rewrote "Black Lives Matter" on the chalkboard, and again, it was crossed out and replaced with "Trump." At that point, Zuckerberg wrote an internal note saying he wouldn't tolerate such behavior. Then it happened a *third* time. He wrote another note, and I went back to the diversity team about having a town hall. This time it was granted.

The town hall was optional, which meant that only people who already cared about such issues or self-identified allies were going to attend. So, in some respects, we were going to be preaching to the choir, which we understood. Most importantly though, leadership was there in full force. However, an event that was organized in the hopes of explaining the feelings and treatment of Black employees, both internally and externally, turned into me and a bunch of our ERG leadership comforting white people who were seemingly having a contest to prove who was the greatest ally. After comforting a third white woman crying after taking the mic to discuss her fight against racial injustice, I realized we weren't really going to get anywhere. What should have been a talk about personal experiences and suggestions for activating one's allyship, like taking actual action and not just hashtag activism and profile pictures, turned into a praise session for white folks doing the bare minimum. They stood up and gave each other rounds of applause for having hard conversations with their prejudiced family members about the election and reading certain books. It felt like diversity theater.

This is the dark side of ERGs: using Black employees for show-and-tell without any benefit to us. What starts as an organic need for community and support can easily turn into a company-driven publicity initiative. The true value of an ERG is using it to advance the needs of the employees and to consult with them when making policy changes or reviewing products and ads before they are shipped, but more often it turns into trotting us out when it's convenient to brand the company as inclusive, as opposed to being truly inclusive and listening to Black people. Big tech can't make Black women invisible internally when it comes to projects, equitable pay, and promotion and then make Black women visible when it's convenient to make the company look good, leveraging their ERG labor with no credit or compensation. Black women are tired of doing more for less and having our kindness and willingness to work hard for our community taken as weakness. Those days are over.

CHAPTER 6

This Is Why I Feel Like an Outsider: And Leave Once I've Worked Long Enough to Put You in My Résumé

> You use up everything you've got trying to give everybody what they want.
> —Nina Simone, singer and civil rights activist

When I joined Facebook, the first thing I did was look for my tribe. It's not like I expected to meet tons of Black people there; I had read the company's diversity report. I knew what I was getting into. But soon, I joined the Black employee resource group (ERG). Through actively participating, being outspoken about how we could improve programming, and helping steer some events, I eventually led it with a team of seven other people. The programming we put on made my heart sing, from a Black Lives Matter panel with Ben Crump to a "real talk" session with summer interns and the first official gathering of every Black employee at headquarters for Black Leadership Day. The name has since changed, but what mattered most was that we created a sense of home for Black people who worked there.

The events were just as much a communal and social outlet as a professional development space. The need to find a space to belong in the midst of what can be an intimidating and unwelcoming environment was deeply felt among Black employees, particularly for the transplants who were new to the area and didn't know where to go or what to do.

The first questions the ERG usually fielded were "Where can I get my hair cut/done?" "Where is a good church?" and "Where do people hang out?" We wanted to make sure Black people felt welcomed and could have a reprieve at work if needed. This is also good for retention: if people can't find a sense of personal engagement within the workplace, then they need to find one outside of it, meaning they spend less time at work events. If employees cannot find a home outside of work, then you're in trouble—they're more likely to quit and move elsewhere. Creating that sense of home, even just through the ERG, encouraged greater ties to the company for marginalized employees and an incentive to work harder, stay longer, and motivate others in the same vein. These actions and emotions influence every key metric of a company's success: revenue, profitability, customer experience, morale, retention, and more. Any company committed not just to diversity but also to its own success would seek either to create a sense of home for their employees or to provide ERGs the necessary resources to do so because it's good for business all the way around.

I recognize that we shouldn't have had to create a space for ourselves to find that sense of community and acceptance, but the truth is if we hadn't, we simply wouldn't have found it. When people talk about diversity, they get stuck on numbers and statistics, what I call "diversity bean counting." They check the boxes: x number of women, Asians, Blacks, Latinx, LGBTQ+, people with disabilities, and so on. But true diversity is about more than just numbers; it has to come with a heavy dose of inclusion. That means a company must intentionally create and foster a culture where we feel we have a seat at the table, not just entry to the room to watch as a bystander.[68] Sometimes, that's all they're willing to give up.

Tech companies might find me and other Black women and convince us to join their ranks, but if they don't retain us, they can't grow us, and if they don't grow us, they won't keep us. They can't keep us if we don't see ourselves reflected inside or *outside* the work community. See, white employees are more likely to enjoy an instant sense of community when working for a tech company because they are surrounded by people just like them. They don't need to find themselves in the community outside the workspace because the inside community already reflects them. We Black women, though, only have the outside community to look to.

Yet big tech hiring practices for employees and suppliers have had deep consequences for the fabric of the surrounding communities, especially where people of color live. The homogeneity of the tech scene has now become so vast that it's spilled into once robust, diverse cities and displaced the existing communities through gentrification. What were once mom-and-pop staples have now been replaced with beer gardens that only play pop music, an unspoken but clear signal as to who their desired clientele is.

I was born in Oakland, California, at the Kaiser Permanente Hospital, where I also had both of my children. Save for short stints in Los Angeles and Washington, DC, I've spent most of my life here. But today, as I walk around Oakland, large swaths of it look completely unfamiliar to me. Just three blocks down the street from that hospital, a new mixed-use retail and residential shopping area has been erected with an organic grocery chain, Sprouts, and a Starbucks as its anchors. Another few blocks down that same street, new tech companies, like Square, driven out by the higher rent in San Francisco and the Peninsula, are setting up shop everywhere. New restaurants and bars have opened to entertain their workers. Never in a million years did I think I'd see a bar with an indoor bocce ball court full of hipsters in the middle of downtown Oakland. Excuse me, "Uptown Oakland," as they have tried to rebrand it.

For Black women in particular, this gentrification has meant that not only are we uncomfortable at work, surrounded by people who don't look like us, but now we also don't feel comfortable *outside* of work either. That leaves us feeling uncomfortable everywhere. The secret among Black women in Silicon Valley was that you came to work for one of the large tech companies, did your time, and stayed long enough to get your résumé stamped. Then you got the hell out of there fast to Atlanta; Houston; Washington, DC; Baltimore; or New York. If we don't feel a sense of community, we will leave as soon as we can. If tech companies could provide a way to create an inclusive community on their campuses and encourage inclusivity through lobbying for resources in the communities where their employees live, that would go a long way to encourage us to stay well past that résumé stamp and, thereby, impact the companies, the local communities they inhabit, and the global public.

Time and time again, tech companies fail to create environments and communities, both internally and externally, that tether people of color to the enterprise. It's a recipe for failing to keep me and other Black women among their ranks. Once, I was working for a company that was seemingly perfect. The office was in Oakland, about two blocks from my kids' school. I liked the chief executive officer (CEO), whom I'd grown to have a personal relationship with and could go to directly, and

I enjoyed the legal team. Until one day I hit a breaking point. I was supporting a sales deal for a perky blond-haired, blue-eyed white woman, let's call her "Karen," who always talked about allyship and women's solidarity around the office but was extremely aggressive and could be nasty when she didn't get her way. I'd had a front-row seat to her getting snarky with others on prior occasions. Everything was always someone else's fault. One early afternoon we got on a call with the opposing counsel and sales head, and she did not tell me that she had lied about the terms she was attempting to shoehorn into our agreement in order to appease the opposing sales head. Well, not on my watch, because we were hampered by certain federal regulations. Toward the end of the call, we agreed to regroup once opposing counsel had redlined the agreement to reflect our changes and the salespeople had come to some sort of compromise. As soon as she pressed the red button to hang up the speakerphone, the situation went all the way left.

In the fluorescent light of the conference room, I noticed Karen was scowling. Her upper lip was curled ever so slightly, and her blue eyes were squinting at me. Then she did the unthinkable. She threw the pen she had in her hand across the table at me. Now, I'd seen her get smart with folks but never violent. Throwing a pen to hit someone is legally assault. Nevertheless, she persisted. She stood up, raised her finger, face fully flushed, and screamed as close to my face as she could get across a wide conference room table, "Why couldn't you just close the damn deal? Just do what I say!" I was completely taken aback, thinking, *I know the fuck you didn't,* but I knew I couldn't yell back at her because she would run out of the room crying and make me the villain when she, literally, was the aggressor. I've seen that movie numerous times, bought the popcorn and a keepsake from the theater.

"What in the entire *fuck* is your problem?!" I asked after dodging her pen like Neo in *The Matrix*.

"Why couldn't you just close this deal? It's almost end of quarter, and I was banking on this."

"Then you should've thought about that before you lied and put me in a compromising position. I took an ethical oath to uphold the law, not actively break it because someone needs to hit their quota. I'm a steward of the company, not your personal attorney."

"Ugh, God! Just do what I asked you to do!"

"Let me tell you something"—which if you know Black women, when we say this, it's a warning shot and the kiss of death in one—"if you ever yell at me and speak to me like this again, or furthermore, throw an object at me because you didn't get your way, I will drag you up and down Grand Avenue by your hair. Throwing things at a person is assault, so I'd be well within my rights to exercise self-defense, and I'm not afraid to get fired for that. Are we clear?" I didn't wait for an answer and left the room. To this day, it is the most unprofessional thing I've ever done. Having someone throw something at you at work when you're at a breaking point will do that to you, I guess. It still makes me cringe, and in my head, I could hear my grandmother's voice telling me she's disappointed and that I represent us all—meaning both my family and my race—when I go outside every day, and I had acted in a stereotypical fashion that made us look bad. I knew I had to get in front of the situation before Karen could spin this to make me appear violent for no reason.

I went to find Karen's boss, a kind and funny Indian man with whom I had a great rapport. After doing a lap around the fourth floor, I found him. "Hey, I need to tell you something," I started.

"Sure, what's up, Bärí?"

"So, I just got out of this negotiation with Karen."

"Okay, did you close it, or how did it go?"

"No, we didn't because she wasn't honest about our offerings and got upset with me for telling her we couldn't sign off on them. She then yelled and threw a pen at me and I told her, 'That is assault, and if you hit me, it's a problem.' I finished by saying I'd drag her up and down Grand Avenue. I just want to be honest. Mostly because I meant it. If she does anything else physical to me again, I have no qualms defending myself."

"Well, hell. It shouldn't have to come to that. I hope we can still get this done."

"No, it shouldn't. So you should speak to your subordinate. I don't know if you're pressuring her, if she just really needs this commission, she's just ambitious, or if this is her general demeanor. Either way, it won't work with me. But let me know what else you need."

It felt cathartic to tell him this, but it also was embarrassing. I was raised better than how I behaved. I never wanted to do anything that would jeopardize my professional reputation, but I'm keenly aware that I can't work in a place that literally doesn't feel physically safe and where someone feels justified in assaulting you because you didn't give them the answer they wanted. Another truism my mother taught me: "Just because you didn't like the answer doesn't mean you didn't receive one."

That was the moment I broke a glass ceiling only to find myself standing on a glass cliff, and it wasn't the first or the last time I'd be standing on the edge, hanging on by my toes. The glass cliff, sometimes called the Black bluff, is the idea that women, particularly

Black women and other women of color, ascend to leadership positions during times of organizational crisis when the risk of failure or burnout is high. This is a notion built upon the idea of what happens when you win a pie-eating contest and are rewarded with more pie and a round of congratulations that doesn't seem genuine. Why would I want *more* when I just gobbled down an entire pie in under a minute? I don't want more work. The glass cliff works the same way. The woman is then promoted into a role that is hard to succeed in. It's akin to being set up for failure. This phenomenon results in disproportionate blame and criticism, higher rates of failure, and damage to their professional reputation. It's company politics and backroom dealing with a side of back-channeling on steroids. Navigating just one of those workplace obstacle courses is like running blindfolded through a barbed-wire maze, let alone navigating all three elements at once. In the case of placing Black women teetering on the cliff, it may even be a matter of attribution or confirmation bias, or worse, both.

The cliff is usually invisible, but there are generally warning signs of the rocky terrain ahead. The most commonly noted are

- unimportance—a role that's been created without sufficient resources or support in order to check a box either for diversity purposes or as a formality;
- impossible tasks—challenges are great, the chance for failure is high, and assignments carry unrealistic expectations and no real leadership support;
- and tasks that are controversial, inherently difficult, countercultural, and come with built-in resistance.[69]

Worst-case scenario, the cliff you're standing on is composed of all three. Legal sits squarely in the middle of all three categories. Just my luck.

Right before the COVID shutdown, I was sitting alone in a conference room in San Francisco, with a great view of the bay, when I realized I was standing on the steepest, most fragile glass cliff I'd ever been on. Quietly gathering my thoughts at the end of my second week of being in a new leadership role at Retirement 101 and looking around the room at a whiteboard full of notes in different color-coded phrases that read like a foreign language, I realized that I hadn't been told the full truth about the scope of my role. A mixture of shock, panic, and fierce anger washed over me to the point that I looked at my reflection in the glass and saw my face was flushed. I was literally hot with anger and emotion.

I turned to my meeting companion and smiled. "May I ask you a somewhat personal question? I know I've only been here a little over a week, but I feel like I'm not privy to some information around the nature of these meetings and any assignments coming out of them."

My colleague, we'll call him Russell, smiled back. "Sure, go ahead," he assured me.

I took a deep breath and sighed. "You aren't coming back from sabbatical, are you?" Meeting with him every day for the past week and change for three or more hours a day didn't seem like something a normal executive team member did. Frankly, when I asked others, they'd said they hadn't had these meetings, so something was clearly out of the ordinary here, and I wanted to know what it was and why.

"No. When I go out next month, it isn't my intention to come back, and you'll be taking over these compliance officer duties," he said. My face slowly melted from my warm grin to a neutral state.

"No one told you I was leaving on sabbatical or about transitioning?" he asked. "I told everyone before Thanksgiving break that I wasn't planning on coming back."

"No, Russell. No one told me that. That's actually material information because it significantly changes the scope of the work I'll be doing and how much of a lift it is. This is a highly regulated space, and you really don't want someone playing around with SEC compliance that is a novice." My heart sank. I'd been in this situation before when something seemingly too good to be true was. Going into a role with one hand tied behind my back was a recipe for disaster—not just for what the company needed but for me personally. I left that night feeling defeated, and I hadn't even finished week two.

I gleaned two huge revelations from that conversation, and they weren't unique to me. First, I was yet again being set up to do more work for less. Taking on the role of head of legal did not encompass the duties of the compliance officer as a colleague was currently filling that role. Considering I'd interviewed and secured the position after Thanksgiving—December, to be precise—the company was well aware of Russell's imminent departure and chose to hide it. Those additional duties weren't even so much as mentioned in the interviews or after I accepted the offer, and they should've been disclosed during the interview process as it likely would've changed either my decision or theirs. The work of the head of legal is not the same as that of the compliance officer, and both are full-time jobs. That brings me to the second point: I am literally doing more for less money. When I negotiated my salary and equity options, I wasn't aware that I'd be doing the equivalent of two full-time jobs. I was at a disadvantage in negotiating because of information that was willfully kept from me. Not cool. Can't win for losing in this scenario, twice over.

I went home feeling dejected, duped, angry, and stuck. I opened my door, changed into a trusty sweatsuit, sat on the edge of my bed, and just let tears stream down my face while the house was quiet and no one else was home. Even still, I locked the door and modulated my volume. No need to scare my kids in case they came home and looked for me. Then I began second-guessing myself. *Did I not ask the right questions? What should I have asked that I neglected to? Did they just lie to me and play in my face? How do I fix this? How can I make them understand the inequity of this?* My mind was racing with many questions but few answers. I also knew that anything I asked could, and likely would, be misinterpreted as me being "difficult" or "ungrateful," or worse, not deserving to be there.

What transpired was a back-and-forth for months over hiring people to build out the compliance function so that I could focus on legal. Both sides were frustrated, and it was the first time I questioned my capabilities. Even though I have never suffered from impostor syndrome, I did feel like I was receiving impostor treatment, through no fault of my own. I was being treated as if I should just be happy to be there and not question the hiring process or what was being asked of me, even as I told them I didn't have the expertise or experience to provide it. I was met with a constant refrain of "Oh wow, we didn't know it was that different or that difficult." "Does this really necessitate the work of a whole other employee?" "You sure you can't just fold this into your regular work?" The answer was clear: "No, I can't because it's a second *unpaid* job."

In my heart, I'd made a decision. However, being raised by a single mother on a public school teacher's salary had my head saying something different. But for my peace of mind, I knew what I needed to do. At the end of the second week, I asked to speak to the head of finance, whom I reported to, the following Monday. I walked into the conference room, laptop in hand, and told him that I didn't think I was set up for success and didn't think this was the right role for me. I also raised my grievances about withholding material information that would have altered my decision. Because it was my birthday the next week and I had a long-planned trip to Paris to celebrate, I wanted all of this off my conscience and fully planned to slide the computer across the table and leave on a positive note. Instead, I was met with a barrage of assurances that I was right for the role, they'd find the help I needed, and it would end up being great for me and for the company. In hindsight, this was gaslighting. Very polite gaslighting, but gaslighting all the same to get me to stay dog-paddling in the deep end of this pool. In the moment, it felt like a vote of confidence, and to the credit of the head of finance, I think he believed what he was saying too. He was a sincere, sweet guy who was the same age as me and had been put in a position that was between a rock and a hard place. Whatever I decided would also weigh and reflect on him. He told me to take the time I needed to think and enjoy my trip, but not to resign and they'd have people for me to interview within ten days. I agreed.

Fast-forward eleven months, and I was still at my limit on tackling a role that just wasn't meant for me and was not a successful proposition. After only receiving one other person to help handle the compliance function and limited use of outside counsel, I couldn't dig myself out of the hole left in Russell's absence—a hole that leadership was aware of prior to my joining the company—and I knew I wasn't getting good internal traction due to resistance. Of course, a fall woman was needed. Not surprisingly, beating my head against a wall for nearly a year proved to be frustrating, and I knew I couldn't be successful. Adding to that confirmation, I'd watched the CEO continuously shed members of our executive team before they'd reached a year in tenure, and most notably, they were parents of young children who either didn't have childcare or whose children needed to be homeschooled during the pandemic. Realizing that my only fault in this was saying yes to a role that I didn't have all the information about made me understand that I was being treated like an impostor because I'd been set up to act like one.

Impostor treatment is what happens when you don't exhibit impostor syndrome when others expect you to, but they treat you as if you should. They clock when you get to the office and when you leave. They observe how you interact with others. They police your speech and tone. They find reasons to question your decision-making and method of work. All of this had happened before, so I should have seen the signs, but maybe I chose to ignore them, and as with a bad boyfriend, I thought things would change. They didn't. I know my worth. I know what I asked for. I know the treatment I should've had, and as my mom said, I "fell for the okey-doke."

The way this is approached, which again is analogous to winning a pie contest, is still not how I would do it. Why give someone more pie when they are already past the point of full? Reward them with something else. Unfortunately, that's not the way it works in the office because the way people look at Black women in the workplace is different from how they look at others. Really different. When we seemingly do the impossible and solve a long-standing problem, we shouldn't immediately receive another one to solve, but it doesn't matter because we are viewed as the world's mule. Companies see a problem, phrase it nicely to make it more palatable, and then ship it off to us so that whatever needs to get done is accomplished, and it doesn't matter if we want to do it or not. Because we allegedly didn't get our jobs due to meritocracy, because we aren't typically a natural "culture fit," we have to constantly go above and beyond to prove our position, our salary, our justification for being in the company, and our overall worth on an everyday basis. That is exhibited constantly while standing on the ledge of the glass cliff. *Great. Give her something else to solve. Let's see if she can do it.*

The problem with the glass cliff is not just unmet expectations, both personal and professional, but the lingering effects it has on a person. Burnout is real, and I know I felt it more than I was ready to admit at the time. All the classic signs were there. Instead of hopping out of bed when my alarm went off, I dreaded getting up. I said a prayer before booting up my computer and often muttered, "What fresh hell is gonna greet me today?" when I opened my email inbox. I tried to tell myself it was just a vestige of the pandemic and working while also being a part-time kindergarten teacher. I knew that wasn't the case when I began to dread every single thing related to my job. Talking to coworkers who wouldn't take my legal advice. Team meetings that constantly moved the goalposts for the definition of "progress." Activities that were supposedly optional, but you always knew someone would notice your absence. And we were doing all of this on lockdown. I didn't look forward to any part of my job. It became so debilitating that when I did have a moment off, in between proctoring kindergarten and my daily workload, all I wanted to do was lock myself in a room and be alone. Truth be told, considering what I'd learned about the role prior to the pandemic, I would've wanted that even without the pandemic. I was drained when I hit the door when I began working there even before lockdown started. The only thing I found myself compelled to do after work was immediately change into sweats, make sure my kids ate something, and then zone out in front of a Bravo marathon to turn my brain off.

As someone who hopped on a conference call three hours

after I delivered my daughter a few years earlier, this was completely out of character. It was hard to admit that I didn't find joy or purpose in my job. And it was causing me not to find joy in life, period. It was clear to me not only that I'd been set up to do two roles at once, one of which had never been mentioned and that I didn't have experience in, but also that I was expected to perfect it in record time. Impossible. Everyone could tell I was irritable, argumentative, and desperately trying to control something within my purview. Even that didn't make me feel better. I knew I was in trouble. This wasn't just burnout but depression.

I'm not alone in this. Those brunch conversations I used to have with my girlfriends who also worked in tech were transported to group texts and us eating together on Zoom, still sharing the same stories. What we needed was true support, which was in short supply. Some of us had kids, and some were single and child-free. The level of support remained the same before and after the additional stress of the pandemic. The constant was that wealthy, privileged white men with stay-at-home wives—who often had nannies of color who were abandoning their own kids to rough it while they worked for these people—didn't understand why we couldn't perform at prepandemic levels.

The reasons why not are simple: Black women are seldom given inadequate resources and support, and more often than not, we're expected to wrangle an impossible task. Add the pressure of being unable to take the bad things that predated us and turn them around quickly and then being blamed for that failure, and we know our future career prospects are put on ice. Shonda Rhimes captures this perfectly in her book *Year of*

Yes, writing, "You don't get second chances. Not when you're an F.O.D. [first, only different]. Second chances are for future generations. That is what you are building when you are an F.O.D. Second chances."[70] That means don't screw this up for the rest of us. Kyra Kyles, the CEO of YR Media, said that Black women are "so worried about excelling because we realize we're not being judged as individuals; we're being judged as part of a collective,"[71] as representatives of the whole of Black people—just like my grandmother and mother told me.

We need the same room for failure and the ability to bounce back as our white male counterparts. We need to have "real intentionality" and "fair parameters" established.[72] We are more than the proverbial "Clean Up Woman" in Betty Wright's R&B classic. Black women "should be brought in when things are going well, so that we can take it to the next level,"[73] not just when something is on a downward slide so that we're blamed for its inevitable failure. Being bogged down by cleaning up messes we didn't make ensures we can't grow. But there are investors, employees, and board members expecting employee growth, and they're not acknowledging that we were "brought in literally to clean up someone else's mess."[74]

When Black women do reach higher positions, we often ask ourselves, *Was it worth all of this?* There were many late nights and early mornings when I agonized over the answer at Retirement 101. In her book *The Memo*, Minda Harts says those nights and mornings are emblematic of the workplace trauma and microaggressions many Black women experience in their careers. She notes that we are laying the groundwork so that it will be seen as palatable for us in the long term.[75] If we make others look good, then, perhaps, they will make us look good at some later point, right? Maybe they will. Most of the time they don't. And that isn't sufficient. Neither is putting us in a role and giving us the title, especially if it's double the work and not compensated as such. Proper allocation of resources, dollars, and sponsorships must be available in order for an employee to be successful. "Equally important," as reported in *Forbes*, "is having adequate resources, whether it's an actual budget to create and run a team, hire an executive coach, or pursue professional development opportunities, not to mention mental and emotional support."[76] Most of all, we need more transparency. "Transparency about what's involved in a role could go a long way toward increasing recruitment and retention"[77]—something that was sorely lacking in my experience and led to complete burnout, which manifested mentally, emotionally, and physically.

Like a lot of my contemporaries in tech, I bought into the strong Black woman trope, the "perception that Black women are naturally strong, resilient, . . . self-sacrificing,"[78] and able to handle anything thrown at them. This was incredibly harmful to my mental health and to the health of my girlfriends in similar situations. Per a 2014 study in the *Journal of Black Psychology*, trying to embody this trope is harmful to our mental health. The study revealed that faithful devotion to this trope "increase[s] the relationship between stress and depressive symptoms" for Black women.[79] I can't speak for anyone else, but I know that was true for me. "Additionally, the pressure to be perceived as perfect and 'have it all together' can lead many Black women in leadership positions to put themselves and their well-being on the bottom of their already lengthy to-do lists."[80] Again, guilty.

Black women are attributed superhuman abilities but none of the support to accompany that. There is no grace afforded us to say, "I need to take a break," or to say that we are logging off for a truly unplugged vacation to recharge. Personally, I've never done that for any vacation. I live in fear of the perception that I'm not available, even when I've rightfully taken time off. By contrast, I've had (white male) coworkers who routinely do nothing but post pictures on Facebook and Instagram displaying the great time they're having, ignoring emails while on vacation. If only.

There is verifiable grooming of Black women not to cause trouble and to just be grateful for what we get while never appearing dissatisfied or wanting more. That mindset keeps us packed into certain work profiles, forcing us to bend like pretzels to do what they want us to do until we get fed up. We have to disabuse ourselves of that notion and ask ourselves, "What do I know I deserve, and is this providing that?" If it's not, look elsewhere. We may not have the same range of job mobility as others, but corporate jobs aren't the only option. With the exodus from corporate work to entrepreneurship and a "choose your own adventure" spirit, "we don't have to make everything work. We can actually go places [or *create* places] where we can thrive and feel supported."[81] I've seen many go into freelancing and consulting, and still others take completely different paths. Some find another corporate job, but a good number of them—at least from my circles—decide they want to find a way to work for themselves so that they don't have to fit in somebody else's box. As my mom and grandmother say, "Everywhere you go, there you are." So, if the issue is always going to be how to assimilate into another office, or the standard of behavior or presence is based on what a white man thinks it should be, that's not going to change depending upon the office. People will still expect the same of me, and whether I provide it or not, the answer is going to be the same because there I go and there I am. If you jump ship to another office but the requirements or expectations are the same, then what are you really doing that's different?

The lesson I learned during the pandemic, which was a shared lesson discussed on Zoom brunches, is if the position you're in no longer serves you, and you are able to, walk away. Don't let being "an example for the race" force you into staying in a situation that is causing you harm and doesn't allow you to make a decision that is right for you. Simply put by my former colleague Cathy, "Don't lose your mind and sacrifice your spirit for these raggedy-ass jobs." Sprinkling Black girl magic shouldn't cost your sanity or your soul. Amen.

CHAPTER 7
This Is What True Allyship Looks Like

> If you have come here to help me, you are wasting your time. But if you have come because your liberation is bound up with mine, then let us work together.
> —Aboriginal activists group, Queensland, 1970s, delivered by Lilla Watson

Big tech pantomimes performative allyship on a routine basis. That train is never late. In fact, it is typically early. Performative allyship is a broad, grand gesture that is purely symbolic but does nothing to improve the plight of the people it claims to advocate for. You see it routinely on social media platforms on Martin Luther King Jr. (MLK) Day, during Pride Month, whenever there's a "blackout" day for a protest, and on Juneteenth. Well-meaning companies will change their avatars and backgrounds to show support for the Black community. They will speak out via press releases in support of racial justice to score public relations (PR) points and espouse their company's commitment to diversity, yet these same companies continue to keep hidden their employee diversity numbers and leveling—in some cases, even internally. They don't hire Black executives or equally pay Black employees, don't promote Black employees at the same rate as their white colleagues doing the same work, don't have Black board members, don't listen to concerns regarding microaggressions and discrimination, and were completely silent about racism up until their hands were forced in the summer of 2020. It isn't true allyship if you only speak out when your back is against a wall. It isn't true allyship if you speak only when *not* saying something would look worse.

In the summer of 2020, when the nation was embroiled in a racial reckoning several centuries overdue, I had to *tell* a tech chief executive officer (CEO) to say something to his employees in the wake of the murder of George Floyd and the subsequent protests.

"Well, I never thought about it," he replied when I made the suggestion to him. He sighed as if I was giving him an optional homework assignment he had no interest in completing. He didn't need the extra credit for his grade.

"With all due respect, you have the luxury not to," I reminded him.

After I worked to coach him on what tone he should strike, he sent me and the head of human resources (HR) a draft of the company-wide email he planned to send, asking for feedback. While his intentions were good, or at least I hoped so, there was no real passion or feeling behind the note. It was mechanical, rote, unfeeling. The head of HR and I hopped on the phone to discuss it.

"Hey, Bärí, did you see the edits he made?"

"Yeah," I started. "I saw them and they are completely robotic. He took out everything that had some emotional touchpoint. Makes me wonder what's the point?"

"Do you think we should add some things back in?"

"I totally think we should. Otherwise, this is incredibly dry and won't land," I assured her.

We kept chatting, and I added some edits and sent it back to him, only to receive a ping moments later: "I took out emotion purposefully. Can we just get this done?! I want to schedule to send it because I'm taking tomorrow off."

I could feel my entire body tense up from my annoyed tic where I vigorously shake my right foot from side to side, my face grimacing. Even though we were on the phone, I could still hear my mom's voice in my head, as always: "Fix your face!" So, I responded, "Just don't send anything then." He asked why not. "Well," I said, "because this reads like you don't actually care. That's fine if that's how you feel. But it would be better if you do nothing than send something that can be interpreted as callous." He sent the note anyway without our edits. As predicted, the internal response, particularly from Black employees, was, "Why did he even send this out?"

I hate to say, "I told you so."

Nothing says *I am an ally and care about Black lives and systemic racism in criminal justice* like telling someone to speed up writing an email feigning empathy for a cause you aren't invested in. This same CEO later signed up to be the executive sponsor for the Black employee resource group (ERG) at his company. It's totally fine that he chose to do that, but he wasn't really invested in being involved and what that entailed. Instead, he'd rather parade around the office or sit in the big glass conference room in his standard issue Silicon Valley uniform of choice. Daily. The care he put into crafting an odd Jobs/Zuckerberg uniform to save time so the company could move at "maximum velocity" seemed more important than diversity or showing basic empathy. If you don't want to do something, don't do it. We can tell. That's the way that things happen, and if you aren't really about that life, we'll know. So don't do it. We can see it.

The truth is *allyship* is not a noun; it's a verb. Allyship requires self-reflection, active listening, and self-education to better understand different perspectives. There is a performative dance that people do, and it's not what Black people who are really doing the work do. So, there may be a Juneteenth-themed meal in the company cafeteria. Ask most of the people sitting here, eating, stereotypically, fried chicken, mac and cheese, collard greens, and sweet potato pie, what the day actually means, what it's for. That goes double for companies that are now giving it as a holiday. You will get puzzling glances and people just happy to have an extra day in the weekend to go to the beach or barbeque. The companies are acknowledging something in solidarity, which, likely, the C-suite and the rest of the employees don't understand, in the name of "allyship." Also, we eat more than just one meal! I made it a personal rule *never* to eat fried chicken in front of others at work, just to prove that point. My husband is incredibly amused by this and tells me, "Go on and eat it. They know you eat it. We all know."

I'm cautious of looking or acting like they think I will because if I do, they'll pat themselves on the back for accepting me and my bringing my "whole self to work." If I don't, it's great because "She's one of us, not like the others." In each scenario, folks think they are being allies. Have I heard both of these statements before? Yes. Do both make me tired? Yes, but in different ways. Even your lunch choice will dictate whether you are too seen or unseen. It is exhausting to have to explain to someone that, really, I do *not* like watermelon. Even with salt on it. The many years I've spent having my mother force-feed me a piece of salted watermelon . . . still don't love it. While this may look like a sharing of culture to some, it can actually come off as patronizing and culturally tone-deaf.

The problem is big tech wants to coast on their laurels of ERG work, the occasional donation to a particular cause or organization, sending an email to acknowledge Black History Month, and a themed lunch, and then their work is done. That is . . . until they want to declare actual allyship.

Well, first, you must define what *allyship* even means. The definition depends on who you ask, but the answers generally hold common themes or actions. To some, it can mean just what I noted above: performative and one-time-only transactions or photo ops to bring awareness to an issue or show support for a marginalized group. To others, it means actually having empathy that turns into action to right a wrong for a marginalized group you are not part of. Effective allyship requires people to understand and acknowledge some hard truths. The first step is understanding the key concepts of allyship—privilege, power, oppression, and marginalization—and how they work together. For some companies, from leadership to entry-level employees, admitting they have a measure of privilege and power just due to their immutable traits is hard to swallow. It's akin to telling someone born on third base that they didn't actually hit the home run they thought they did. I can understand the issue. You are telling me that I actually wasn't a beneficiary of the meritocracy I espouse everyone else should be held to. It's humbling. People don't like to be humbled.

One of the hardest parts in this process is realizing that you may be complicit in wrongdoing... that is, if you didn't actively do it yourself. The second hardest part: How did you exacerbate or promote the misdeeds? And the worst part is the third part: Did you actively promote this as a positive? I'll save you two minutes of googling. Yes. An example might be saying a backhanded compliment like, "Oh, look, you made it against the odds." That's one way to view it. Yes, most people might expect that would be a positive viewpoint to share. It is... on the surface. However, if you ignore racial issues around socioeconomic circles, finances, educational opportunities, network access, and colorism, it can all be seen as a wash, while also making that person "special" and "different"—"not like the others." Worse yet, some employees think they are active allies, but if you ask Black women colleagues, they will vehemently disagree.

In 2021 the *Women in the Workplace* study by LeanIn.org and McKinsey & Company surveyed sixty-five thousand employees from a little over four hundred companies. They reported that 77 percent of white employees consider themselves allies for women of color, yet only 39 percent said they follow the adage "If you see something, say something" when they observed discrimination, and only 21 percent advocated for advancement or new opportunities for women of color. Notwithstanding the 77 percent of white employees viewing themselves as allies, per the 2020 iteration of the same study, only 45 percent of Black women believed they had strong allies at work. Furthermore, only about a quarter of Black women believed it's mostly accurate that Black women have strong allies in their workplace.[82] The overwhelming majority of us don't believe we have allies, which isn't a shocker.

I've experienced the phenomenon of white folks calling themselves allies; most often, white women feel a sense of camaraderie due to shared gender. Sharing a marginalized identity would seemingly make one empathetic to others and lend itself to understanding. Until it doesn't. When I was head of legal at a start-up, I had to work quite often with the head of people, whom I affectionately referred to as "Workplace Wendy," an affable white woman. We worked together regarding performance improvement plans, separation paperwork, offer letters, and any personnel complaints. Often we would be in meetings and she would eagerly try to engage me around personal topics, which initially felt friendly, but the more it went on, the more it felt like a passive-aggressive way to go on a fact-finding mission. One day while we were in a meeting I had organized to discuss a process I'd created for HR requests and contract review, I admired her freshly dyed pink-and-purple ombré hair. The conversation quickly devolved from talking about hair changes and clothing preferences into a passive-aggressive discussion about the new processes I had put in place.

"This is so great! I know this will help us get organized. I just wish that I had more input and that we could review this a little later."

"Why?" I asked. I hadn't collaborated with her on any of her HR policies, even the ones I told her she should ensure the company has, as this was her first time heading the department and not just handling recruiting.

"Well, I just think I should look at it with fresh eyes a little later, and then see if I think I can add something to improve the contracts process. Maybe also show John and Sharon."

Again, "Why?" I asked. One of the leaders in product, let's call him "John," and a leader in the design department, let's call her "Sharon," didn't typically make contractual policies or determine the appropriate process for requesting, retaining, and tracking contracts. She mumbled and stuttered something under her breath before mustering up a solemn "Never mind."

Fast-forward a couple months, and I was fresh off presenting a ten-minute talk about the dangers of biased artificial intelligence (AI) and biometrics at the Recode Code Conference in Scottsdale, Arizona. There are very few adrenaline rushes I get outside of sharing information that people haven't considered and doing it in a straightforward but humorous way. On stage before the now CEO of Amazon, I also made sure to be styled in an outfit I absolutely loved that summed up my personality: bright orange sleeveless blazer-style V-neck blouse, snakeskin midi skirt, metallic pumps, with short white nails, slicked-back bun, large hoop earrings, and snakeskin glasses. Delivering that talk was a huge high for me, and I got many comments from and made connections with people who were impressed by the information and my casual yet informed delivery. So, imagine how hard and fast I came down when I had a meeting request from Wendy, with John and Sharon copied and invited, as soon as I returned home.

    Reading the invite, which had the subject line "Policy," I knew this was going to be an attempted three-way bullying session to get me to change my policies and processes. Not up for discussion. What startled me, but was not surprising, was the passive-aggressive way this meeting came to be. Instead of talking to me personally, or to the CEO (who had no idea this meeting was happening), they had talked among themselves and decided to follow the Golden State Warriors motto, "Strength in Numbers." Unfortunately for them, they got the wrong one.

    I was working from home the day of the meeting, which was strategic on my part. Being in the same room would likely have heightened any tension as they knew I wasn't pleased with how this meeting was plotted and planned, nor did I want to discuss the topic. It was déjà vu for me again, seeing three white people sitting on one side of a table, even on Zoom, and me on a side all to myself. Note, too, that I was wearing a white T-shirt and my hair in crochet braids—which, to me and ostensibly to my co-workers, is peak Blackness. None of them had ever seen me like that before because I always showed up with my hair in a bun or with curls, and I think seeing me representing my Blackness in a way that didn't even pretend to be palatable was unnerving. Dare I say "aggressive"? It wasn't intentional, but it set the tone regardless.

    They began by complimenting me on what they'd heard about my presentation at the conference. *Great. So, let's get to getting. We all know why we're here, so no need to gas me*, I said to myself. As they each started to discuss what they didn't like about my contracts policy and process, I listened and felt my shoulders rise and my ears start to get hot. When I am bothered, the first thing that happens is my ears immediately get hot, and I have to fight the urge to start rubbing them. The more they spoke, the more heat traveled from my ears to my hands, then to my feet. My foot was shaking rapidly under the table, back and forth, to work out unnerved energy. At that moment I was pleased that we weren't all in the same room. I'm sure they were too because the more they spoke and I didn't react, with neither words nor facial expressions, the more they began to stutter and muddle their thoughts. I wanted to be respectful and hear them out, but I could tell that my silence was worrying them. I waited for a lull in the conversation to vocalize an observation.

"First, I appreciate the kind words about my Recode presentation. I'm glad you heard nothing but good feedback. Thanks for sharing that, and your support is welcome. Now, thank you all for sharing your concerns about the policy. While I appreciate that you may have issues with me putting structure in place because it wasn't present prior to my arrival, this is actually better for the company, and for us all, in the long run. Everyone will understand there's one process, how to initiate it, and it also helps with record retention, which we'll need for more funding rounds and legal compliance. Also, the two of you, Sharon and John, never said anything to me about taking issue with the policy. So, perhaps you should have come to me first before you all decided to team up to ambush me." I laughed to deflect any perceived tension, then continued. "You also have to acknowledge the optics here. Let's note that I'm the last Black woman left here at the company. The other two we had are gone. One left due to frustration, and the other was essentially pushed out with constructive termination. Telling the last one here, who has been in her field for eleven years, how to run her function is unprofessional, particularly because I don't tell you all how to run HR, product, or design. Yet somehow you all feel entitled and well within your rights to tell me how to do my job when you've never done it. You have all of these ideas and suggestions, but you all couldn't talk to me individually. Why? Now, I wonder why you all feel this is in your purview. Why is that? I'm open to feedback, but you didn't approach me. And did you consider how this would be received?"

Dead silence. I couldn't see anything from their elbows down, but it looked like everyone was wringing their hands. They looked at each other and took turns looking askance at me on the screen before John finally spoke up. "Bärí, I'm really sorry. I don't think we considered how this would look or how you would feel. And you're right. You've never told us how to do our jobs, and we shouldn't have tried to tell you how to do yours."

"That's correct, because I trust you. I know that you are professionals, and you know more about your function than I do. I would never overstep my boundaries and tell you how to do your job, especially when I don't know the first thing about it. Will I offer suggestions? Sure. But I will also offer them to you directly. I don't need backup to give my opinion on how I think something may or may not work. As a colleague, I hope that you have the same trust and respect for me as I do for you. Part of the reason why the other two ladies are gone is because they found that lacking. This experience right now is feeling much the same."

I looked at the Zoom and noticed Sharon had her head down and Wendy was looking at her with sympathy. Then I heard sniffles and a soft wail. Sharon was crying, and my immediate thought was, *Ugh, here we go. This is now going to morph from her assuming responsibility for wrongdoing to me having to comfort her because she feels guilty and doesn't like being told she's wrong.* The weaponization of tears is a classic play. I've seen it before in the workplace, also when someone did something blatantly disrespectful to me, and if I didn't immediately comfort them for crying about their own wrongdoing and guilt, then I was seen as insensitive and angry. I could already hear how this would be retold: "Bärí made her cry." Can't win for losing. After each person then went around and apologized and said they had made a mistake and told me I was valued, we ended the call, but not before Sharon made sure to tell me how much she appreciated me as a colleague, my perspective, and that she was an ally. She was incredibly sweet and genuine. I believed her. But the dynamic was never the same, though, at least for me. The trust was gone, and so was I about four months later.

There is also the problem of co-opting an issue and turning it into something that centers the non-Black person and their participation, or the narrative shifts to their comfort and making them feel welcome to participate. It's akin to wanting a participation trophy. No matter how poorly you do, or how you don't contribute anything to the team or the result, you still are rewarded for being engaged, even if it's damaging.

White women have taken over the experience of "women at work," even when our issues are not the same. It's automatically conflated to centering their experiences. Take the example of what I like to call the "Girl Boss era," which peaked around 2015. It essentially glorified women putting ambition and career ahead of family concerns and applauded them for participating in hustle culture. The prime example was former Yahoo CEO Marissa Mayer, who was lauded as the second coming of Sheryl Sandberg. When Mayer only took two weeks of maternity leave and had a nursery built next door to her office, many praised her dedication to work and wondered why more women couldn't do the same.

Well, for one, Black women are not in similar positions of authority. White women have been able to attain more visible leadership roles and are often seen as the "safe" face of diversity in tech, particularly in predominantly white and male tech companies. Several factors are at play—proximity to power, cultural norms and familiarity, and network. White women have historically held more privilege and power than other marginalized groups, and certainly more than Black women, and that affords them greater access to leadership roles and opportunities to advocate for diversity and inclusion. This proximity to power is on full display when looking at who runs tech companies and who they would feel most comfortable working with. If you have to diversify, someone who reminds you of your wife or sister is, by default, more of a "culture fit." This plays into cultural norms. Tech, like many other industries, is dominated by white men, and the image of the white, educated, middle-class woman has been used to promote an appearance of diversity that is more palatable and marketable and viewed as "mainstream." It allows for a company to diversify without challenging any societal norms.

Additionally, white women are often more visible and have greater access to resources and opportunities to promote diversity and inclusion in tech than other marginalized groups. This is due, in part, to their relative privilege and access to power and influence both within organizations and society as a whole. Because of these factors, white women have the ability to be more vocal in advocating for diversity in tech without receiving as much negative backlash or scrutiny as Black women. It would be great for them to use that privilege to be active allies and advocate for greater inclusion for us when it comes to hiring, promotions, equal pay, resources, and concessions for greater work-life balance rather than the opposite, which I experienced at Facebook. When I was looking to switch teams before I left, I had to do a presentation. Part of that presentation offered an idea to create an opt-in checkpoint to view explicit content instead of autoplay. Another woman who I had to share the document with, who staunchly referred to herself as an "ally," hijacked the idea to leapfrog me and secure the position. Two months after I left, the checkpoint was launched. So, no, lady, you aren't and weren't ever an ally. But that doesn't mean no one can be. It just requires that, in some cases, you put the issue above yourself.

It is imperative to recognize that elevating white women as the face of diversity in tech can obscure the experiences and challenges of Black women and what it takes to survive, let alone thrive, in this industry. To promote true diversity and inclusion in tech, efforts must be made to address the unique barriers and challenges we face and to elevate a diverse range of voices and perspectives. Co-opting the narrative of being a woman in business with white women as the gold standard sets unrealistic expectations for Black women without the same resources. In fact, it undermines and invalidates how hard we work to receive the same visibility and attention to our issues. While some white women see this as allyship and advancement, it just adds another layer of pressure. True allies would use their voices to argue for greater parity for Black women and understand the unique issues we face when trying to advance.

Recently, there has been a continued diversity ally malaise. See, that's the thing about "allyship": you can opt in and out when you want to if the issues of the marginalized group don't affect you. When you get tired of hearing about something, you can choose to no longer pay attention or participate. If only it were so easy for those of us who have to live it. We can't just put our neatly packed luggage down when we log on to Zoom or walk in the door. However, that seems to be just what some companies want us to do.

I did some consulting work for a company in 2022. At that point in time, there was a merger and acquisition with another group of people coming over from a large, very established telecommunications company with set rules, traditions, and employee benefits, from employee resource groups (ERGs) to having Juneteenth off. Well, at an all-hands meeting, a Black employee asked how the ERGs would turn over and be managed after the merger. No response. A white woman asked; still no response. Finally, a white man asked. There was a response, and it wasn't one most people wanted to hear.

"Any [company] Slack user can create a new Slack channel, although channels should be consistent with our values and focused on moving the company and our mission forward. They shouldn't be tied to any particular identity or social movement." So, that basically makes ERGs extinct. But how I took it? *Shut the fuck up and just sell the product. Worry about your humanity and rights on your own time.*

Like, why would you think this doesn't fit a value? Do you not care about company culture? Are employees just robots without emotion? Sorry, but I can't leave my Blackness or womanness and femininity when I log on to the VPN. Perhaps this is something other people can do because they don't have to justify their existence on a daily basis. There isn't an identity coat check at the door, nor is that something Black women can do. Having conversations with members of the existing Black ERG was enlightening. All those members had already decided upon hearing that statement that it was time to look elsewhere for a job where they would be supported holistically. I told them to tell me if and when they found that place.

This is the exact opposite of a demonstration of allyship or making your marginalized employees feel welcome. Equality is not equity. Treating us like "everyone else" doesn't quite work because we have a different lived experience that carries over into all spaces, including the workplace. That notion is causing some companies and their funders to demonstrate "diversity exhaustion."

Diversity exhaustion is the feeling of being tired of hearing about diversity, equity, and inclusion (DEI) and fatigue with doing the work it requires. Rank-and-file employees have been seen complaining about it on Blind, a social media app primarily used by tech workers, which allows people to be as candid as they desire. In the comments there's an undercurrent of feeling that representational diversity isn't helpful since the real value is in diverse ideas—cognitive diversity rears its head again—and not just race, gender, ability, or sexuality. These employees are tired of having diversity forced on them. There's another form of fatigue in which companies are frustrated with the lack of progress with their DEI efforts, no doubt because proper allocation of budget and resources haven't been afforded to those doing the work. With that frustration and other social diversions, companies have been quietly backtracking on all of the pledges and promises they made during the summer of 2020 now that folks aren't watching. *The Plug*, an online publication, in conjunction with *Fast Company*, created a comprehensive guide recapping all that happened a year and a half later, and what stuck out was that most of the people and companies that had pledged didn't stick to their promises or didn't share updates because there *weren't* any to share.[83] Sure, a few smaller companies had something tangible to report, but no big tech companies had any big updates. What they did have was an ongoing fight, arguing for the right to self-audit their progress. That's not how this works. That means letting companies cherry-pick the best out of what they did or didn't do, so maybe they won't say how many people they promoted because that was negligible, but they *will* share how many people they hired, even if they're all on the base tier. How is that beneficial in terms of actual change?

With other issues paramount and most diversity departments and initiatives tagged as overhead, budget cuts and deprioritization come for DEI first. If something isn't valued as a business imperative, it's on the wrong side of the budget. Despite loud commitments of solidarity and support for Black communities in 2020, the tech industry seems just fine overlooking the business argument for hiring and retaining Black employees and prioritizing DEI and belonging. This is why, as part of diversity exhaustion, many companies have fired or let go of much of their diversity staff—they're tired of figuring out how to do this because they can't find a way that's palatable and makes it look like they've actually *done* something.

The second part of this exhaustion is something we've already discussed: the definition of *diversity*. The lack of a singular, consistent definition is killing diversity departments because now tech companies are "solving" diversity by expanding its definition. Whether that's diversity of thought (yes, it's a real thing) or geographical diversity (he's from Idaho *but* he's a Democrat, or he's from Sweden *but* he speaks Spanish!), they all ignore the issue of representational diversity, which means hiring, listening to, *and* incorporating ideas from people of marginalized communities, be it women, people of color, LGBTQ+ people, or people with disabilities. It's no wonder why people are so tired of diversity—it's not getting solved because no one is doing the real work. Companies do the bare minimum of what will make *them* look the best, not what's best for the industry. What tech needs is a common baseline. What is the industry's definition of *diversity*? We need a singular, solid definition that every company is beholden to and from there, in a show of authentic allyship, shift DEI's allocation on company balance sheets and tie it directly to their performance.

CHAPTER 8

This Is What Happens When We Don't Have a Seat at the Table: Technology Gone Bad

> Research shows that diversity improves problem solving, productivity, innovation, and ultimately the bottom line. We need the female perspective in technology.
> —Regina Honu, CEO of Soronko Academy

The dawn of the internet and subsequent technological advances promised the democratization of voices and experiences as well as greater access to information and opportunities for social and economic advancement. Social media was evangelized as the main tool to give voice to the voiceless and as a vehicle for making the world more open and connected. Sounds good, right? We certainly assumed good intentions would facilitate action and positive experiences. In her 1994 book *Teaching to Transgress*, scholar and activist bell hooks argued that the internet had the potential to be a "revolutionary tool" for marginalized communities. hooks asserted that "If we can develop a culture where using the internet to access information and create knowledge is seen as a liberatory practice, then we can begin to create the conditions for the development of a new kind of intellectual who is not bound by the constraints of traditional power relations."[84] While the advances of technology have yielded some positive results—the use of social media for community organizing that took Black Lives Matter from a hashtag to a movement, for example—it has also been weaponized due to a lack of Black women sought out as contributors from product ideation through implementation. Despite the fact that Black women are active and engaged users of technology, and often early adopters and influencers, they are underrepresented in positions of power and influence in the tech industry. According to a 2017 study by the Kapor Center, Black women made up just 2 percent of leadership roles in tech companies and were more likely to experience bias and discrimination in the workplace than any other demographic group.[85] Our absence from leadership roles is manifested in how products are created and how the poor treatment of Black women online is proliferated and deemed acceptable. Tech companies can proclaim good intent all they want, but until we see representational diversity in product creation and strategies to protect Black women from online treatment that further marginalizes, suppresses, and harms us, they'll always be lagging behind.

I travel a good deal for work, so I've become intimately familiar with airports and Transportation Security Administration (TSA) scanners. Unfortunately, I've also become just as familiar with pat downs. See, my naturally curly hair tends to set the scanners off. No, I don't carry explosives or weapons or hide bottles with more than 3.4 ounces of liquid in my hair, even though I'd like to (but ask me about my strategy to pack so many conditioners that often a few will be confiscated for being "too many").

It turns out the machines, designed by straight-haired white dudes, were not coded properly to recognize hair like mine.[86] Considering these scanners can see through to my *skeleton*, the fact that they can't see through my hair is a problem. And that's the least of my worries about what technology can do. Do I think about these issues? Yes. It's even worse once I pass security and get inside the terminal. I dread going to wash my hands and having to wave my hand at least three times under the soap dispenser sensor for it to turn on and another three times to get the paper towel dispenser to work. Why doesn't it work? These dispensers use an optic light sensor to detect when a hand is there. The darker the hand, the less light that bounces back to the sensor, which means I must keep waving. It's a minor nuisance, but these little things gradually add up and influence larger, more consequential, everyday life disturbances like racial profiling, policing, creditworthiness, and surveillance. The huge issue is that racial bias has been encoded, whether purposefully or accidentally, into the products we use every day.

In 2020, as reported by *Business Insider*, the TSA asked vendors "for ideas 'to improve screening of headwear and hair in compliance with Title VI of the Civil Rights Act.' That law bars federally funded agencies and programs from discriminating—even unintentionally—on the basis of race, color, or national origin."[87] The good thing about this is that the TSA *was* aware of what their technology was doing, how it affected people with natural hairstyles, and how it could impact the organization—it's always the bottom line with funding. Their proactive decision to ask for help was likely born of the fact that the TSA has a transportation security screener workforce comprised of almost 27 percent Black employees.[88] Surely, those employees had experienced the same biases and had something to say about it. Something doesn't have to be intentionally coded to be harmful, but those building the products still give zero consideration to the potential harm they could have for Black people. The difference here is the TSA listened, likely to their Black women employees. If only tech companies would employ the same philosophy when it comes to arguably one of the worst product creations for Black women: the internet.

For all the promise of the internet bringing a greater sense of utopia, it's just a replica of real-world problems with the same offline dynamics, and Black women are again the canaries in the coal mine. The problem is that the sense of a "universal user" is not a person, and definitely not a Black woman. The default user is whoever tends to build it: a cisgender, straight, able-bodied white guy. While the argument centers on math being the foundation of an algorithm, the functions the math performs are solely based on the programmers' coding, which incorporates their interpretation of data, language, and parameters. This means that anyone else's experience and existence are automatically othered. I spoke with Dr. Safiya Noble, a professor at UCLA, and she noted how this narrative is deeply flawed: "People believe technology is objective and neutral, based only on math. It doesn't have a value system, so how could it possibly be discriminatory? Well, computer language is a language, and language is subjective and up for interpretation." That language enables the constant othering of Black women online. Even in our separate corners of the internet, the ubiquity of online violence and systemic racism is evidenced by social media, radicalization, and the abject co-option of Black creators' content.

As an avid Twitter (now X) user, I have my own experience as part of the 84 percent of Black women who have been harassed, trolled, doxed, or ridiculed online.[89] In fact, the very process of responding to an X thread about writing this book and its content subjected me to being called everything but a child of God and pressed some lovely individual to find or guess my email address and send me this cheerful message (*sic* all, naturally):

> Why is it that you dumb, low IQ MONOS think it's OK to force diversity where there's mostly white people, but you don't go to black countries and force white people to fucking be there? Diversity forces low iq, unqualified people like you into positions they don't deserve. People like you should be forced to see surgeons or other people like that who have not been qualified for their job because your dumb cunt ass thinks that other people should be forced to hire or see them. Also, you're mad at Manchin for not voting the way you want him to, fuck you, this isn't China, not yet. There's only one end to this madness, you and your ilk gtfo this country, ie, we ship all you to Liberia, and you leave all of our technology, and everything we created behind. You're not culturally appropriating our things. There is also the prospect of dividing the nation, then watch as your side turns to shit, just like everything you touch. The final solution, would be war, and thankfully, you people have openly identified yourselves as anti American, racist pos. White countries have the highest levels of emigration, because people want to come to our countries to use our money and take away everything that we do great. Meanwhile, everywhere that black people go, education goes down, and crime goes up. Lying cunt.

Truly delightful! The best part of this message is the irony of calling me "low iq" while simultaneously butchering the English language.

It wasn't the first time I received hate mail after being trolled on X. Trolling Black women for shits and giggles by intentionally being cruel can go so far as using digital blackface, actively cosplaying as a Black woman online, reinforcing stereotypes by either cosigning or exhibiting them, spreading disinformation, subverting communities, and upending movements. The process of actively undermining the presence of Black women and our ability to challenge ideas, critique arguments, or effectively engage in community building and organizing in peace affects our representation in product creation.

Identifying systemic harassment and abuse is frustrating when you constantly need to describe something others can't see or understand, and even worse, when they straight-up deny it. The thinking is, *If we can follow, collect, scrape, and aggregate data and train everyone using our product, how could we miss something important?* My answer: "You don't even know what to look for or how to look for it because it doesn't apply to you." The attitude is one of superiority that embraces the notion that an issue's relevance is only valid if it alters the model of the "average" user. No one else matters. So, good luck to them.

An additional way systemic racism is exhibited online is internet radicalization. While the radicalization of average users (i.e., white men) is now woven into tech's story, the focus has not shifted to the experiences of the victims but instead to the feelings and mental health of the perpetrators. On the flip side, the media has long been keen to call any violence perpetuated by Black folks a cultural problem, and social media is no different. Both act as if Black people aren't susceptible to mental health crises.

In 2017 in Portland, Oregon, Demetria Hester, a Black woman, was attacked by Jeremy Christian, who followed her off a light-rail train.[90] When the police arrived, they questioned

Hester—asking for her identification and acting as if she were the perpetrator—while Christian sauntered off unquestioned. Later that night, "he was charged with murdering two men who were defending two Black teens from his racist Islamophobic attacks."[91] Hester testified at the trial, saying all could have been prevented if the police had just listened to her seventeen hours prior. But instead, they dismissed her and let a man, currently serving a life sentence without parole, walk free to spew his hatred and menace others. The issue? Christian's past is inherently digital; if one searches his name and "Portland" he has almost a million Google results, all focusing *on* his radicalization and the makeup of his social media profile, not where that radicalization ultimately led him—to Hester, who was a complete stranger at that point. No one noticed that online harassment can and does lead to in-person attacks, nor did they realize the significance of his online radicalization leading him to attack someone like Hester, whom he didn't know anything about other than that she is a Black woman. What was on his computer? What websites did he frequent? What message boards did he engage with that reinforced his beliefs and provided the false entitlement that it was not just okay but *morally right* to attack Hester and, later on, two Black teenagers?

Meanwhile, Hester's coverage of two hundred thousand results when searching her name on Google is only digital as far as the articles that covered her attack and arrest. Without a digital record to see how these instances are connected, leading to their eventual outcomes, these attacks show that we are not taking this pattern of harassment and violence seriously and prefer to treat them as outlying, isolated incidents, as opposed to an escalation of what can happen if there are no consequences for behavior like Christian's.

This behavior has been documented for as long as we've been

online, from dial-up AOL chat rooms to BlackPlanet to Myspace and every platform after that. Genie Lauren notes in the foreword to *#HashtagActivism* that hashtags, in general, were initially mocked as performative activism without the action, but nothing could be further from the truth. The basis of all hashtags is to bring awareness and visibility to certain movements and causes, be it BlackLivesMatter, MeToo, HeForShe, BringBackOurGirls, etc. But to the point of systemic racism, let's look at the first two. #BlackLivesMatter and #MeToo were developed in response to continued narrow-minded reporting on critical Black concerns, and while both demonstrated their impact on Black people, they also brought them to the attention of people unaffected by such concerns. They were created specifically by Black women to do what the internet and social media promised us. But again, social media platforms fail. MeToo was co-opted, and the majority of Black Lives Matter hashtags have to do with Black men. It's a double slap in the face to Black women: they're victims of the circumstances that led to creating the hashtag, and even then, they're not the focal point in their own activism.

Lauren found this out the hard way. A front-end web developer, Lauren is widely recognized for her activism on Twitter (now X) using the handle @MoreAndAgain and her involvement in the success of Black Twitter, particularly in social justice cases. In 2020, inspired by recent uprisings, she created #BlackLibLit, a safe space for Black people to come together to read and discuss fiction and nonfiction works that tackle the issue of race in the United States and across the world. Back in 2013, she was named among *Ebony* magazine's Power 100 and *Jet* magazine's first annual 40 Under 40. That's no surprise, however, considering that year Lauren "was instrumental in stopping a juror on the Trayvon Martin murder trial from making a macabre profit grab of a book deal"[92] on her experience as a juror and why she voted not guilty. Upon seeing the news, Lauren tweeted the agent's information to her three thousand followers, urging them to contact the agent and spread the word. She also launched an online petition to stop the book deal, which was successful within hours, garnering 1,343 signatures. But not long after that, X deleted her entire account for unclear violations, and despite Lauren's appeals for reactivation or, at the very least, an archive of the content she had created, she received nothing but the same automated response. Ten years, encompassing 530,000 tweets and an immeasurable impact on countless social justice movements, down the drain. What kind of message does that send, not just about the racial implications of Martin's murder but on who can take unfavorable action and go unpunished?

Another example is Tarana Burke, a sexual assault survivor who created #MeToo in 2006 to empower other young survivors of color and draw awareness to the magnitude of sexual assault and harassment in the workplace. What comes to mind when you see #MeToo? A skinny white female celebrity. Hollywood. Neither of which had anything to do with Burke's original experience. So, what happened? Answer: lack of allyship. Allyship is understanding a unique issue and using your voice to advocate for it. This may have been how the co-opt for #MeToo began, but it got overrun by innate arrogance and entitlement that led to its popularization in 2017 following the Harvey Weinstein allegations. Now, do I have anything against using it to expose Weinstein's behavior? Absolutely not. I am happy he's going to die in jail. But that was not the point. Burke's original intent was to create awareness of women's experience of dealing with sexual harassment and sexual assault in the workplace—it didn't have to do with the entertainment industry and not specifically white women's experience in it.

It was a Black woman's experience, and it got shafted with the attitude of "Oh, that sucks. But look what happened to *us* on a larger scale." You all remember Loki's flippant reaction when he learned of Asgard's destruction and the meme that followed: "Yes, very sad. Anyway, it got me thinking . . ." This is the exact attitude that those who took over #MeToo exhibited. Burke has spoken out about her shock and distress in discovering the celebrity-driven social media storm following Alyssa Milano's tweet, which garnered reactions from 4.7 million users worldwide within a day. And had it not been for the persistence of Black Twitter, Burke would likely have remained uncredited and unseen as an ambassador for her own message.

So, what's the big deal about allyship now that Burke has been credited? She's been in *TIME*, she is listed as the founder of #MeToo, she's done multiple speaking engagements about the roots of the movement, and Harvard conducted a case study on her. Isn't that enough? No, it isn't. Burke is credited *now*, but she wasn't initially because of the lack of allyship. It was Black women who took up the call to demand credit be given where it was due, and it was only through constant reassurance and repetition that people did. Burke's name on the #MeToo Wikipedia page doesn't necessarily translate to women, particularly white women, knowing where the movement came from. The celebrity image of #MeToo hasn't changed from its co-option, and Burke has commented on this, saying in a talk at the University of Chicago, "When people hear me, they want to talk about court cases and Harvey Weinstein and R. Kelly. That's bullshit. That's just smoke and mirrors to confuse you."[93]

In the case of #MeToo, Black women were the allies their white counterparts claimed to be, but this is not a one-size-fits-all situation. It is not that others should be barred from joining a movement such as #MeToo; we need and want allies, but there is something to be said when allyship only goes as far as adding yourself to a cause and then slapping an entirely new face on it. So, yes, join us. But use your voice to advance our cause, not take over.

As technology advances, so too do its shortcomings. Nowhere is this more prevalent than in Web3 and the Metaverse. Web3 is the newest unregulated iteration of the World Wide Web and incorporates concepts such as blockchain technologies and decentralization—a free-for-all, which, to me, sounds like the road to anarchy. The Metaverse is a virtual reality space that embodies characteristics of actual experiences of people and their environments *and* simulates sensory experiences—it's a better version of The Sims come to life. Both platforms offer the same promise that the internet once did: democratization, greater opportunities, and an escape, so if you can't live your best life in your real life, just make an avatar that can.

If only it were that simple. "Better" tech typically means worse issues, as evidenced by the Metaverse's problems, which are just virtual manifestations of what happens in both the real world *and* online. The rub is now the experiences are a mix of virtual interactions with real-life sensory experiences. Take Chanelle Siggens, for example.[94]

No one puts on a virtual reality headset expecting the worst. So, imagine Siggens's surprise when, while waiting in the virtual lobby to play Population: One, her avatar was approached by a male avatar, who, within minutes, sexually assaulted and ejaculated on her. Unable to differentiate what was real and what was pseudoreal, Siggens experienced the same physical responses she'd have in real life: adrenaline rush, accelerated heartbeat, even sweating. She reported the user account, only to be met with an automated response saying punitive action had been taken. But whatever that action was, it didn't stop it from happening to her again just an hour later.

Siggens's experience triggers a barrage of unanswerable questions about safety. The same issues that we've faced in Web2 are aggravated in Web3. Black women on social media self-report having post-traumatic stress disorder (PTSD) and experiencing other kinds of harm from being trolled and responding to the things they see written about Black people, particularly Black women, on the internet. It isn't just about hate speech and anti-Black speech online but also what many Black women feel as an imperative to respond if it comes across their timeline. In addition to PTSD, racial battle fatigue and depression result. Now, add to that virtual sexual assault, which we already see in Web2 when timelines are flooded with violence against Black bodies and the sources of mental anguish for Black women are seemingly inescapable. There is a lot of emotional labor in engaging with social media for Black women, while cishet white men can seemingly just have a good time. Web3 is supposed to be a space where we can live our best lives, and instead it results in more abuse with actual physical ramifications. Researchers say the harassment, assaults, bullying, and hate speech already running rampant in virtual—and augmented—reality games are neither easily quantifiable nor easily prevented or controlled. Bad actors in the Metaverse are hard to identify because incidents occur in real time and usually are not recorded, and behavior such as what Siggens encountered can be more severe than online harassment because of virtual reality's all-encompassing, sensory-heightened digital environment.

In a phone call between us, Dr. Safiya Noble articulated this well:

What did the other person have to be thinking and enacting in order to engage with her avatar in this way? While experimenting with these technologies, there's not enough study around the psychological and physiological responses to these experiences—and of course, if you ask a Black woman about these experiences, we'll tell you we're all gonna be dead if it doesn't change.

The irony is that the Metaverse is continually advertised as a place to be your best self. Well, to those in some depraved corner of the web, their best self is to live out their worst fantasies. And this so-called safe haven isn't safe at all but actually encourages such depravity because it gives people another avenue to be anonymous, enabling them to act on their worst impulses without any repercussions because it isn't "real." We are creating an ideal playground for every Dr. Jekyll to become Mr. Hyde, encouraging a space for people's egos and ids to live. You can be buttoned-up Brad from eight to six, have a break to eat dinner, then from eight to eleven, you're buckle-up Brad from *Mad Max*. The Metaverse allows people to do that at will, like the next thing on demand. We already get on-demand food, on-demand rides, and on-demand entertainment, so why not this too if it's just the cosplaying of victimless crimes? Now, that is a dangerous way of thinking, and although the Metaverse was meant to efface all that, it has done just the opposite. Talk to Siggens or any woman who has experienced a similar situation, and they will let you know that there *are* victims, even in the Metaverse.

In discussions over safety, tech companies talk about implementing guardrails around not just consent but how avatars can and can't interact with one another. However, it's unfortunately all too normal in tech to talk about doing something and leave it at that, which was exactly what Meta's chief technology officer, Andrew "Boz" Bosworth, did. In an employee memo reported by the *Financial Times* in 2021, Bosworth wrote that moderating what people say and how they act in the Metaverse "at any meaningful scale is practically impossible."[95]

If companies have resigned themselves to this lost cause, should we even engage? What is the potential harm or the legal implications? I can never take off my legal hat, and the Metaverse has huge legal risks. Separate and apart from being another vehicle of harassment and ridicule, there are no regulations around it. Which means, just like social media and the rest of Web2, Web3 doesn't owe you anything. Don't look for protection from the government or the companies, but then, when did Black women ever really rely on the government or tech companies to protect us?

———

If Black people couldn't rely on the government or companies in the past, they certainly can't rely on them now as the world changes in the name of better technology. As we've seen, some of the best technological advancements are also the worst if they don't operate with guardrails. The worst, to me, comes from the use of artificial intelligence, better known as AI—and not to be confused with Allen Iverson. In regard to AI, there are no guardrails because shipping fast doesn't account for them. Or contemplating litigation. Or weaponization. Or really anything that may stop a company from being first to market while simultaneously being first to harm. The idea of a system that pattern matches and determines your future and fate, without any regulation or transparency, is more than a notion. It's the premise for a dystopian movie where pattern matching using old discriminatory data and predictive analytics combine to create disastrous outcomes for Black women. The scariest part is that it isn't a movie; we're living it.

AI technology has exploded in the last few years. I first heard whispers of it in 2016 when I was at Facebook, of how we could use it for content moderation. And my concern was, and still is, that if the humans doing this work are not well versed in cultural cues to understand internationally or even regionally what content is acceptable versus what is offensive, how will we train a *computer* to differentiate? Humans are picking the datasets for AI, so we're training them erroneously and making it more efficient to take down the wrong content, and therefore the wrong *people*, based on that content. Add to that, the people controlling these datasets, nine times out of ten, are not the people who will be affected by the algorithm. I was not a fan of the idea, but even after I left Facebook and joined StubHub and then All Turtles, AI was there. It was embedded.

Initial product creation talks are fresh, exciting, and somewhat down to earth. There weren't, at least not at StubHub, any grand idealizations of AI—all we wanted to do was use it for ticket purchases. We spoke of it in service of our existing products, not to replace people or make other products obsolete. It was about facilitating ease of use and creating efficiency. But some of that efficiency is cost savings, and the biggest cost at a company is labor. So, when AI is already being used and the efficiency issue gets raised, it's easy to predict the company's next "natural" course of action.

Much is made about the use of technology to make life easier, but at whose expense? Often, it is at the expense of those *not* in the room. This happens not just in hiring, which we all expect, but also in firing and layoffs. Automating layoffs isn't entirely new, but the recent adoption of the practice by some larger and more influential companies, like Facebook, is very curious. Having reported their first revenue decline in late July 2022 since going public a decade prior, Facebook decided to employ austerity measures in September 2022, including using an algorithm to get rid of contractors placed via Facebook's multimillion-dollar deal with Accenture. Reportedly, Facebook used an undisclosed algorithm to lay off sixty contractors "at random" in the content moderation and business integrity departments. The irony of choosing to cut people in those areas isn't lost on me. Those are arguably two of the most important departments in terms of what is allowed on the platform, how it's regulated, and the ethical obligations, if any, the company decides to implement. Furthermore, the company went one step further, announcing that it would make large cuts to the team responsible for ethical considerations of Facebook's products. In AI's current state, people can write and do whatever they want at the whims of a twenty-five-year-old engineer, who likely hasn't been exposed to diverse people, so they definitely won't know our history or the proper information to include to determine content moderation, which has even greater consequences in other areas.

Going forward, AI has expanded into even more important roles. At All Turtles, the company's entire premise was about building products that incorporate and use AI technology and then using them in different capacities, which, on the surface, sounds ideal. For example, in health care, using AI for pre-diagnostics or with elder care is a great example of "tech for good," but there's always the scary dystopian possibility.

In genealogy, products such as AncestryDNA and 23andMe are wildly popular. People love genealogy, and who wouldn't want to learn more about who they are? Genealogy is especially important to a demographic of people whose ancestors were stolen from their homeland and plopped down here and who have no understanding or knowledge of where we actually come from. What is our real language? Our culture? Our name? "Williams" sure as hell isn't my real last name. There's a large demand for genealogy tests, particularly from Black communities. All you have to do is spit in a tube (per AncestryDNA) and mail it in, and you'll receive your results in a matter of weeks. Ideal, right? Well, it started out that way, but that's not how this fairy tale goes.

Let me preface this by noting a key difference between AncestryDNA and 23andMe. With AncestryDNA's spit-tube process, you're getting a breakdown of your ethnicity. That's it. *And* there's an opt-out process (if you read the fine print, and I'm part of the 0.5 percent that does) to disallow the company from using your information for other purposes. Most people won't, but the important thing is they have that choice—one 23andMe didn't always offer, and is not the default setting when, arguably, it should be. With 23andMe, you're receiving genetic information: Are you predisposed to cancer? How likely are you to get Alzheimer's? All the shit that, first of all, I don't want to know in the first place. But the bigger issue is 23andMe was sold to a biomedical company, which means your genetic information is now in the hands of people who could use it to inform health-care decisions, develop new drugs, initiate recruitment for clinical trials, etc. I remember seeing a Twitter thread started by a young white woman doctor who said that in her medical textbooks, in a section for how to treat patients of different ethnicities and how they might react, Black peoples' reaction was written as something like, *No, we don't want medicine. We're just gonna pray and wait on Jesus.* Bottom line: don't give Black people pain medication. She was incredibly surprised that this level of stereotyping was taught as appropriate patient care. That's the kind of crazed notion that can come out of handing over your genetic information—people will assume that not only are you predisposed to certain diseases and ailments but you can tolerate levels of pain. I don't know about you, but this seems like a gateway to malpractice.

An even scarier prospect is how ancestry companies can unintentionally perpetuate the United States' history of using Black people as guinea pigs in medical experiments. Biomedical companies are baiting us with the lure of finding out who we are and what cultural practices we lost, but they're hiding from us the fact that they can and will do whatever they want with our medical information and DNA if we don't understand what we're choosing to opt in to. What began as a fun and cool scientific way to help everyone understand where they came from has morphed into a grim, full-circle moment of genetically stereotyping people.

There are, and were, lots of cases for AI where it is intended for good, but creators don't factor in the issue of *where* all the information is coming from. For years the industry was too focused on expanding the reach of what this tech could do—the Valley was drunk and high off excitement and too lustful and greedy over the perceived power of AI to recognize and acknowledge, let alone solve, the abuses that have run rampant.

Shall we name a few? Criminal justice, profiling, policing, and sentencing, all by way of algorithm, are what keep me up at night. Yes, unjust racial profiling and resulting racial disparities in the criminal justice system certainly don't depend on AI. But when you add it to an already racist system, as many law enforcement agencies across the country are—including my own in Oakland and those in major cities like Miami, Los Angeles, Philadelphia, Atlanta, and New York—things get even scarier for Black families.[96]

AI works by distilling a large volume of information down

to simple concepts, categories, and rules and then predicting future responses and outcomes. The rub is it's a function of the beliefs, assumptions, and capabilities of the people who do the coding. AI learns by repetition and association, and all of that is based on the information humans, who hold all the racial and often specifically anti-Black biases of our society, feed it. I'm torn between working to advance this technology as an attorney and being fearful as a mother of what these advances mean for my two young children, especially my son. The same technology that's a source of excitement around efficiency and opportunities in my career is being used in law enforcement in ways that could mean my son, who is thirteen now, is more likely to be profiled or arrested or worse for no reason other than his race and where we live.

These shortfalls of AI technology are no secret. Despite this, state and local law enforcement agencies have begun to use predictive policing applications fueled by AI like HunchLab, which combines historical crime data, moon phases, location, census data, and even professional sports team schedules to forecast when and where crime may occur and even who's likely to commit or be a victim of certain crimes. The problem with historical crime data is that it's predicated upon policing practices that already disproportionately focus on Black and Latinx communities, as well as those who live in low-income areas. Shocker, I know. The true conundrum is posed in a *Science Journal* question: "Are associations utilized by AI software responses to existing facts, or are they reflections of the accrued biases and beliefs that are baked by the coders into the code itself?"[97] I would answer that question with another question. How could it *not* reflect who is making the technology?

With police profiling in the past, predictive technology perpetuates and exacerbates the problem, sending more officers after people who are already targeted and unfairly treated by police. I don't have to narrate what we've seen over the last few years, from Freddie Gray in Baltimore and Mike Brown in Ferguson to Oscar Grant, who was killed by someone I would call "cop adjacent," in my hometown. Add to that the Justice Department's reports on Ferguson and Baltimore and the findings of Breonna Taylor's murder in Kentucky, and it's to be expected that criminologists have raised red flags about the self-fulfilling nature of using historical crime data to inform AI.

This is happening right in my own backyard. A 2016 study by the Human Rights Data Analysis Group resolved that if the Oakland Police Department used its 2010 record of drug crimes information as the basis of an algorithm to guide policing, the department would have dispatched officers "almost exclusively to lower income, minority neighborhoods."[98] Never mind that public health–based estimates imply that drug use is much more widespread, taking place in many other parts of the city where my family and I live. A lot of drug use can be found in the wealthier enclaves in Oakland and Piedmont, but those areas aren't policed nearly as much. But what else is new?

I don't live far from those "lower income, minority neighborhoods"; even if I wanted to, it's in my blood, and I frequent them often. This proximity has also led to me being a victim of both intentional and unintentional crime. Those maligned neighborhoods include the barbershop where my son gets his hair cut and our favorite hoagie shop. Because of this, I don't allow him to walk ahead of me in certain places, and the only place I'll allow him to ride his scooter is on our block. Why would I let him have free rein given that simply setting foot on those sidewalks makes him more likely to be seen as a criminal in the eyes of the law? I'm not in the business of setting my son up for failure. The risks are even more serious (and unavoidable) for those who can only afford to live in the neighborhoods that AI would most likely lead officers to focus on.

AI is being used in every step of the criminal justice system. It tells law enforcement when and where to police and profile, uses facial recognition to identify alleged criminals, and implements sentencing technology to determine sentences and bail eligibility. But it doesn't stop there.

One of the scariest things about AI is just how pervasive it has become in a relatively short time frame. We see it not only in policing and criminal justice but in health care, job recruitment and displacement, housing, and education.

Health care is a minefield, and Black folks don't have the best track record with the health-care system, let alone with technological advances in medicine. Need an example? The Tuskegee syphilis experiment was an unethical project conducted by the United States Public Health Service to see the ramifications of letting untreated syphilis wreak havoc on nonconsenting and uninformed Black men whom they lured with promises of food and clothing.[99] Want an example of Black women used as government guinea pigs? Look no further than Henrietta Lacks. Her death from aggressive cervical cancer led to experiments with her cells, again taken without consent, which later were instrumental in curing polio, creating the human papillomavirus (HPV) vaccine, and understanding certain forms of cancer treatments.[100]

Now, you would think since Black folks have been a fertile ground for experimentation, AI advances would be able to provide better health-care options for Black people. Wrong. Historical data used to predict who needs care, how much, its duration, and expense are thrown together in a blender, and the results are undiagnosed, overdiagnosed, or completely ignored illnesses. Historical data continues to undergird the algorithms that spit out these conclusions, and it typically excludes diverse populations. This leads to skewed results. I have some experience with this myself. As I perused Twitter in 2019, I saw a tweet from a doctor about an AI algorithm that could successfully predict predisposition for cancer by upward of 70 percent. Intrigued, I found the original author of the study and slid into his DMs.

"Hello. I was reading your study findings and found them fascinating. How large was your sample size?" I asked.

"Thank you! Glad you are interested. The sample size was seventy," he wrote back. *Hmmmm*, I thought. I knew that the research had been done in New Zealand, which is generally homogeneous, save the Māori population.

"How many people of color are part of this study? Do you have any Black patients?" A day passed before he finally wrote back and said no.

So how, then, would I come to trust or rely upon this technology when it was created without my demographic's input or participation? Here is another case of life or death based on centering the lived experience of white people. I understand—it is New Zealand and all—but I wouldn't want that technology to be responsible for diagnosing me. And that's not the only problem. Algorithms determine who is prioritized in health-care treatment even if you are diagnosed correctly.

UnitedHealth sells a product called Impact Pro, which helps hospitals identify patients "most likely to benefit from high-risk case management services," according to researchers.[101] The intent of the algorithm is that "the cost of a patient's past health care use [and associated costs] will help predict future health-care needs."[102] The problem is that the algorithm was undergirded by looking at patients' medical histories and how much it cost to treat them. So, it didn't actually predict medical need, but cost. What researchers found is that cost and need are not synonymous. The UnitedHealth algorithm outcome "assigned comparable risk scores to white patients and black patients when black patients were substantially sicker."[103] Yet those who spent more were fast-tracked for certain hospital and insurance-covered programs, while those who didn't continued to deteriorate.[104] Even more damaging, because cost is the determinant, the dataset used isn't considering that access to health care in lower-income communities is often seen as a luxury, with lower-income households often choosing to delay care due to expense. If it's March 31, and rent is due April 1, you'll pay your rent and worry later about paying the copay to address that nagging cough you have.

AI has stamped tracks over every aspect of our lives, and for Black people especially, this does not bode well if tech continues to overlook their data, refuse to update it, and dismiss the need to fact-check. Which is exactly what I told Congress when I appeared before them in February 2020 to give a testimony on the impact of AI in the financial services sector.

Financial services aren't the first thing that jumps to mind in conversations about AI's drawbacks, but AI shines a light on and takes part in the systemic racism built into this industry, coming back to the same issue as policing: datasets and fact-checking. Who's fact-checking the fact-checkers? Answer: no one. There's the rub. If you're creating any product based on historical data, you *have* to check that data. How old is it? How stale is it? Where did you source it, and are there any updates to those sets? Are they being incorporated? You can think of this data retrieval almost like a buddy system—they're found first and based on what someone else uses. No one is going out there and asking the people affected by these algorithms; no one is truly thinking this process through enough to make it fair. One of the first questions the congresspeople asked me was what the definition of *fair* is. What does it really *mean* to be fair to people?

There are thousands of definitions of fairness. But from my standpoint in terms of financial services, I don't consider it fair to employ AI, which uses biased, outdated, and racist financial data, to determine—for example—someone's creditworthiness for a home loan. Why is that? Well, the algorithm is using data from 1968, and there was a ton of redlining then, so AI will automatically presume, based on the credit history of Black people *then*, that those numbers will still be prevalent in 2024. Which is essentially saying that time is stagnant and there's been no progress and absolutely nothing is different. The *law* is different. Women couldn't hold credit cards unless a man cosigned for them until 1972, yet we don't see AI withholding them from women today. Using information that predates our current time frames automatically makes AI's algorithms faulty; we need to take into account the laws that have changed because that alters all our data, which, in turn, changes the algorithms for how we treat people.

So, the question then becomes, how do we insulate people from the misuse of this information? How do we put up guardrails around how we use and program AI? That's where the AI Bill of Rights comes into play.

I worked on the AI Bill of Rights in conjunction with Georgetown University two years before my congressional testimony. Together we drafted a bill that addressed how it might look to ensure algorithmic bias does not reoccur in emerging technology, but we were forced to stop when lockdown hit. During that time, however, the White House picked it up to create their own version, which is promising because it at least starts the conversation that technology cannot go unregulated, as much as that isn't something companies want to hear.

In October 2022 the White House published the *Blueprint for an AI Bill of Rights*, which includes a nonbinding road map for the responsible use of AI and identifies five principles to "guide and govern the effective development and implementation of AI systems with particular attention to the unintended consequences of civil and human rights abuses."[105] The *Blueprint* was met with mixed reactions. Janet Haven, executive director of the Data and Society Research Institute, applauded how it "breaks ground by framing AI regulations as a civil-rights issue," while Daniel Castro of the Center for Data Innovation railed against it entirely, saying, "Existing laws that protect Americans from discrimination and unlawful surveillance apply equally to digital and non-digital risks." Others, such as Surveillance Technology Oversight Project's executive director, Albert Fox Cahn, say the *Blueprint* isn't enough and urge bans and legislative action on the most invasive technologies and worst offenders, including policing.[106]

Even with the principles, one of which is algorithmic discrimination protections, the fact that this blueprint is nonbinding and has no actual checks and balances for regulation is disheartening. Sure, we can *tell* companies that their algorithms can't discriminate by using irrelevant data, but again, who is fact-checking the fact-checkers? The rub is that these companies are making the work out to be much harder than it really is. Use updated records. Do the work to attain the most up-to-date information. But people don't want to do that, so they'll take shortcuts and go the path of least resistance to use what's easiest instead of most accurate. This comes back to people in tech, especially those in management positions, not knowing what to look for and having the attitude that if something doesn't apply to them, then it's not worth considering. *That* is something big tech needs to address before any real progress can be made on rectifying the ramifications of AI technology, and we can start by diversifying the workplace and listening to the voices and experiences of marginalized communities. And as we've seen from experiences like those of Dr. Timnit Gebru, the ex-Google artificial intelligence computer scientist, that fight is still ongoing.

Gebru's paper "On the Dangers of Stochastic Parrots: Can Model Languages Be Too Big?," which she cowrote with those in the AI division at Google, argues that the systems used by ChatGPT and other products are making a grave mistake by "accepting large amounts of web text as 'representative' of 'all' humanity," which further entrenches tech's way of thinking from an affluent white male perspective.[107] It will leave no room for other voices, which Google ironically proved with their decision to fire Gebru after she refused to withdraw the paper or remove the authors' names. But that didn't stop her from fighting the good fight.

As the founder of the Distributed AI Research Institute, Gebru continues her work to pull the attention of the industry and media from fears about AI destroying humanity to seeing what effects current AI technology is having on our communities, and the exploitation and fatal imbalances it is causing. She's doing it by homing in on one of the paper's key contentions: AI is not magic.

It's easy to forget, or dismiss, this notion. But maybe tech wants us to believe that AI is magic, because, in Gebru's words, "that means you can abdicate responsibility: 'It's not me that's the problem. It's the tool. It's super-powerful. We don't know what it's going to do.'"[108] Sorry to burst the bubble, but that's not the way this works. AI is eye-opening and jaw-dropping at times, but we cannot disillusion ourselves into thinking it wasn't wholly constructed by humans. We *have* to remember that, and we have to remind big tech of it too. Building AI systems with certain characteristics for profit and comfortability (keeping the white standard) is the problem, and that means the people behind the creation of those systems are too—looking at you, management and chief executive officers (CEOs).

In May 2023, proponents of AI regulation rejoiced when an unexpected move occurred: Sam Altman, CEO of OpenAI, publicly called for establishing laws around AI. But what most people don't know is the night before he was supposed to testify to Congress on behalf of said regulations, he also hosted a "puppet magic show" dinner for various senators and congresspeople to wow them with all the great things AI can accomplish.[109] Well, why the hell would he do that? Two reasons. The first is to have guardrails so that if he does something with AI systems that goes wrong, he can't be indicted or sued. The second, bigger reason is that these policymakers and lawmakers don't actually *know* what they're regulating. It's a lot easier to listen to someone in the field tell you how you should create these regulations, but that, of course, comes with its own pitfalls. Is it really wise to be guided in terms of regulation by the people making it? These CEOs are never going to tell you to regulate AI in a way that harms what they're building or their ability to line their pockets. Never. That goes against the most basic element of human nature: self-interest. Altman and others have absolutely zero incentive to stop AI innovation because even in the simplest of cases, like streaming subscriptions, advertisers will continue to pay them, and they will continue to make money off providing you with show recommendations provided by an AI algorithm.

Did Altman feel pressured to testify before Congress? Maybe. Could you make the argument that this was his punishment for not acknowledging regulations were needed from the start? You could, but I would shoot a counterargument right back: it was a weak-ass punishment. It's like giving your kid a time-out when they're misbehaving but then asking them if they want cookies or ice cream. In this case, he chose both. He played to optimism—*Let me show you what this can do!* He played to caution—*Regulate this, it's a danger!* No one can argue that he didn't play devil's advocate, but you also can't say that he didn't heavily skew one more than the other. *Regulate AI, but regulate it based on what I showed you it can do.* This shit is chess, not checkers, and when you come up against an opponent like AI, you're going to need more than some out-of-touch CEOs to guide you. But those people are few and far between. No one is filling the gap, and when that happens, everyone else becomes collateral damage. It's not just Black women but everyone of color, LGBTQ+ people, people with disabilities, poor people, anyone without personal direct access to decision makers—everyone who doesn't have the means to rail against this machine.

You can see why safeguarding AI is such a problem in that we need to see where it can go and what we can actually do to protect ourselves and our communities. There are numerous iterations of this AI Bill of Rights, now including the *Blueprint*, but it's concerning that we still haven't developed anything concrete. This is not to say there isn't a lot of forward movement, but we must remember the catchall that big tech has always lived by and shows no signs of giving up: there's only so much getting ahead when you're already behind.

The call is coming from inside the house in the Valley. These problems are a symptom of the tech industry's pattern of prioritizing product launch speed while deprioritizing the lives of users in general and racial minorities in particular. That, in turn, reflects the absence of diversity in Silicon Valley, especially in leadership and policymaking positions. When there aren't enough diverse perspectives at the table during the ideation, creation, testing, and launch processes, you end up with products that do not work equitably for everyone—products that can actually disrupt our lives and perpetuate the painful everyday experience of discrimination. Innovation is at the core of the careers that allow me and my husband to provide a good life for our family. The same innovation, if not used properly, could take it all away.

CHAPTER 9
Blind Spots and Big Dollars: People and Profits

> The most common way people give up their power is by thinking they don't have any.
> —Alice Walker, writer and activist

Black women are the consequences and collateral damage of the pitfalls of tech. Voter suppression at a micro level is against Black people—period. Disinformation tells them that Democrats don't care anyway, so why bother voting? Technology is used to hype propaganda and disenfranchise us. Facial recognition is profiling in our communities, and even if the results are incorrect or yield false arrests, it is still being deployed in major cities without our knowledge or consent. So, don't complain about mistaken identity when a city talks about fighting crime. Educational algorithms looking for "ideal students" overlook first-generation college students, who are disproportionately Black people and immigrants of color.[110] At every level you see suppression and denial of opportunity and profiting from erasure and exploitation of Black women via technology.

When we are not at the table, it's easy for companies to develop blind spots that have unintentional ramifications for minorities, fail to see how they are leaving the door open for bias or overt discrimination to creep in, or simply make products inoperable for certain people. I've experienced this myself.

When Facebook acquired Oculus, I was excited to try it out. Walking over to the Oculus building, I chatted with another coworker about what types of games we could play. With vigor, I put the headset on and waited. And waited. And waited some more. Nothing happened. I asked a colleague for help with the headset and told him mine didn't seem to work. He came over and readjusted the strap. I waited again. The headset never worked. When I asked what was going on, my colleague told me the censor couldn't detect my head through my hair.

―――

These blind spots extend to content creators and how platforms monetize the content they do *not* create, instead falling back on the axiom that they are providing a platform for creators to promote their content, and there is not only no attribution to the creators but no monetization for them as well. Facebook first created its self-service ad platform to satisfy clients who wanted to select who saw their ads. This meant people advertising jobs and housing could specifically select certain demographics. It wasn't long before some users only targeted white men between the ages of twenty-five and forty for jobs or eighteen- to thirty-year-old white men for their housing listings. So, while Facebook built what customers wanted, it also enabled them to discriminate against people of color, women, and older people and allowed corporations to break employment and housing discrimination laws. Had any of the people this discriminated against been in the room, these blind spots and others could have been avoided.

In 2019 Ancestry.com released an ad that was received with

rightful outrage, creating undesirable public relations (PR) results. Set in the nineteenth century, the ad depicted a white man holding an engagement ring and encouraging his Black lover, an enslaved woman, to "escape to the North" with him. This bastardized version of the Thomas Jefferson and Sally Hemings "love story" ended with the closing sentiment, "Without you, the story stops here."[111] When I saw the ad, I thought, *Who was in the room when this ad was signed off on?* Surely *someone* there knew the exploitation of slavery isn't a good way to sell services. But as it went, it wasn't just the product that was rebuked. Marketing campaigns without cultural nuance can yield backlash that damages the brand and business for years, and once Black Twitter got ahold of it the next day, the commercial was taken down.

Similar was Facebook's Cambridge Analytica fiasco in 2016, when the company improperly accessed and used the private information of some eighty-seven million Facebook users.[112] Then candidate Donald Trump had the ability to buy access to millions of potential voters' phone numbers and demographic information while dissuading others with disinformation about another candidate's record and the locations of polling places; all of which gave him a head start on voter depression and suppression. Being so plain about lowering voter turnout by singling out Black and brown folks was very telling. For one, Trump campaign operatives and supporters told us that voting for Hillary Clinton wouldn't change anything. But on top of that, they also gave out the wrong voting date, which meant they understood to some extent that Clinton and Trump were not the same, and they had to have a secondary measure to ensure they were protected in case the previous message didn't hit. This digital privacy abuse also revealed that when people are sold to advertisers as a product, what users share can and will be monetized and used against them, and it was only possible because no one was in the room to point out how the use of their data might impact marginalized groups. And they also ignored people who raised those flags *cough* and shut it down before it could be brought to higher levels.

Encouraging low voter turnout through questionable means is a long-standing political strategy, but enabling it with technology just makes it worse. Cambridge Analytica's ability to target marginalized groups of voters was only possible because Facebook overlooked the potential for a nefarious organization to do so. In the face of a long and glaring history of such attempted exploits, this oversight is a symptom of an industry culture that prioritizes speed and deprioritizes the lives of users in general, especially racial minorities. It is a direct result of the absence of diversity in Silicon Valley, especially in leadership and policymaking positions. Conference rooms full of white tech executives—even those of different genders, ages, and presumably political beliefs—can fall into these mistakes via complacency, privilege, and unacknowledged blind spots. Some would call that a feature, not a bug.[113]

———

Technology controls every facet of our lives: how we bank, what ads we see, our credit scores, police presence in our neighborhoods, and where and how we vote—so what happens when these technologies are created without a diverse set of viewpoints? We end up with faulty products and blind spots that have unintentional but grave consequences for marginalized people. Case in point: Facebook Live.

When Facebook Live was due to be launched, we were all excited. I was fully behind the product, but that didn't stop me from pointing out an obvious blind spot. Someone could easily disrobe on Live or tape themselves in the commission of a crime. When I asked if there was a kill switch for the feature, the answer was, "No one would use it in this manner." The answer was naive at best and flippant at worst.

I gave an example of sex workers. "Y'all realize that on the platform we also can send money through Facebook Messenger now. I've used it myself a few times to send money for my annual Christmas gumbo catering. So if I can go on Live in a closed group, and Facebook Messenger allows people to receive money, what, exactly, is stopping me from setting up a webcam business on the platform? Especially if the rent is due tomorrow."

My teammate replied, "But no one would do that, and if they do, we'll fix it on the back end because it needs to get shipped."

Wrong answer. Not having people from diverse socioeconomic and ethnic backgrounds sheltered these product developers from the realities of life and use cases for their product that they couldn't fathom, let alone conceptualize. If you've never been poor, how would you know what people will do for money and attention? If you've never known or been related to someone who participated in a gang initiation, how would you know that they would document proof? I wanted to respond with, *We ship shit and don't think we need solutions for when it goes wrong.* But understand that this doesn't mean they necessarily disagreed. They mainly responded that way because they were under tremendous pressure due to their deadline. Does that excuse their reason? No, but it is important to understand. Even though I brought forward problems that I saw and they went *Mmm,* that didn't mean they didn't see it. It was more of a "We don't have time for this." Problems might get fixed on the back end but not always because others think they are viable or worthy.

While it was nice knowing the issue I brought up wasn't

dismissed out of pure blindness, it didn't stop what came next. Shutting my concern down before it could be taken to the highest person led to a result I anticipated but dreaded: seeing the murder of an older Black gentleman in Cleveland six months after launch and increased requests from law enforcement for copies of feeds and videos. So, the way this is done, you have to decide what you are designing. What problem are you solving? Who is it a problem for? What are you building? Who are you building with? Not everyone will use a product the way the developers do, and testing with diverse populations is a necessity, not nicety. This experience reminds me of the one adage my dad drilled in my head: "If you stay ready, you don't have to get ready." That is arguably the best lesson I learned that applies not only to basic life skills but especially to tech designs and scandals. Tech companies aren't staying ready but instead deciding to get ready "on the back end" at our expense, all because of the perceived race to be the fastest to produce, the fastest to profit. Never mind if it comes at the cost of people's lives.

"Market first, ship fast, fix later (if at all)." That should be tech's motto. Their companies have always been about profit more than their people. Yes, they may purport to care about their employees with their "Come as you are" mantra, but we've seen little of that is true. "Come as we *expect* you to be" is more accurate, as is "Come and do what we want when we want." There is no room for what anyone else wants—the company's wants win. So, if the company wants us to ship out a product before it's properly tested, we will. If they want us to fix its problems on the back end, we'll do it. And if they want us to prioritize profits over ourselves and keep quiet, we will—right?

It's my sincerest hope that we won't anymore.

I understand that speaking up isn't simple. It *sounds* simple, just like making a business case for diversity. If you want to make more money and produce inclusive products that serve larger markets and avoid PR disasters, then listen to marginalized people and implement their ideas. But as a person of color, you have to jump through hoops that are on fire and covered in barbed wire just to get in the door. Once you're in, you have to fight to be heard and then fight harder to see your ideas implemented. The last hurdle? Getting credit for having done all those things and the outcome. Don't dare complain or point out how the company is flawed for not listening. Whistleblowing could be the nail in the coffin that was once your career.

I struggle with that every time I write an article, or even this book. My friends and family love that I stand up for myself and my community, but they worry that it's perceived as complaining. "Are you going to get in trouble?" is my mom's constant question when I tell her I raised an issue at work. It comes from a place of love and protection, but at whose expense?

Whistleblowing has taken center stage in the last few years while employee activism has gained footing inside big tech companies. Whether protesting government contracts at Microsoft and Amazon or attempting to unionize for greater employee benefits and protection, people are exhibiting the courage to challenge the status quo. But when that happens, who is heard and who benefits? Take Frances Haugen, for example.

Haugen was a Facebook product manager who was privy to internal studies on how Instagram use led to the rise of low self-esteem, self-harm, anxiety, and depression, particularly in teenage girls. The ramifications? Less engagement, fewer eyeballs on ads, and less revenue. So Facebook said, *That sucks, moving on.* But when Haugen blew the whistle, she was rewarded with compensation by the Securities and Exchange Commission (SEC) (which is given when it's verified that what you're whistleblowing has related stock issues) and more, which Dr. Safiya Noble articulated: "With respect to whistleblowers, I have to raise my eyebrows with this white woman getting the equivalent of ten million dollars to basically do a world speaking tour and a book deal, when, instead, many of us that talked extensively about wrongdoing lost their careers, and they were certainly not put into her position."

Her words both lift my spirits and weigh me down. They were a true summation of the juxtaposition of what Haugen had to say and what I, or any number of my friends, had to say. Hell, we couldn't even be listened to internally, let alone be the star witness in multiday Congress hearings. This further propelled questions I had been struggling with in terms of legitimization. Who gets to blow the whistle? Who is believed? Who is revered for it, and who is reviled? It is reminiscent of Elizabeth Holmes, who was allowed to lie for years and bring in hundreds of millions of venture capital dollars, while I'm not allowed to tell the truth for free. I've been writing articles about my experiences for a while, and it didn't yield a distinction from *TIME* magazine as one of the hundred most influential people in the world. This all goes back to the adage "Don't shoot the messenger." Well, you can feel free to unload a whole clip on the messenger if she's undesirable. When it comes to profits over people, if the messenger is a Black woman, be prepared for that choppa to spray.

In the last few years, there have been several instances where tech companies have had to reckon with putting profits over people. Shareholder, stakeholder, and employee activism have gained a foothold in the industry, and they aren't letting up. A good deal of this activism has been built off the backs of Black women's emotional labor, strategy, and vocal support. Amazon publicly learned this the hard way.

Timed bathroom breaks. Stepping over a dead coworker, literally, in Ohio. Productivity standards set by robots. Welcome to working in Amazon warehouses. I was horrified to read how Amazon ended up on the National Council for Occupational Safety and Health's "Dirty Dozen" list.[114] Taking directives from your robot overlord (I mean manager) means you are timed for the quantity and speed of your "picking" (selecting and packing items).

Amazon's initial work-around was to use their technology to eventually phase out the humans, which, to me, is just perverse. Determining people's capabilities based on how fast a robot works is asinine. If you are a business and can't hire using discriminatory reasons, but you're basing your measurements on a literal robot, how is that *not* discriminatory? Someone tell me. You are measuring speed and efficiency, not competency, and using a robot that doesn't have to go to the bathroom, eat, take breaks, or take months off if it breaks a limb. Imagine what that means in terms of how businesses then judge employees. It's like asking your microwave, "Hey, how fast can you take my kid to boxing class?" Hello, you're asking a microwave. It can't do that. But that's the equivalent of what Amazon asks its workers to do. Amazon's focus on automation and robotics will cut down on humans working in warehouses, which, in turn, cuts costs and comes at the expense of Black workers, including Black women. It kneecaps their ability to rise in the ranks if they still have a job at all.

Enter employee activism. In March 2020 Amazon opened

a warehouse in Bessemer, Alabama, a predominantly Black area twenty miles south of Birmingham. Paying fifteen dollars an hour with benefits, it was a good job for the area. The warehouse workers consisted of 85 percent Black workers, the majority being Black women. After enduring the working conditions for several months and with the onset of COVID-19, Jennifer Bates, a warehouse worker and learning ambassador (an employee who trains new workers), prepared to be David to Amazon's Goliath. Amazon was wielding its endless resources to ensure that the majority Black workers were convinced they didn't need to unionize. Using technical, economic, and cultural means, Amazon required warehouse workers in Bessemer to attend anti-union meetings after hiring anti-union consultants. The gist of their argument was that unionization wasn't necessary because the workers had all they needed. Who cares about being surveilled or having to empty your pockets to make sure you aren't stealing when you have good hourly wages and some benefits?

For Bates, that wasn't enough. While she acknowledged that Amazon could significantly increase benefits and pay above fifteen dollars an hour, a humane work environment exhibiting dignity and respect for the workers was her primary motivation. The intersection of race, class, and gender has solidified in a material way in Bessemer. It wasn't enough for the products Amazon makes and sells to be used against the community Bates is a member of, but they exploit the people who help distribute them. With grueling ten-hour shifts and the need to constantly walk around the warehouse (the length of fourteen football fields) to do her job, Bates was inspired by the civil rights movement to aspire to start the first United States–based union in Amazon's history. Invited by Senator Bernie Sanders to give testimony to Congress, Bates detailed her work environment to the Senate Budget Committee on March 17, 2021, just a year after she began working at Amazon. In her prepared remarks, she noted that "Amazon brags it pays workers above the minimum wage. What they don't tell you is what those jobs are really like. . . . From the onset, I learned that if I worked too slow or had too much time off task I could be disciplined or even fired."[115] Her testimony created an onslaught of press coverage about Amazon's warehouse conditions, and the day after, Bates was stripped of her ambassadorship. A National Labor Relations Board hearing officer later determined it wasn't due to retaliation, but the timing sure seems convenient. In addition to being stripped of a role that had meaning for her, Bates was also shunned within the workplace, with coworkers reluctant to talk with her lest they be labeled as troublemakers.

With Amazon enabling scare tactics through holding mandatory meetings, posting flyers in the bathrooms, texting employees to warn them against paying union dues, and branding Bates with the proverbial scarlet letter, they successfully persuaded warehouse workers to vote against their own interests. No doubt the characterization and whispers around Bates influenced the outcome. After two rounds of voting, Bates and her coworkers' efforts to unionize failed. And despite becoming a national symbol of workers' rights, she wasn't rewarded with a book deal, invitations to tech conferences, or a multimillion-dollar speaking tour. In fact, Bates received the opposite. She was banished back to anonymity while Amazon ramped up its efforts to make more of Bessemer's employees obsolete. No need to worry about workers' rights and workplace conditions when the workers aren't real. It's easier and cost effective, and it solves that pesky problem of humane working conditions.

Bates's frustrating example triggers questions about what we're doing, or not doing, to combat inadvertent employment discrimination. It's a little late for that, as Bates asserted in her testimony;

we're already on the back end again. But that's the crux of the issue. We've *always* been on the back end, just as we were with Tesla and its self-driving cars that ran over pedestrians of color.[116] Tesla and Amazon are just the bigger, meaner, more devastating versions of what can happen when companies refuse to use their research and development abilities to test products properly—that's how basic, seemingly inconsequential pieces of tech can evolve until we've got self-driving cars running people over and powerful companies displacing a core workforce because how dare they not be able to live up to the speed of a robot's work rate?

It's boggling to think that the government hasn't, and isn't, thinking down the road about how to tackle artificial intelligence (AI) from a policy standpoint and what to be mindful of so that we're not inadvertently making things worse. Because, believe me, things are going to change fast. People are always going to be people—if you have bad knees, you usually have them for the rest of your life—but robots can continuously be improved. AI will be exacerbated. It's already being trained on human touch and vision; soon it'll learn emotional intelligence to a certain capacity, and all that combined with robotics is scary as hell. And what will be the cost, not just economically but also from the standpoint of how businesses run, how we advance as a society, how the current workforce will pan out, and how policies must adapt to them? I, for one, don't want to be judged against AI because it's not made to be judged against my personal standards, or even against the aggregate of people like me. I'm not interested in that, and I don't believe most of us are.

There is a huge risk associated with being vocal in the workplace. It doesn't just affect your current job but extends to potential future employers. I know that feeling all too well. Last year I sat in an interview with a founder chief executive officer (CEO) for the role of, ironically, diversity officer. He was nice enough and seemingly interested in my previous supplier diversity work at Facebook and how I started and led employee resource groups, which his company didn't currently have. But when he spent the first fifteen minutes dancing around the subject of my writing without actually asking me about it, my attorney sense went on alert. There are certain tells, especially in negotiations, that we are attuned to. You can understand what people don't want to lose based on how hard they negotiate for certain things.

"So," he began, "I googled you and found some of your articles. They were really interesting. Gave a good look at what the inside of these companies are doing, or not doing."

"Thanks," I said. I perceived the sentence to be a compliment.

"I guess . . . what I'm wondering is . . . are you going to keep writing?" he asked.

It reminded me of the phrase *If you threaten to lie on me, I'll just tell the truth on you.*

"Yes, I don't have any plans to stop. I've been really transparent about my desire to keep writing, and I said that up front while interviewing at my last two employers. No one seemed to have a problem with it." When I left Facebook, I was adamant about being transparent about writing articles that often critiqued the perils of lack of diversity in tech and the subpar products that yielded. When going on interviews, I told people where to find my articles and asked candidly if it would be a problem for me to continue writing. I didn't want to be forced to stop writing or only write things that would benefit the company. I'd already been lectured on avoiding topics that could implicate the company or encourage people to make comparisons between what I wrote about and where I worked. Enough of that. I write what I want.

"Well, what's going to stop you from writing about us?" he questioned.

"It should actually be my job to ensure there's nothing going on here that I would want to cover," I replied. It was an honest answer. I understood they were just getting started on their diversity program journey, but it seemed crazy that he was asking me to be the head of diversity while questioning *why* I kept writing about diversity. All of that just made me wonder, *What exactly do you have to hide?* If the point is for me to come in and uncover what needs to be fixed, I'll do that. But you have to grant me the ability and the leeway to do so, and this man seemed scared. And the bigger conclusion wasn't just that he was scared but that he didn't want me to *know* what he was scared of, which only told me they knew the things they needed to fix and just weren't amenable to them. Well, guess what? I'm not amenable to that. I'm not a mascot or a cheerleader. I'm not a beard for diversity.

Truth is I don't want to work somewhere that would give me writing material, and to accept this role, I had to feel comfortable that I'd be given free rein to eradicate anything I saw that I would write about at any other company. Fast-forward a couple weeks. I'd already discussed salary and equity and provided names for references. Imagine my surprise when I was told that, unfortunately, I didn't get the role. It wasn't the first time, nor the last. Could I have lied about my intentions? Sure. Would I have felt good about it? Absolutely not. It's a bad way to start a relationship, and make no mistake, deciding to work for a company is forging a relationship. Better for folks to know what they are getting with me than lie to them and pull a bait and switch. I've been on the receiving end of that stunt before.

Putting profits over people doesn't just occur internally; it's also happening externally. Silicon Valley and its companies' models are about extraction. No "addition" is seen as a positive unless it creates greater engagement. Content creation exposes another side to this myth. So many products we see coming out of tech corridors have become household names because of Black content creators, and yet they are the least recognized and the least able to monetize their content but are the *most* likely to have that content weaponized or appropriated. These are spaces where we could actually drive and have influence in popular culture on our *own* terms, but they've built these systems in ways that we aren't able to effectively use for our own gain.

While the founders and creators of social media apps—from Mark Zuckerberg at Meta to Evan Spiegel at Snapchat to Jack Dorsey at Square and formerly Twitter (now X)—have typically been privileged white men, the biggest adopters and trendsetters on their platforms are Black women.[117] Regardless of the platform, though, the dynamic is the same. A Black woman will create something unique on X, Instagram, Snapchat, or TikTok, only for someone (usually a white woman) to copy it and see it go viral, leading to endorsement deals, exposure, and most importantly, credit for something that was stolen. The first prominent example of this is Peaches Monroee. She was the Vine creator who coined the phrase *eyebrows on fleek*. Other people adopted this phrase, co-opted it, or monetized it, with anything cool deemed "on fleek," except for Peaches. By the time she learned of the buzz, it was too late. It was already *out there* in the lexicon. It didn't matter who made it anymore. And the rub is not only are there simple attribution issues, but there are now tools, such as otherside.xyz and vicariously.io, that curate social media accounts and lists specifically to track what others are doing. These tools curate and collect diverse dances, slang, and experiences without having to interact with, hire, or pay Black creatives directly. Worse, they work without proper context or acknowledgment of the creator but always with full pay to the person who copied it. Look no further than Jalaiah Harmon.

Harmon created the Renegade, a viral TikTok dance, as a fourteen-year-old living in Atlanta. After the video was uploaded to Instagram, one of her twenty thousand viewers copied it and put it on TikTok. From there, many influencers re-created the dance, and those with larger followings were given credit as well as the lucrative endorsement deals paired with it.[118] Addison Rae was one of the biggest beneficiaries, even appearing on *Jimmy Fallon* to teach him the Renegade amid an entire lineup of dances she had co-opted from other Black creators.[119] It was only Twitter's backlash that prompted her and Fallon to apologize, though the latter insisted they had acknowledged Rae was not the original creator, and yet still failed to mention Harmon.[120] Besides, an apology is a mere slap on the wrist compared to what Harmon lost out on had she been properly recognized from the start.

To receive credit for a viral sensation also means to receive endless opportunities. All of this plays into monetization and ownership. While you may have created the dance, you effectively licensed it to the platform without limitation when you uploaded it, and you can't "own" a dance in any legal sense. This is akin to not being compensated for your ideas, particularly when they drive revenue for the business, whether internally as an employee or externally as a user. The knife is further twisted when you realize the people being paid for your creation don't look like *you*, which makes it seem that it's more about not *wanting* to pay you for your efforts. You're expected to hand over your creations while others "refine" and monetize them at your cost.[121] In the summer of 2021, in response to Harmon's and many others' work being stolen, Black TikTokers mounted a digital walk-off. The effect was instantaneous: Megan Thee Stallion's new hit single "Thot Shit," which was poised to break TikTok, was a flop. The power of Black TikTokers did not go unnoticed, especially as white creators struggled to produce virality on their own, leaving the platform with only "mediocre lip-syncs and unimaginative . . . dance trends."[122] TikTok responded by instituting a series of "rules" for crediting creators, none of which have been vigilantly monitored enough to create a level playing field for Black and white creators. There is yet to be recourse for those seeking credit or a way for them to sue those who steal their content, but the strike was still a step in the right direction because while it did not create lasting change on the platform, it *did* temporarily prove their value.

Perhaps the most egregious offense on the part of tech companies is using technology not only to discredit and avoid paying Black creators but to erase them entirely. Capitol Records even signed an AI-generated rapper (though they dropped it within two weeks of signing it). FN Meka, a virtual rapper, was the creation of a non-Black-owned AI company, Factory New, with "lyrical content, chords, melody, tempo, sounds, etc." partially created with AI.[123] It didn't just stop at digital blackface with its aesthetic but made sure to say the N-word in its lyrics. Like in all societal transformations, but arguably more so with technological advances, power expands and contracts. Revolutionary change means there's variability regarding who holds power in the end, threatening our sense of inevitability. The problem here is the potential for greater erasure entirely. This is about silent observers becoming loud perpetrators. It isn't limited to music. Levi's came under fire recently for using AI-generated diverse models on their website. The brand worked with LaLaLand. ai, a digital studio that makes customized AI models for companies like Calvin Klein and Tommy Hilfiger to "supplement" their human models.

Avatars used to "supplement" Black culture were used prior to the influx of AI. Anyone over the age of thirty-five likely remembers the Black Entertainment Television (BET) video show host Cita. While voiced by a Black woman, it was a computer-generated host, complete with current slang, talking to viewers in a deliberately sassy voice. Black folks aren't absolved of their participation in the name of cost cutting either. But what AI is evolving into isn't just some cost-cutting measure. It's far worse.

Stepping into a lab to create something already in abundance is co-opting an identity, using it to make money, and intentionally excluding the people you are stealing from. The diversity AI can provide will always be fake—let's not sugarcoat that these are computer-generated avatars of inclusivity. Are brands using Black AI models for pieces when they only photographed a white human model engaging in digital blackface? Are digitally created rappers using African American Vernacular English and in-group epithets engaging in digital blackface? More than that, are Black models being exploited in the name of technological advancements? While on photo shoots, some models have been subjected to body scans that brands can use to create digital replicas of their bodies to model clothes.[124] There are legal issues in denying them the rights to their body and those rights being assigned to a company, meaning the models were losing the rights to their image and likeness. Imagine losing the intellectual property of your own body. That's what is happening.

With the current movement to train AI to use open-source systems to figure out how to have more realistic and more human interactions, we are in danger of losing property over all kinds of work. It starts with AI-generated avatar models; then it turns to using ChatGPT to write scripts that are a mishmash of four people's work. Is that a derivative work, and if so, how do you compensate those authors? Imagine that script was for a movie. It isn't that far off; just look at how Levi's created their multicultural models. They had the training data and some sort of AI software. That's *all* they needed. That's all anyone needs. Movies are no different. You can use any generative AI for background or computer-generated imagery (CGI) to create a location, so there's no need for location scouting. You don't need actual footage. You don't need actors or actresses because, as Levi's demonstrated, you can create characters off of datasets. You might have a character using datasets of Angelina Jolie, Jennifer Lopez, and Regina Hall; a third of each, and *poof*! Character complete without using any of those actresses. Rinse and repeat until you've got an entire cast, and then you've got yourself a whole-ass movie that is hundreds of times cheaper to create. So, what's stopping you from mass-producing them? This begs another question: What does it mean for people's livelihoods? Using AI this way could decimate an entire industry and then some. It means putting people out of jobs or, at the very least, drastically changing the way writers and actors earn their money. How would they make a living? How would they get compensated in the earlier example—do Jolie, Lopez, and

Hall each get a third because they were each used as inspiration? Or does the cut depend on how *much* of their likeness was put into the training data in comparison to the others? There are so many questions, and the answer to all of them is nothing is set in stone. It's a damn free-for-all. What's more, it takes the earlier content creation problems to a whole new level because people are not creating the content; they're running a system that serves to co-opt language and displace actors and writers. Which leads to co-opting an entire culture.

I'm not exaggerating. It's not just entertainment for entertainment's sake. But again, it starts with something small enough that most people won't realize it can easily turn drastic. An example of this was a debate on Black Twitter over two Black movies, *The Wood* and *The Brothers*, about which one people would watch first. Seems pretty innocent, right? Just wait. There's a reason why Black people love these movies. They are cultural touchstones; they capture the authenticity and inside culture of what it means to be Black in America. They're full of inside jokes, references to certain times, places, songs, events, and little cultural in-group markers that you either get or you don't. And when I saw the discourse on Twitter (now X), it made me think, and fear, what might happen to these conversations if AI continues unchecked. They could disappear, along with their actors, writers, directors, and costume designers. All anyone needs to do is fill in the blanks: speech patterns, elocution, diction. The movies themselves could vanish, only to be replaced by mass-produced, AI-generated ones that don't have an ounce of cultural nuance or, more likely, have an inauthentic take based, again, on who is coding and where they're getting the training data from. This leads to the danger that AI can not only displace people but could actively change the cultural narrative of a specific group.

When I think about AI in this context, I am more than fearful for our cultural future. Someone could easily make a mirror of one of these movies and use it in such a debate, telling us that it is emblematic of our culture *and*, worse, prey upon the younger generations who haven't seen the originals. They'll think, *Oh yeah, okay. That is Black culture.* No, that's a sixty-year-old white man from New Jersey telling you what he thinks your culture is. It's kids from Inglewood in 1999 telling you what Black culture back in the eighties was like, and who the hell are they to know? They aren't part of the community or that decade. They literally have no basis for creating this other than the fact that they have the means and the technology. That, to me, is the scariest part because technology raises all of us. It is certainly raising our kids. And now we have something completely generated telling them what our culture is or reflecting it without anyone of that culture contributing, implementing, or distributing it. If that gets shown to people who are not intimately aware of certain cultural touchstones, you can bet your money that it *will* signal the start of the end of that culture. My son, for example, wouldn't confuse an AI-made *The Wood* or *The Brothers* because he's seen the originals, but what about others? What about different forms of content? That I worry about—and as AI advances, it is all too conceivable—is that he and his peers could fall for shit like this in as little as five years.

As evidenced by the earlier examples of Monroee and Harmon, much of what drives American culture, especially in terms of popularity, is what Black people say is cool. We all have touchstones, whether it's TV, music, or movies, but now there's an ability to create all that and more out of thin air. If AI can provide a way to automate that or "create" it, people can easily put signifiers on content to make it *look* as if Black people said something was cool. There's no telling what can be promoted about people without them knowing about it, or what could go around "representing" cultures from the point of view of someone who doesn't know what they're talking about. That's the greatest concern: someone not in a culture telling you what your culture is and then shipping that out to you and everyone else, making you the messenger of that creation without your awareness or input.

To make matters worse, consider how, for most of the world, American culture is exported to every other nation—and the idea of doing that *without* involving the people of that culture is terrifying because it means anyone can define any culture for themselves and make it what they want it to be, whatever is most palatable to them. Does that remind you of anything we've seen before? Yeah, it should. It's a modern, technologically advanced version of colonization; it means doing away with language, cultural markers, cultural references, food, and history. It's content creation gentrification. It's using technology to make us question our own culture, and it's a message to Black communities that they aren't needed.

To me, that's the scariest possibility of our future. And it's already happening.

The irony isn't lost on me that technology that is blind, offensive, and discriminatory is called out on the same platforms that censor Black voices via unfair content moderation practices and give Black women post-traumatic stress disorder (PTSD) with a barrage of misogynist speech. That's the rub. Tech has a way of hurting us when it should be helping us, and that gap is largely due to our absence at the point of origin. But there are ways to mitigate this, starting with the uptick of employee protests.

In addition to unionization for more humane working conditions, employees are on the front lines fighting for a say in how companies deploy their products, and to whom, to ensure they're not being weaponized. Big tech companies have seen more of this activism in the last few years, with protests regarding issues ranging from facial recognition products sold to governments to virtual reality products used to train soldiers to be more "effective" at their jobs. I'll leave it to you to discern what that means. It isn't a coincidence that as the workforce gets younger and "woker," corporate social responsibility and diversity are colliding. Per a 2016 Gallup survey, "millennials struggle to find good jobs that engage them." The bulk of this lack of engagement is due to not finding their work purposeful.[125] This shift in generational workers also meant a shift in internal discussions in the workplace, dovetailing with the election of Trump.

After the 2016 election, a growing number of employees at companies like Facebook, Google, and Amazon began to change their thinking. When their CEOs seemed eager to kiss the rings and adjust for Trump, their employees began to actively speak up about their products being used for harm, particularly to marginalized communities. Companies pledged not to build databases identifying people by race, religion, or national origin. Keeping such promises, however, would require more than talking to one's manager about surveillance or the security state.

In June 2020 Black Facebook employees staged a virtual walkout over lack of content moderation on the platform and the need for diversity in the leadership making those decisions. Zuckerberg has always had a public standpoint of being hands-off with regard to policing what people post, including then President Trump. So, much to the ire of Black employees, incendiary posts blasting the Black Lives Matter movement protests in the wake of the murder of George Floyd abounded. Trump's post stating in part, "When the looting starts, the shooting starts" was the last straw, especially after Twitter applied a notice to his tweet, saying it violated terms of service regarding violence.[126] In response, Facebook employees circulated petitions and threatened to resign due to the lack of content moderation, and several wrote publicly about their unhappiness on Facebook, Twitter, Medium, and elsewhere. Employees described the ire as the most serious challenge to Zuckerberg's leadership since the company's founding.

According to Tech Crunch, "Zuckerberg responded to internal frustration and escalating clashes between protesters and police by announcing that Facebook would donate $10 million to groups fighting for racial justice in the United States."[127] That amount seemed paltry for a company with a market capitalization of over $650 billion at the time. Also, throwing money at a social problem when hypocrisy abounds inside is perceived as disingenuous, at best. Hurting the general populace impacts the bottom line of big tech companies, and having Black women in the room during everything from product conception to content moderation would have saved them big dollars—and lawsuits. Tech executive Annie Jean-Baptiste spoke about a teammate who summed this up perfectly: "If you're talking about 'them,' there had better be some 'theys' in the room."[128] Without them your product is inherently flawed.

At the core of product creation, according to Jean-Baptiste, tech companies should consider who the "user could and should be. It's not about completely doing away with the target customer or user you had initially focused on, but about widening the pool" of who that user could be.[129] There must be an acknowledgment that everyone has unconscious biases, which are born out of how we perceive and are perceived in the world, because our minds use mental shortcuts for decision-making. Acknowledging these biases and the fact that images of creators are *not* the same as the "average user" will shore up many of the blind spots that run amok in tech. Responsible creation requires asking, "I don't represent everyone around the world, so how do I get those different perspectives in?"[130] As Jean-Baptiste says, "I identify as a Black woman, but I don't represent all Black women. So how do we make sure that 1) we're not pegging communities as a monolith and 2) we're getting those potentially historically marginalized perspectives into our product design and development process?"[131]

Jean-Baptiste's research has found that this process should have four essential inflection points: "ideation, user research and design, user testing, and marketing."[132] The problem with incorporating diversity is that diversity, equity, and inclusion (DEI) always centers the moral case: "It's the right thing to do." We know that doesn't appeal to companies; if it did, I wouldn't be writing this book. Instead, the appeal should focus on the business and monetary aspect, which I know from personal experience can be a success. It all comes down to creating "a shift, from seeing these groups as underrepresented to having a ton of cultural and economic power."[133]

When I made the business case for supplier diversity at Facebook, I focused on the spending power of diverse groups and how they want to use products created with them in mind. Aside from the monetary aspect, there is also the new ROI: return on influence. Just as Black content creators are monetizing social media platforms and the companies that advertise on them, companies need to disabuse themselves of the notion that *underrepresented* means "powerless." "Black and Latinx consumers . . . have trillions of dollars in purchasing power,"[134] and women decide the bulk of household spending. Never mind the cultural cache of Black women who start and lead cultural trends, so ensuring that our needs, wants, and use cases are rooted in products is just smart business. Bring us in and bring us in early.

Advocacy starts from the inside and begins with who is sitting at the table. It includes implementing community-based participatory research in the discovery phase to allow the community to "lead at the outset, in terms of what their goals, needs, and challenges are, versus having them come in and provide perspective later in the process"[135] or after the product has shipped. We've seen how that goes. Now it's time to be the advocate, and companies can start with three easy-to-implement solutions:

Be proactive about bringing all the voices to the table. Ask yourself how often people from marginalized communities are in the room when decisions are made and hard questions are asked. Do the decision-makers listen, and then do they implement those ideas? Ideas are fantastic; execution is better. Also, please understand that one person is not a spokesperson for their entire race. We aren't a monolith. Seriously. Having the stamp of approval from the chief diversity officer isn't good enough, particularly when that person may also be fearful of dissent at the risk of losing their job. Making decisions shouldn't be left to one "representative" but a collective.

Deliberately ask yourself how you can be an ally. Be a Trojan horse. If you are in rooms where underrepresented voices have not been invited, find ways to advocate for them. When creating a product or looking to solve a problem, ask yourself if the solutions presented would work for them. An example of this in my own work is when I inquired about a new app that required the user to look at their phone to unlock it. I simply asked, "How does a blind person use this?" No one had an answer, and why would they? No one in the room was blind.

Carefully consider whether your product or new feature may have unintended negative consequences or can be used for nefarious purposes against marginalized people. This is imperative if you are dealing with AI technology, which is used to determine creditworthiness, policing of communities, surveillance, and housing. If you aren't sure what those negative impacts could be, test your products with people from different backgrounds and lived experiences and take their feedback seriously.

What's stunning is the sheer number of tech transgressions we've seen in the past few years: misuse of private user data, subversion of democracy via voter suppression, spread of disinformation due to lack of content moderation, taking investments backed by foreign funds, and continued reluctance to amplify the voices of diverse content creators to address these blind spots. The problem, as always, is having a homogeneous group of people in the room making decisions that affect the lives of heterogeneous populations around the globe. One size does not fit all, and sacrificing an entire group of people for profit while choosing to disregard them is even worse. In fact, being profitable and being principled is only as hard as business leaders make it. Being both can lead to greater profit.

CHAPTER 10

This Is What Tech Is Doing to My Community: You Can Disrupt Without Gentrification

> But in the end, they take spaces, redo them, sell them for a certain amount of money, while the people who have been there are displaced. And in some cases, the people of color who are there are perceived as enemies by white newcomers.
>
> —bell hooks, *Homegrown: Engaged Cultural Criticism*

I remember chuckling to myself when I learned Google was starting to offer a shuttle service from an East Oakland Hills church, about a three-minute drive from my house, to their Mountain View campus. But I should've looked in the mirror because not too long before that, I was driving to a park-and-ride station in Castro Valley to hop on one of those white unmarked shuttle buses to Facebook's Menlo Park campus. Once I left Facebook to go to StubHub, I was a regular commuter from a bus stop near my house, taking the transbay bus to the San

Francisco headquarters. The irony was palpable. In some respects, I'd turned into what I loathed most: a native who acted like a gentrifier.

First, it is important to understand what I mean by *gentrification* and *gentrifier*. *Gentrification* is a term created in the 1960s by British sociologist Ruth Glass to label the phenomenon of middle-class professionals moving into working-class neighborhoods in London with more desirable prices.[136] A *gentrifier* is a person or group of people moving into a historically low-income, urban neighborhood, contributing to gentrification, which often results in the displacement of longtime residents. It isn't used with a positive connotation but as a pejorative. Gentrification is gleefully self-unaware at best and counterproductive at worst. It's essentially newcomers pushing out native residents and businesses to make way for people who can spend more money on new constructions, overpay home asking prices, and demand neighborhoods bend to their whims instead of integrating themselves into the neighborhoods they've moved into.

One way gentrification demands this change is through transportation. Many big tech companies like Facebook have company-operated, WiFi-equipped buses to transport employees to and from their homes in Oakland and other areas surrounding San Francisco. In doing so, these companies and workers have effectively insulated themselves from anything actually in Oakland, the city they claimed to have moved to for a love of the neighborhoods, the culture, and the people. Constantly putting themselves in positions so they don't have to interact with any of the things they supposedly "love" says otherwise.

So, how does transportation lead to unfair demands for neighborhoods to bend? First, turning my city into a bedroom community for those in Silicon Valley who can't afford San Francisco or don't want to live in the suburbia of Menlo Park does nothing for those of us who are natives or have been here for decades. While we can appreciate the tax base, the rate of rent increases is eye-popping and far faster than building affordable housing to keep those natives—who also, by the way, handle a lot of the gentrifiers' services, from dry cleaning to cafés—in the city. If tech companies want to encourage their employees to live in Oakland, they should open offices in Oakland, pay their taxes in Oakland, and encourage employees to live, work, and play in the city. Busing folks in and out every day does just the opposite. For one, it means these employees never get out to interact with Oakland—all they know is what they see from bus windows. Second, they don't *need* to interact with local businesses because, for example, Facebook has everything on campus, from dry cleaning to doctor and dentist offices to nail salons to take-out boxed dinners. They provide so many day-to-day amenities in a blatant attempt to make people work more and disassociate from the communities they live in. If people can get all their chores and errands done at work, they will. They won't go out after work or on the weekends to their local restaurants or service businesses, and if they *do*, the tech bros are going to look for a way to displace them and have them replaced with chains. They're going to demand the neighborhood bend to their desires instead of trying to fit into what already exists. Busing is the worst possible outcome for everyone . . . except those on the bus. It took being a part of that problem to realize I wanted to work toward a solution.

I remember seeing a white woman jogging with a dog in an area of West Oakland lovingly called The Bottoms by natives but now known as Prescott to newcomers. Seeing her jog with this dog on a leash around sunset made me say to myself, *Welp, it was fun while it lasted*, because I knew what was coming. Gentrification in Oakland has been a complex and controversial issue for many years. Oakland, like many Bay Area cities, has experienced significant gentrification in the last decade as more people move to the city in search of affordable housing and tech-oriented job opportunities, whether in the city or nearby. One of the primary drivers of gentrification in Oakland has been the tech industry. As tech companies have expanded their operations in the Bay Area, many workers have moved to Oakland in search of more affordable housing, resulting in the displacement of native Oaklanders. Four main drivers contribute to displacing natives and longtime residents, and I've seen them all up close:

1. Rising housing costs: As tech companies have moved into Oakland, they have brought highly paid employees who can afford higher rents and housing prices. This has led to a shortage of affordable housing and rising housing costs, making it difficult for many longtime Oakland residents to continue living in the city.

2. Gentrification of neighborhoods: The tech industry has also contributed to the gentrification of many neighborhoods in Oakland. As more tech workers move in, they often bring higher incomes, displacing longtime residents and bringing subsequent cultural norms that can change the character of neighborhoods.

3. Displacement of local businesses: The tech industry has also contributed to the displacement of many local businesses that cater to low-income residents. As rents increase, many businesses cannot afford to stay

in the area, leading to the loss of community spaces and the displacement of residents who rely on those businesses.

4. Tech transportation: Many tech companies provide shuttle buses to transport their employees from San Francisco to their offices in Oakland. This means no need to drive and take stock of the city, notice what small businesses there are, or stake out your next haircut place or sandwich shop. Provided transportation negates the need to socialize and explore. Local businesses have always depended on the foot traffic of the people living in their neighborhoods, but they can't anymore: old residents have been displaced and new ones get their services at work. I'm guilty of being a beneficiary of this one.

Additionally, gentrification in Oakland is linked to broader issues of economic inequality and racial segregation by concentrating wealth and resources in certain areas of the city while leaving others far behind. The San Francisco–Oakland area was labeled the fastest gentrifying in the country and has been since 2012, per a 2020 report published by the National Community Reinvestment Coalition, using data from the US Census Bureau. It ranked cities on the rate of gentrification during a five-year period ending in 2017.[137] Oakland was hit hard, with a Black population dwindling from 35 percent in 2000 to 24 percent by 2017. The culprit? The tech boom created a great number of positions but not the housing needed to accompany the rate of job growth. The displacement that's followed has many natives and longtime residents angry and eager to pump the brakes on the culture shift within the city.

The culture shift raises two issues that people tend to want to ignore in this proud blue-collar city: racism and classism. While the case for reparations has been made for American descendants of enslaved people, there is certainly an argument for something similar to be allocated to survivors of gentrification. Yes, I said survivors. It takes a lot to stay in a place that used to feel tailor-made for you and now looks and feels like a stranger. Big tech moving into these communities—both in offices and employees residing in Oakland—played a huge part in that shift.

Oakland has always been portrayed as San Francisco's gritty little sister with a chip on her shoulder, and rightfully so. It is home to an incredibly diverse population, from Chinatown in downtown Oakland to the predominantly Latino Fruitvale district to the Black center of town in Deep East Oakland, and it has been jarring to see people who previously would, or did, live in a heavily gentrified San Francisco now descend upon the city. Once they come east and set up camp in Oakland, after being priced out of San Francisco, they proceed to do the same thing to the people already there. The same "kick out the natives and take the land" spirit exemplified in what some call Oakland's new renaissance is what America was founded on. Now, it's just extending into urban centers after white flight is no longer in vogue and people would rather be closer to the action and shorten their commute. Those who remain, like me, have to not only learn to navigate an entirely new city but deal with survivor's guilt.

Many gentrifiers brought with their move a sense of intellectual and monetary superiority and a desire to get the neighborhoods they now occupy to bend to their will. My go-to example of this in Oakland is a Black church, which has served the community for seventy-plus years, being hit with a potential five-hundred-dollars-a-day noise ordinance violation letter for their choir practices due to a neighbor's complaint.[138] My answer to that is much like the pastor's, who responded, "If you come around a nursery, you're going to hear babies crying. If you come around a church, you're going to hear noise." This is a perfect example of the entitlement shown by newcomers who don't respect the communities they are entering but instead want to change them completely. The irony is many of those same newcomers moved to Oakland because they "loved the diversity" and the culture, but at every turn they want a Starbucks to replace a local mom-and-pop and a new sandwich shop to cater to their desire for "artisan" sixteen-dollar sandwiches. It's easy to spot the newbies in the shiny new bar that plays only rock music and has an indoor bocce ball court that replaced a beloved local dive bar or that took over a formerly abandoned space while complaining about the hip-hop-playing club a block and a half away. But that's just part of the story.

The larger issue is the idea that these communities were not worth investment prior to new residents moving in. With these gentrifiers, suddenly it's a race to spur economic change in a "historically disinvested neighborhood—by means of real estate investment and new higher-income residents moving in—as well as demographic change—not only in terms of income level, but also in terms of changes in the education level or the racial make-up of residents," according to Berkeley's Urban Displacement Project.[139] With the new residents come rent increases. With the rent increases come the hard reality that the neighborhood is no longer affordable for the majority of the people who look like me. And if there is one thing about gentrification and desirable areas, as activist Darrell Owens says, "where white people want to live is where Black people cannot live, and where white people don't want to live is where Black people end up living."[140] With that, it is changing the soul of

Oakland, block by block. New restaurants, bars, and stores are usually seen as the main markers of gentrification. However, the displacement of the previous residents is more impactful and harmful. Many people characterize gentrification as an investment, but if lower-income people aren't displaced, then it isn't gentrification because they're able to participate in the community revival.[141] The problem is the revival isn't for them, nor was it ever intended to be.

Naming practices are also sacred to a place and its inhabitants. Gentrification often renames neighborhoods to make them more palatable for wealthier new arrivals. The resulting erasure of names and their significance to the existing community is a blatant indication that this space is no longer yours, and your status there is not tenable at best and unwanted at worst. New names whitewash a neighborhood in order to imply it's desirable and safe and to distinguish it from what it was previously. Sometimes, new names are just real estate marketing tricks to birth a more exciting place name. It has been jarring, to say the least, seeing neighborhoods that I remember frequenting with my mother as a kid (downtown Oakland to shop at I. Magnin, which is now closed, or Sears, also closed) now being referred to another name, Uptown, to appeal to a completely new demographic. Uptown is the remixed name of what is really part of downtown Oakland, following the city's massive gentrification project in the early 2000s to renovate the Fox Theater and build ten thousand new units of housing around Grand Avenue and Telegraph—most of which is completely outside of the price range of people who previously lived in the area. The irony isn't lost on me. Again, it is by design.

If you build it, they will come, but this isn't exactly a field of dreams. While it's easy to put all the onus on newcomers, the blame can be shared, and should be, by companies that aren't hiring or are firing and laying off Black women in the area. As a Black woman, I am all too familiar with the adage "Last hired, first fired." It's starting to feel that way when just walking around my hometown, which is unrecognizable in some parts. It's akin to the tech industry's long history of displacing jobs predominantly held by people of color, especially Black women, whenever disruption (man-made or not) rears its head. We are the last to be hired but the first ones out the door. Also like the tech industry, there isn't a dearth of talent in Oakland; there's a dearth of opportunity. Never was this more glaringly obvious than during the COVID-19 pandemic, which disrupted tech companies' business strategies and necessitated furloughs and layoffs. With those pandemic-led layoffs, companies ripped off the temporary, cosmetic fixes they'd hastily slapped over the diversity initiatives, not that they had done much in the first place. Once they saw it was okay to do away with the programs, they wasted no time in removing them.

The numbers tell the tale. According to the Bureau of Labor Statistics, in April 2020 women comprised approximately 55 percent of the 20.5 million jobs lost.[142] A glance at the list of people recently laid off at big tech companies, such as Airbnb, Uber, Meta, Google, X, and Lyft, from fall 2022 to spring 2023 reveals that women and people of color took a big hit once again. This setback will have deep consequences for the long-term economic and employment health of Black women, which was trending poorly as it was. As several 2019 McKinsey studies have noted, women and Black and brown people tend to predominantly work in service roles, which are quickly being automated. In fact, almost five million Black Americans will be displaced by automation by 2030—from office support to warehouse and production work industries.[143] We are overrepresented in jobs most likely to be affected by automation and underrepresented in those that are most resistant to automation-based displacement. Automation, artificial intelligence (AI), robotics, and job elimination were already diminishing the livelihood prospects of Black women. The pandemic expedited this practice and made things worse.

The real inequity here is how these cuts are made and who makes them. Not all layoffs are created equal. After several high-profile workplace discrimination cases in the 2010s, some big tech companies started to formalize the criteria used to make layoffs, though it still creates disparate impact. The two criteria are "last in, first out" and their department. Service-oriented and administrative roles, marketing, sales, recruiting, human resources (HR), and diversity are usually first on the chopping block and are predominantly comprised of women.[144] Black women are doubly at risk. Add to the formalized criteria the unspoken criteria, which often has to do with culture fit and relationships.

When looking at the broader workforce, Black and Latinx workers are more likely to work in lower-paid, consumer-facing service jobs that limit their ability to work remotely, according to Elise Gould and Heidi Shierholz, an economist at the nonprofit Economic Policy Institute and the former chief economist at the US Department of Labor, respectively.[145] When tech companies shifted their workforces to work remotely during the pandemic, they furloughed, or got rid of entirely, many of the support jobs that kept that workforce operating smoothly, from office support to food and wellness centers. As tech companies realize they can do more with less, those marginalized people who were made redundant may never get their jobs back. With software as a service, virtual assistants, and robotics handling factory work, economic instability is a threat for people of color, especially Black women—in addition to the onslaught of discrimination they face at the hands of that very technology in their everyday lives. In fact, per Layoffs.fyi, which is tracking layoffs in the tech sector, as of the end of January 2023, "more than 1,000 tech companies laid off nearly 160,000 workers last year, . . . and another 185 companies have cut some 57,000 tech workers since the start of [2023]."[146]

The tech industry has set up a system in which Black women and other underrepresented minorities are the product, consumer, or both. Very rarely have we created what we're using, been asked to contribute, or been given credit when we do. If you don't have to pay for the product, then *you* are the product. We aren't actively creating the technology, but we also aren't participating in making the strategic and policy decisions that have significant economic consequences for our communities. Never mind that we can't even reside in those communities anymore due to being priced out. In that sense, the tech sector doesn't just reinforce economic disparities with its lack of diversity—it actively exacerbates them. Tech is driven by a desire for efficiency that will yield higher profit margins, less overhead, faster product cycles, and greater convenience for customers, but it comes at a steep human price. And that needs to change.

First, tech companies must recognize, own, and understand how they are complicit in creating the economic instability and social climate that affects some racial groups disproportionately over others and takes away our ability to live in the areas that used to be ours. Aside from the shuttles taking gentrifying residents of "Uptown" Oakland to such far-flung locations as Menlo Park and Mountain View, contributing to traffic and the gig economy by way of ride-sharing, DoorDashing, and Instacart messengering, tech hasn't offered much to locals. In fact, it takes more than it gives, which is symptomatic of not identifying with the landscape. While tech companies were born here, they don't identify with being *from* here, and there is a clear difference between the two. Because of that, the actions of tech founders and their employees who transplanted to the Bay Area, and Oakland specifically, to create and exploit opportunities here, shouted to us locals that *what* was here was desirable, but not *who* was here. Their wealth came quite literally at the expense of locals. City governments bent over backward to provide tax breaks, like the notorious Twitter tax break that cost the city $70 million in revenue.[147] Uber and Square bought into the old Sears building, Uptown Station—there's that remixed name again—promising more Oakland-based jobs, only to completely abandon the project when the pandemic hit. It was later purchased by a Singapore-based investor.[148] When the project was abandoned, the damage had already been done. Upon the announcement of Square's arrival, Oakland experienced one of the fastest rent increases in the country. According to *The Guardian*, "The area's monthly median rent for a one-bedroom has risen to more than $2,300, requiring workers to earn $50 an hour to stay afloat," and in 2018 "US federal housing officials classified a six-figure salary as low-income in the region."[149] Imagine $100,000 being "low income." Now, picture who draws that salary and remember they would be classified as "low income" by that standard.

Big tech companies need to implement steps to mitigate the impact their disruptive strategies have on underrepresented minorities. Public-private partnerships are a start. By offering job retraining and new skill acquisition in the five categories most prone to displacement—office and administrative support roles, sales, production and warehousing manual support, transportation/trucking, and food preparation and service—they can mitigate almost 60 percent of the risk to the Black workforce. This is where the "reparations for Oakland" come into play.

For starters, tech companies could actually pay their fair share of business taxes, which would underwrite some of these programs. If companies are committed to their espoused values of diversity, equity, and inclusion, as seen plastered all over their websites and collateral, then they must focus on the talent who already live in Oakland, not actively look past them. I know, I know. I've heard it before too: "It's hard to find good local talent. Where did they go to school? If they didn't go to school, which coding camp were they part of?" No answer is really ever good enough. While tech companies are doing everything they can to broaden the definition of diversity so as to have more employees to count among their diverse ranks, none consider local geography as a component of diversity. That is the exact opposite of what I did when creating Facebook's supplier diversity program. I recognized that as the company continued to expand and eat into more and more of East Palo Alto, not only were residents displaced, but so were their companies. In order for them to stay local, they needed us to patronize their businesses. There is always the excuse of progress being slow and the need to be patient. But almost ten years after big tech companies began releasing diversity reports, how much longer do we need to wait? If you create the talent you need, the wait will be shortened. To eradicate or at least alleviate these inequities will take collaboration across the private, public, and social sectors to promote and pay for job training, retraining, and up-skilling opportunities. These, too, could offer tax benefits for tech companies if funding for these programs comes from their philanthropic efforts (a tax write-off itself).

It is a win-win for all, but most of all for the Black and Latinx communities that find themselves on the outside peering in while descending further into poverty. This phenomenon is particularly glaring in the heart of big tech's locale, the Bay Area and Silicon Valley in California, where those displaced because of big tech's gentrification and inflation effects live in tent villages along the side of the road by the dozens. There is an opportunity to promote and use "tech for good" and finally deliver on a promise Silicon Valley made a long time ago. This is how we make it happen.

CHAPTER 11

This Is Why I (And Other Black Women) Leave

> Reclaiming my time. Excuse me, what he failed to tell you was when you're on my time, I can reclaim it.
> —House Representative Maxine Waters

I can name the exact moment I knew it was time to leave Facebook: the afternoon of June 1, 2016, within eight months of returning from maternity leave.

I had been working there for a couple years. With my manager, the microaggressions were too frequent and the growth opportunities too few. My manager and two other lawyers in the department had decided to rescope my work prior to that to placate another (non-Black) woman who had similarly threatened to leave (notice a pattern here?)—a fact I learned after the rescoping—leaving me with work that wasn't challenging and wasn't as interesting as what was removed from my plate. Worse yet, that news was delivered to me on my day off while I was relaxing at home on a Thursday before I was headed out of town for a long weekend with my husband, Jaime.

My cell rang, and I saw my manager's number. *Nothing good*

can come of this, I thought. I was correct. No one calls you on your day off unless something is wrong or they are stemming the bleeding of something. We all learned this by watching the movie *Friday*, when Craig, played by Ice Cube, got fired on his day off.

"Hi, David. What's up?" I asked.

"Oh, just wanted to quickly touch base and we can discuss this more on Monday, but there are some changes to how you'll support some departments. You will have to allocate more time to others in a trade-off with one in particular. We think Wendy [yes, it's a different one, and that's her real name] should lead there with Labs."

"Why is that?" I asked.

"Well, she has telecommunications experience that you don't have."

"Why is that a problem now? It hasn't been for the last two years," I reminded him. "Do my clients know you're doing this? Are they aware of that change?"

At that moment, Jaime brought me a glass of wine because it was around three, it was my day off, it was five o'clock somewhere, and he heard my voice elevating. As someone who has known me since age thirteen, he heard my tone and knew what it meant. It was peak *This isn't going to be a polite conversation*.

"We really think marketing needs handling, and the way you've wrangled other departments would be great for this."

"Okay. That's all well and good, and I'm already working with marketing. But I still want to work on this business."

"Oh, you can! But Wendy will just take the lead and you work with her and what she assigns you."

"You're serious? You must be kidding me. I was doing this before you both got here. Again, do the clients know you're doing this?"

"No."

"So, then why are you doing this? And if she leads, is there now a reporting structure to her? I need to understand what I'm working with." Jaime came in with another glass of cabernet sauvignon at that point because an hour had passed and I was still talking loudly.

"Well, there will be a dotted line."

"I *know* you're lying!" The facade of professionalism had dropped, African American Vernacular English was in full effect, and code switching had left the building. "So, now I serve two masters? (Pun intended.) Because that's what I hear about this, and you haven't given a solid reason why. Clients don't know. So, they didn't ask for nor approve this change. You're cherry-picking requirements and decided to placate her. What is this and why?" My head was spinning and my heart was racing at this point. *I've already seen how this worked with my teammate, so I'm not going for the okey-doke. Try it with someone else.*

"It gives you a chance to work with her."

"Okay, and she's nice. However, I didn't ask for that, especially if this means she now controls work I was doing autonomously. If you are trying to low-key give her a direct report, just say that. Or if she wants this work in her purview, say that. But I'm not with the work-arounds and the slick words. Also, you could've done this on Monday and not killed my long weekend and trip."

At that point, the doorbell rang. My mom had come over to see my baby daughter and my son. She heard me yelling from my bedroom, down two hallways, and asked Jaime, "Who is she speaking to like this?! Why is she yelling?" He told her it was my manager, and she told him to be prepared for me to be unemployed by the end of the call. Little did I know, my mom was there for a good ninety minutes while I was still on the phone, played with our kids, and eventually left. Jaime heard me after my mom left, still loud, came back in our bedroom, and left the rest of the bottle of wine.

I eventually said "Have a good weekend" to David after three hours. I was determined not to let this occupy my thoughts for my quick getaway weekend. I was wrong.

Monday came, and when I questioned how and why that decision was made, I was called angry by the same man who'd asked me if my husband and I had gotten into college via affirmative action and who'd tried to touch my hair once after inquiring how it "does that." Cue the "angry Black woman" trope. I don't subscribe to that angry Black woman trope because it doesn't apply. Saying what I want and what I deserve isn't a trope. So, go away with that line of thinking. Because I don't exhibit a placating "I'm just happy to be here" attitude, I'm deemed angry. I should've known better when I got a calendar invite for me, David, Wendy's boss, and the vice president of our group. Why this required three people, I don't know, but the subject line said something like "Team Dynamics." Great. We were going to have a team meeting about the "new team dynamics." Only interesting thing . . . Wendy was MIA for this meeting.

Imagine a Black woman sitting across a table from three white folks who outrank her, discussing this new structure and being chastised for not being joyful about having her beloved clients and work ripped away, all while the person assuming this work, and the focus of the meeting, was nowhere to be found. The word *angry* was repeatedly bandied about. Never mind that I had a calm tone and was merely asking questions, which they never directly answered. Because they were trying to evade my questions, my even daring to ask for explanations was an affront to their sensibilities, even as they were playing three-against-one. That entire meeting was a masterclass in gaslighting a Black woman to think something is wrong with her. I was sitting directly across from three people who negated me and my clients' preferences and priorities, espousing the virtues of what they were doing and why it was "for the best." Best for who? Wendy? It certainly wasn't best for me. None of it made sense. In fact, it only got worse when we decided to rescope my work further for "optimal" results. "She's going to control this piece of business now and will assign things to you . . . Give her the custom templates and playbook you made so she can start working with clients . . . Be a team player." Nevertheless, David persisted. To this day, I don't know if he was toeing a party line or doing this on his own accord. Neither would surprise me.

What he said next in a one-on-one meeting led me to reach the conclusion I needed to move teams or leave, declare that conversation over, and walk out. My favorite and most challenging work had been rescoped and reassigned. We met once a week to discuss what I was working on for the team. I was still supporting about nine to ten departments, even though they'd reallocated some of my work to Wendy. I asked him about additional resources in terms of hiring; if we're rescoping, let's do it holistically. The new person was going to take three or four of those departments to relieve me, but I wasn't going to manage them. If this person was going to take my departments and I would need to train them, why couldn't I manage them? My boss said I wasn't ready for management because I was "too fired up" about things, whatever that meant. Then he asked me why I thought I could be a lead counsel *and* manage. He then tried to juxtapose my position with that of my colleague—a guy who had the same amount of experience, fewer credentials, and degrees from lower-ranked schools and who other colleagues had told me had used me as a guinea pig for his own advancement.

I first started with my résumé: I graduated from UC Berkeley in three years; proceeded to get two master's degrees, a JD, and a privacy law certificate; and had the same number of years of experience as my colleague despite doing all of that. I also did this while having a family. I told him that when I started working at Facebook, I reported to a lead counsel who had been promoted to that role only three months prior to my arrival. He'd never managed anyone until the manager who hired me (who was also his manager) quit, and he used that as a power play. I then ran down the list of accomplishments that I'd had there (supplier diversity, employee resource group [ERG] work, back-to-back great reviews, a promotion, the building of a drone, the training programs I'd created) and how I'd done arguably twice as much in half the time, even considering a maternity leave.

"Well, it's not a one-to-one match," he replied flippantly.

"Clearly. No, it isn't," I said. "Mostly because I have done all of this while also having two kids and with less Facebook tenure. So, not sure what you mean. I run a household, am always available, and am here before the rest of you every morning, and still answering emails and working while y'all are out."

"Yeah. But you need practice first to manage, and you can practice on the intern this summer." Of course, the intern he was referring to was the Black woman from Stanford Law who I had to lobby to hire just because others were unfamiliar with her historically Black college and university. Once I got over the fact that he had just dismissed and dehumanized this woman as a pawn for my own advancement, I could get to the core of my issue.

I noted that my teammate who had previously briefly been my manager also had no management experience, even with an intern, prior to me reporting to him.

"Well, life's not always going to be fair" was his response.

"Okay. So, then, this conversation is over." I was never going to win in this environment under his thumb. I excused myself, telling him that this conversation was unproductive and should end. He noted we still had twenty-five minutes left, and I said he could reserve them and we could return to what we were both doing. Then I went to the bathroom and cried for the first time in my career. Hiding in a bathroom stall and sobbing as quietly as possible was a low moment. It was a moment I never thought I would experience. I stayed in there for about ten minutes. When I came out, I was met by the head of human resources (HR) legal, the last person I wanted to see. It was just a reminder that HR is there to support the company's interests, not the employees'. No good would come of me reporting this incident. There would be a halfhearted investigation, no wrongdoing would be found because he didn't yell a slur in my face, and then I'd still have to find a way to work with him. Even the thought of it all was arduous and made my teeth itch.

It is truly exhausting when all you want is to do your job well, but you can't because you are spending your time justifying your humanity or proving your right to be there, trying to include yourself in work or social functions to the point of asking for basic professional courtesy. I was tired of being undermined by coworkers who were having meetings relevant to my work without me, having people wanting to "check" my work before I submitted it, and casually being asked how I felt about yet another unarmed Black man being shot.

These experiences are not unique to me or Black women at large. A 2022 Lean In study found that 36 percent of Black women have had their judgment questioned in their area of expertise, and 38 percent and 59 percent of Black women, respectively, said they don't have substantive managerial support or allyship at work.[150] "Mouthy" Black girls don't get the spoils of white tech bros or even their female counterparts. Instead, we get derision, asked how we were recruited into the company, and compared to a less-credentialed colleague with the same years of experience—in my case, the less-credentialed colleague had threatened to quit (just like Wendy) if he didn't receive a promotion, which he promptly did.

These experiences in which we are disrespected and are *made* out to be the bad person, the angry Black woman, or the unreasonable one are transformations that rot us from the inside. And they are by design, says Aerica Shimizu Banks, founder of the intersectional equity consulting firm Shiso. Banks led policy counsel at Pinterest, but after only thirteen months, internal prodding around her diversity, equity, and inclusion (DEI) and pay equity efforts led to the company blackballing her. But unlike most Black women who are encumbered by external pressures and a lack of backup resources, Banks didn't go quietly. She felt her silence would be complicity, that it would do a disservice to others in a similar situation. She refused to sign, saying, "Keep your money," and went out in a blaze of glory in a Twitter thread detailing her experience.

"That's what they want to do, is kill you," Banks said in an interview with me. "Like death by a thousand cuts. Cuts are the microaggressions, which is the term everyone prefers because they don't want to say what they really are, and that is attacks. Racist attacks. They're not actually micro. They may be tiny cuts, but they all have the effect of killing you. And that's what this disrespect is because it whittles away at your humanity."

Death by a thousand cuts sums up *precisely* what I felt with my Facebook manager. They will wait you out because they've got time to waste; they've got energy to spare. Guess who doesn't?

If a company is going to do these tiny things over and over and *over* again until I'm physically and mentally exhausted and considering going on antidepression medication for the first time in my life because the place where I spend forty-plus hours a week is constantly disrespecting me, then why would I stay? I'm bleeding out, and no one, especially not HR, is going to help me.

When I sat down with my manager that day in June, I was already riding on cut number 999, and his comment about life not being fair was number 1,000. That was my tap-out. I wasn't allowed to write or speak without sign-off from both my department and the diversity department, which really wasn't an approval so much as checking I wasn't taking what could potentially be an opportunity from someone else who some might feel was a better ambassador. I wasn't allowed to help other companies with supplier diversity efforts or recruiting suggestions. I thought a break was in order so that I could reclaim my time and do the work that moved me. I wanted to pick my projects and the experiences that came with them. I felt I had to leave to gain a certain level of freedom that I couldn't have in a gilded cage.

In the last week of November, I talked with Colin, the general counsel at the time, who had already relocated to Washington, DC, but was in California for an event. He didn't know about any of this—not my talk with David or the struggles I'd experienced trying to find another team to work on. But someone had let him know I was thinking of leaving, and being the strategic, sweet, kind man he is, and my football buddy, he made it a point to come to me himself. He came up to my desk wearing the Black employee resource group (ERG) T-shirt from the inaugural Black@ ERG event, which I had saved for him because he was instrumental in supporting it, and asked me to walk with him.

Colin and I have always had a great working relationship,

and we had developed a friendship. My first week coincided with a pop culture moment focused on a gentleman with a gorgeous mugshot who was dubbed "the Fine Felon." I posted about it on my Facebook page one night. The next day, Colin swiveled his chair in my direction and said, "So, you like felons, huh?" I laughed, and he smiled. A wonderful friendship was born. We talked about football, hard topics in politics and race, raising kids, and just life. I once gave him a copy of *Between the World and Me* by Ta-Nehisi Coates when he said he was going on a long flight, and he read it and came back and told me what resonated and that he'd given it to his son, who was also thirteen at the time—the same age as Coates's son who he had written the book for.

So, perhaps our rapport was too good because those above me and below him, which was like four levels, often seemed threatened. Someone in my position shouldn't have that access or that good of a relationship. But maybe that's why I didn't go to him directly—I didn't want others to think I wasn't going through the proper chain of command even though I had enough of a rapport to be able to go straight to the decision-maker. But in hindsight, I should have taken more initiative to tell him sooner that this was happening and ask if he could do anything. I didn't want to put him in such a precarious position, and by the time he knew the full scope of what had gone down, it was too late. My mind was made up, I had an offer in hand from StubHub, and Christmas was in a matter of weeks, so there quite literally was no time for him to implement whatever changes he could to get me to stay. Within weeks of our chat, I was gone. To this day, I love Colin. He is, undoubtedly, the best person I've ever worked under. It was my fault for not taking advantage of his wisdom and support sooner, and to this day I still enjoy texting trash talk during football season and having esoteric tech-oriented legal discussions with him.

Moving on to another company that gave me freedom was . . . well, freeing. I became a writer, a consultant, and a coach for start-ups on diversity efforts at an accelerated pace. Burnout is real, and you can't pour from an empty cup. So I understand why Black women choose to go their own way and leave tech companies behind. Given the treatment we receive—the lack of inclusion, mentorship, and sponsorship—many leave for the perceived greener pastures of entrepreneurship.

And we are leaving in droves. While the number of women-owned businesses grew 21 percent from 2014 to 2019, businesses owned by Black women grew even faster at 50 percent. Black women have also "started 42% of net new women-owned businesses, which is three times their share of the female population (14%)."[151] Y-Vonne Hutchinson is part of that 42 percent.

Hutchinson is an attorney; a cofounder (along with Erica Joy Baker Astrella and others) of Project Include, a nonprofit working to provide transformative diversity and inclusion solutions to tech companies; and the founder of the diversity consultancy ReadySet. She was an international attorney who grew tired of being excluded from social functions, work excursions, and the opportunities for other work that resulted. Hutchinson shares a common sentiment of so many of us: "I don't feel like I left, so much as I was pushed out." Constructive termination due to lack of inclusion is real and routinely dismissed, ignored, or unrealized. Initially working as a consultant with good traction, she realized financial security was tenuous at best. She decided to go back to working for someone else while taking a page out of my grandmother's book and doing what she had to do until she could do what she wanted to do. She was uneasy with the decision, and a welcome lunch the first week at her new organization convinced her she'd made the wrong decision and it was time to go. Already.

> I went to lunch. It was an office full of white women, and I started at the same time as another white woman. I felt so out of place, so excluded, and not a part of the team. It wasn't actively hostile, but it was still actively exclusionary, and I was talked to off of the side of the table. It was clear. If this is how it started, I didn't have any delusions about it being different going forward. I felt so uncomfortable and out of place, and they weren't engaging me in the conversation. There was a clear feeling of "I'm never contorting myself again to fit in. I'm not going to put myself in a position to be miserable at work again." I was there for two weeks and then I left. I knew. It was my breaking point. I'm either stuck here for years and [will] be miserable and hate myself, or I can go off and do my own thing again. Might be broke for a little bit longer, but I can't take this. In that moment, I was choosing myself. It was worth it. I had already seen and experienced this before.

I paused our interview for a moment because this sounded familiar. She continued:

> My last boss before moving to the Bay, when I was working at a nonprofit in Nicaragua, he dated his subordinates. He was a white man. He had angry outbursts and [was] just a really bad person whose messes I had to clean up as head of legal. So, I said to myself, *If he can do it, I can do it.* I had a moment of thought

when I left and had the example of a really toxic, not great individual running an organization and doing it off of the backs of people [who are] actually passionate about the work. If all it took was his charisma and sense of self-importance, then surely I could do it on my own with actual skills. Black women are the largest entrepreneurial group in the country. Now, I have one of the biggest DEI firms in the country at this point. My goal is to make other people's working environments better. This work is about facing and undoing part of my own trauma and creating an environment that others don't deal with the same level of garbage I had to deal with.

Hutchinson's experience isn't unique, and her answer to dealing with toxic environments by leaving is a common refrain.

We end up going it alone because we're weary of being used and passed over. Black women are judged on actual results and records, whereas white men are judged, hired, and promoted based on potential. Another luxury afforded to white men in tech: failing upward. *Failing upward* is the term for the phenomenon in which individuals, often white men, are promoted or given opportunities despite their poor performance or failures. While there aren't thorough statistics on failing upward, several studies have documented disparities in leadership positions and employment outcomes for different demographic groups, including white men. When it comes to funding companies and garnering venture capital (VC) dollars, the idea that these men have gotten where they are due to "luck" is egregious. It completely disavows the notion that the only reason Black women aren't successful within companies or with funding their own companies is because they haven't been lucky. Well, easy to say from a privileged position. If you go to the right schools and have the right network and pedigree, you make your own luck. It isn't so much luck as people will constantly give you chance after chance despite you racking up failures. My friends and I often call on a Black woman proverb: "God, grant me the confidence of a mediocre white man."

A perfect example of failing upward in tech is the curious case of the cofounder of WeWork, Adam Neumann. Neumann cofounded WeWork in 2010 with the mission to create a community-driven, shared workspace where entrepreneurs and businesses of all sizes could work and collaborate. He eventually expanded this mission to include living in a dorm-like fashion in pods and communal spaces with WeLive. Neumann and his wife had kids, so they took this vision further with schools styled WeGrow. It all went wrong when Neumann lost billions of dollars of equity for investors and employees in a botched 2019 initial public offering that revealed the company's rapid growth was fueled by heavy spending on real estate leases that far exceeded any potential for profitability. Additionally, the ethics of Neumann's management style and governance were questioned when it was exposed that he had used company funds to purchase personal items, including a Gulfstream jet, and enriched himself by transferring ownership of the "We" trademark to a holding company that he controlled called We Holdings LLC. This meant that Neumann, rather than WeWork, owned the trademark to the company's name, giving him even greater control. He had to step down from the company he created in 2019 in one of the most embarrassing tech implosions on record. Nevertheless, he persisted. In 2022 he was rewarded with a $350 million investment by Andreessen Horowitz, one of the biggest names in VC, in his new venture, Flow. Even Andreessen couldn't ignore his horrible track record, with a sugarcoated acknowledgment in the press release that the firm "love[s] seeing repeat-founders build on past successes by growing from lessons learned."[152] That's one way to put it.

Dr. Safiya Noble and I had a chat about this when I told her I had joined the cofounding team of a Web3 start-up. Her response? "There have been a handful of Black women that have raised more than one million dollars in a round." I told her I knew and had seen most of them in a *Vanity Fair* spread of the Black and brown women who had raised that or more. To their credit, it was a two-page spread, so more space than expected. But that was also the sad part: it fit across two pages.

"White women still have a hard time raising [capital], but it isn't nearly as hard," said Noble. "The gall and the 'fuck you' temerity of these women, and especially white men—they are able to go back to the well and get more VC funds, and Black women can't get a penny out of these folks. It's part of a structural response to Black women in the Valley, either as whistleblowers or people with great ideas that are overlooked. It's all the same."

She's right. For Black women, failure is fatal, and even with cofounders who are a married white couple, I know it will be an uphill climb to fundraise for the start-up I'm assisting. As I keep saying, Black women have had to do more with less inside of tech companies in order to be recognized, but that doubles to get their companies off the ground. Start-ups with female CEOs get 2.7 percent of all venture funding, compared to 97 percent for white men. And the stats are even more discouraging for women of color. Black women lead fewer than 1 percent of the women-led tech start-ups in the United States, receive only 0.2 percent of venture funding, and have funding rounds averaging $36,000. Compare that to white men's average raise of $1.3 million.[153]

I've definitely seen this attitude when looking for mentors and sponsors inside and outside the office, and I've even spoken out about it publicly on CNBC. I went to a VC forum a few years ago, and someone raised their hand to ask a venture capitalist onstage what he looks for in someone to mentor, sponsor, or fund. His reply was, "I look for people that remind me of myself." Of course, he was a straight, able-bodied, wealthy white man. The first thing I thought was, *Well, hell, I'm screwed then.*

The problem with tech is it is a homogeneous industry fraught with casual racism and sexism. This is also why if this gentleman were to decide to mentor or fund a woman, it wouldn't be me. He could easily find a white female counterpart, likely an alum from the same school and socioeconomic background, without much effort. The cultural cues would also be similar, if not identical. That would range from grooming and appearance (so, natural hair on Black women would be seen as foreign or something to explain) to activities and hobbies like golfing, swimming, and fishing to knowing when it's appropriate to interject in a conversation at a networking event or forum, when and how to properly exit a conversation, and how well the conversation went to initiate follow-up. Even something as seemingly innocuous as pop culture references may not be shared. All these cultural cues that people of the same racial and socioeconomic background tend to have in common means that Black and brown people can easily be left out of the mix in large numbers.

Though I might share the same interests as that VC at first glance, I doubt he would entertain that assumption, let alone ask me to find out. More often than not, when I've been in situations where I meet VCs, or even someone at a conference or panel, the person I'm chatting with and trying to build a rapport with will exclaim excitedly, "Have you met so-and-so? I should refer you to them!" as if it were a wholly original and ingenious idea. The person is always Black. Bonus if they end up asking if I know Monique Woodard, a Black woman VC who is already my friend. That usually draws a sly smile and an affirmative, "Yes, I know her."

I mean, I get it. Maybe they think they are doing me a favor by making me more comfortable with people who look like me, instead of recognizing that I may be more partial to *their* work based on complementary interests or areas of expertise and not just skin color and cultural experiences. Hell, maybe I want to expand my network. I'm trying to step outside of the familiar and my comfort zone, even when it's clear the feeling isn't mutual. Was this even a thought to them?

For many Black women in tech, leaving large companies and the nonprofits that serve them and trying to go it alone is the answer. The rub is trying to get funding for their new ventures. VCs or other investors may have a consistent philosophy or set of criteria they apply when deciding who to invest with, but often, the unacknowledged criterion that trumps all others is "someone who reminds me of myself." This is certainly a huge problem if you aren't a white man, considering white men dominate and fund the industry.

With an unwelcoming investing landscape, Black women are finding their own innovative and creative paths, circumventing land mines of sexism, sexual harassment, and prejudice when fundraising. The same grit that leads Black women to found companies also informs the way they bootstrap and find funds. Unlike their white counterparts, Black female tech entrepreneurs are less likely to have a safety net or family to support them.

While others might be able to raise a "friends-and-family round," that's not an option when your friends and family don't have the means or disposable income to invest in your future. These are things we speak about privately and not in the open. That's why seeing someone like Neumann get chance after chance, even after spectacular failure, is a slap in the face. It just hammers home that potential pays if you're a white man, but your track record better be spotless if you're a Black woman.

Some of the methods we have to fall back on include using crowdsourcing platforms, joining training programs and incubators like Pipeline Angels, and pursuing much smaller friends-and-family fundraising rounds. Many of these programs often do double or triple duty by training women on how to properly pitch in addition to awarding funding for their businesses and teaching women how to be investors and set themselves up to serve on boards. Training women how to effectively pool their resources, bankroll businesses, and make wise, discerning choices will not only transform their individual financial futures, the future businesses and women they fund, and corporate boards but could change the course of the tech industry without any influence from the larger established firms. That kind of global impact on technology and trade could change the game.

CHAPTER 12

We Would've Stayed Had You Done *THIS*: How Tech Companies Could Have Made Us Want to Stay

> I was once afraid of people saying, "Who does she think she is?" Now I have the courage to stand and say, "This is who I am."
> —Oprah Winfrey, producer and author

"There's no diversity because there's a pipeline problem" is nothing more than an excuse. Study after study has proven this claim false. It is an excuse for companies to blame others rather than look at themselves and solve the problem internally because, yes, the problem lies with *them*. Tech companies don't want to do the hard, dirty work; they want everything to be fast, uncomplicated, and shiny. The problem is doing that means, in the short term, they are silencing voices and perspectives. In the long term, they are further cementing systemic racism and spreading disparate impact by continually creating products that harm marginalized communities.

We've answered why Black women are leaving tech en masse. But as we've seen, the lack of diverse voices in this industry doesn't hurt just us; it hurts society. It's in everyone's best interests if more of us could join *and* stay. So, there are two questions we still must answer, clarified by CTO Linda Brooks in *Forbes*: "The first to answer: how can we get more Black women to join the tech industry? The second—and maybe even more important—is, once hired, how can we ensure that they stay?"[154]

If and when a company decides to look at themselves to answer their diversity issue, they will notice the same set of answers keep cropping up, born out of their own self-constructed barriers to entry. This is because an organization's failure to diversify is almost certainly one or a mix of the following: lack of variety in recruiting, invisible job descriptions and requirements, and inflexible working schedules.

———

Tech executives seemingly think that employee recruitment is a one-time occurrence. It is not. As Brooks says, "It is the responsibility of employers to ensure that their recruitment efforts reach diverse prospects to not only bring on candidates of all backgrounds but retain workers by making them feel safe and understood."[155] It is a continual process that includes the interview, the offer, pay equity, leveling and promotion, retention, and discernment with layoffs. It is a complete life cycle. Tech companies would be well served by listening to the simple wisdom of Black grandmothers—then maybe their diversity and retention numbers wouldn't be abysmal. But before you can get help, you have to first see and acknowledge that there is a problem. Then, you have to understand that you don't have all the solutions on your own.

The problem is multifaceted. First, we have to look at why Black women aren't staying, which, nine times out of ten, is the environment. If the goal is to retain more Black women, then you have to provide us with an environment that is actually welcoming of us. As someone who regularly surprises others with my presence in work environments, I know these environments are uncomfortable. Likely any person of color in tech has an example of this. "Oh, you don't want to go to happy hour and play bocce ball? Then you're not a team player." *Well, maybe it's because I spent eight hours with you and want to go home to my real life.* There's a cultural disconnect woven into these workplaces stemming from the lack of diversity. If there were more than a handful of Black women, the culture gap would be smaller, maybe even gone. But there are rarely more than a handful because these companies don't actually have target goals for diversity; they have amorphous goals and no real metrics to improve for their diversity hiring, which means they don't have anything to measure for—so you don't know what you don't know, and you're not going to allocate the necessary resources to diversity in recruitment and retention. The circle continues. So, step one? Have a target goal, have metrics to determine how you can reach that goal, and then allocate the resources needed to hit it. Anything else tells me you're not serious about diversity.

The second step is recruitment. The majority of tech hires are referrals, and it's not hard to guess who people refer: those who are like them. This similarity can be anything, from age to ability to race, gender, sexuality, religion, or socioeconomic status, which leads us straight back to the ever-looming myth of meritocracy. It has an interdependence on a certain cadre of schools—usually schools with low minority matriculation and storied pedigrees. Think Stanford, Harvard, MIT, Brown, Yale, Princeton, UC Berkeley, and Caltech. Schools aren't a competency—where someone went to college or graduate school only tells you that they test well, not that they possess practical skills or knowledge to successfully perform in a workplace—but they are treated as such. Since I didn't go to Stanford, I can't possibly relate to the majority of my department who did—the inside jokes fall flat, as does my ability to relate. In an industry where people want to be surrounded by familiarity, this is a stark disadvantage. But what should that have to do with my job or any other Black woman's? It doesn't. Success in the role doesn't have a direct correlation to my undergraduate school, much to some's chagrin. Though, as we've seen, companies will *still* use this notion to keep the recruiting pool small and exclusive.

The way tech companies structure and implement their recruitment and hiring processes compounds the issue of low diversity numbers. So, tech company, you say you want to find more Black women to hire into technical roles? Then why are you recruiting at MIT, Stanford, and Berkeley? The first thing wrong with this strategy is that you are recruiting from schools with very low Black matriculation, period—let alone those majoring in science, tech, engineering, or math (STEM). North Carolina A&T is a historically Black college and university that graduates thousands of STEM majors a year. If you want to find Black candidates, start there. Or Tuskegee University or Alabama A&M, or Spelman and Morehouse, who do joint programs with Georgia Tech. The first issue is *where* these companies are recruiting from. There is neither a STEM problem nor a pipeline problem. The main problem is they don't care to look outside of certain schools for their talent and human capital, and they don't ask for help discerning where else to look. Talent is everywhere. Access is not.

Recruitment includes the systems a company uses to assess potential candidates, which hearkens back to the idea that the promises and perils of artificial intelligence (AI) are wonderful *if* they're equal trade-offs. The problem is they're not. "What people don't often realize is that there are many decisions being made about them that already use AI," said Dr. Rumman Chowdhury in the *New York Times* article "Eight Big Questions about AI," "like [AI] being used to parse résumés, and also the fact that these résumé-parsing AIs have been shown to reflect human biases and discriminate against women and people of color."[156] AI is great for efficiency in the sense that you can quickly determine who you want to whittle your candidate pool down to, but the concern is who is creating these algorithms and what datasets they're using to make those determinations. We cannot let our desire for efficiency outweigh the need for equity.

As more of recruiting is designated for automation, there's something to be said for having a human touch in the process. Humans can look at each candidate holistically; AI cannot. AI allows you to put in keywords and key numbers such as grade point average (GPA) scores, and it will automatically weed out whoever based on that data, which is great for efficiency but not for diversity. Say there are two candidates: one with a 4.0 GPA who did nothing but code in their room and the other with a 3.3 GPA who worked all four years to pay for college. I don't know about you, but I'd be more impressed by and inclined to pursue the latter candidate. When it comes to the ever-changing tech industry, those intangible skills, like the ability to be flexible and pivot when need be, are instrumental. They can't be taught. So, with that in mind, let's take another look at the first candidate. They've got a flawless GPA, but they're also probably used to just doing one thing at a time. They haven't demonstrated, so far as we can see, the ability to do more than that and succeed, so how would they survive in a fast-paced, evolving environment like tech? That's the kind of question AI may not be able to conceive, let alone answer.

Ignoring those questions speaks to why so many Black women never make it through the recruiting process, and that is because recruiters aren't often looking at the extenuating circumstances. GPAs and school qualifications don't tell anyone's full story. We have to look deeper and consider outside factors like jobs, internships, extracurriculars, and caregiving responsibilities. I don't know many Black women, myself included, who did not work during college in some capacity, whether that was work-study freshman year or a full-time job with school part-time. To me, there's value in that—you worked a whole job and still got a 3.3 GPA? That's not easy. On the other hand, I would wonder why you *don't* have a 4.0 GPA if all you did was go to school and stay in your room coding. But if you didn't experience that, then it wouldn't hold value for you. It's the recurring iteration of the same issue: if you don't know about it, then it doesn't matter, and It speaks to the narrow-minded thinking that pervades the tech industry. This is where the importance of checks and balances comes into play. Recall my struggle to hire the Black woman from Stanford Law because my colleagues didn't know Spelman. Granted, humans have implicit biases, but in this case, my coworker was the negative AI system based on an old dataset, so to speak, and I was the counterbalance saying, "But look at this." If we had been using an AI system coded on biased data, she wouldn't have been hired.

There's a catch-22 in recruiting for tech. They want somebody with tech experience, but you can't get tech experience without tech experience. Somebody has to go first in terms of hiring you, and the answer is to look at them holistically. Consider transferable skills from different industries. Many moons ago, I worked in advertising before attending law school. But here's the thing: as a tech attorney, much of my job isn't that different from advertising. It's still client service, just with internal clients instead of external. I still do the same things: hand-holding, project-management, telling clients what we can and can't do, making sure we have good communication, and figuring out creative solutions. Those are all transferable knowledge and skills. Would an AI system have been able to deduce that and apply it to the job application to make an argument for it? Unlikely. Looking holistically at a candidate involves stepping outside the frame of what people think someone in tech should be and look like, and that won't happen unless the people coding for those systems are doing it.

The problem is circular—without fair representation that advocates for an inclusive environment, companies will not retain diverse employees, and companies will not have fair representation if they don't widen their recruiting pool and examine the systems with which they recruit candidates. So, first, get your metrics down and set goals. Second, look internally at how you screen candidates, evaluate whether you're looking at them holistically or not (and implement different strategies if it's the latter), and actively work to incorporate more schools and companies to recruit from. These initial steps are crucial to not only getting Black women and other diverse candidates into the mix but retaining them as well.

———

Another problem with the retention of Black women in tech is living up to invisible job descriptions. Unspoken qualifications are danced around in a job description but not articulated clearly. This starts with the actual description as written, as it is the first point of contact line when recruiting Black women. If folks were honest from the gate about what the role entailed, we could make better, informed decisions about what role to take and know when *not* to take on a role that would ask us to perform two jobs for the pay of one.

Everywhere I've gone, with the exception of Facebook, where it wasn't as blatant, I took on what I like to call being Black America's help desk. If there was any employee resource group (ERG) issue or there wasn't an ERG or a diversity department to begin with, it always fell on me. "Hey, can you help us with <insert anything to do with a diversity topic>? How do Black employees feel about this?" Well, first of all, you're asking me to take a poll of the eight other Black employees *and* be a snitch. Second, you want me to figure out how to fix it in addition to all the actual work I have to get done. It's asinine, but that's how it always went. I was the de facto diversity department because these companies were too public relations (PR) conscious to not care but too cost-conscious and indifferent to make tangible differences to "justify" hiring an actual diversity person and they wanted to use diversity initiatives to "quell the natives." They were only looking for their own personal do-boy or do-girl to reassure the executives that they were making the right decision on something internally controversial about their diversity efforts.

The ironic part is I *wasn't* listened to most of the time, and from brunches with my girlfriends, I learned I wasn't the only one. At Facebook in particular, "Raquel," in the diversity department, almost seemed to go out of her way to shoot down our ideas. She kept repeatedly telling us no. *No, we can't have Black Lives Matter shirts. No, we can't have a town hall. No, we can't have a locked ERG discussion board so that our bosses can't peek in on us to see what we actually go to one another for help about.* Well, you can bet nobody is going to come in and post anything substantive. Why would they ask about how to navigate a toxic boss when they know their boss can just hop in whenever and see what they're posting? Raquel's rebuttal was always the same: "Why can't you just have a conversation with your boss or HR?" Girl, come on. Nobody's doing that, and you know why. She reminds me of the colloquialism "It be your own people," what with the number of times she actively tried to stop us from implementing our ideas. You would think in these roles that your job is to advocate and be helpful, but it isn't—you're just the first in line to be thrown under the bus if what you're bringing up doesn't suit the needs of whoever you're answering to. So, while I didn't like it, I understood it. Raquel has to eat too.

I wouldn't have accepted many of these jobs *if* these companies had been up front about what they were really looking for in these roles. Don't just mention the legal work if you really want the person to be legal *and* a diversity officer; hiding half a job or a full-on other job never works out well, and it will only lead to depression and burnout, as evidenced by my time at Retirement 101. It's no wonder they're having such a hard time retaining Black women—no one would stay under such circumstances where you're being told you're needed and then aren't listened to 99 percent of the time.

Job descriptions are not written to truly articulate what it takes to be successful in a role. When I've given seminars on diverse recruitment and consulted with tech companies, I tell them that diversity starts before sourcing for a role. The first thing that should happen is to properly scope out both the role and what it should feasibly grow into in two years. If someone won't grow past this role in two years, perhaps you don't need a full-time employee. Once this is discerned, how is the company crafting the job description? First, cross off any perceived gendered or exclusive language. I've seen more than my fair share of descriptions that have asked for "ninjas" and "rock stars." Right there I'm turned off. What is a ninja or a rock star? I can't say, but what I can translate from that descriptor is it sounds like a man, for one, and the language itself is coded and dripping in a vernacular I would never use. Just reading that makes me feel like it isn't a fit culturally. And maybe that's the point. If I read the description and conclude that I wouldn't fit in there, I'm not going to spend my time applying.

The fix for this is to focus on the skills and qualifications required for the job rather than creative wording. Job descriptions are often written in a way that discourages looking at a candidate holistically. Rarely do I see a job requisition that separates what I call "must-haves," "nice-to-haves," and "moon shots." In layman's terms, that's what is absolutely required, what would be helpful, and what is likely impossible to find. Every bullet point on a job description isn't necessary to be successful in the role, but they are not separated out in a way that makes it easier to weed folks out of the candidate pool. So, if a company is asking for a rock star, how many qualified candidates are they turning away simply by using that terminology? More than they like to admit.

There's an oft-quoted but mythical Hewlett-Packard internal memo noting that men apply when they meet just 60 percent of a role's qualifications while women wait until they meet closer to 90 percent of them. A *Harvard Business Review* article referencing this reveals there are additional complexities at play.[157] For starters, due to race and gender I wouldn't doubt it if Black women make sure they have every single qualification, if not more. I know I've read every single job description I've ever applied for multiple times. Women are judged on results, while men can squeak by on potential. Black women? You have to be better than both. Sometimes that isn't even good enough. So it may seem silly to say that I, or other Black women, won't apply to a job that describes their ideal candidate as a rock star for fear of not meeting its qualifications, but it isn't. There is some kind of personality or characteristics that this company ascribes to a ninja that they are not actively articulating. How can we possibly know if we hit them when that information is deliberately withheld, and who knows what other invisible descriptions exist? Recruiters for that company should ask themselves what their definition of a rock star is. What intangible qualities and distinguishing qualifications make up a ninja in their eyes? Then lay them out there so potential candidates don't have to guess their meaning. Be up front and transparent, and qualified candidates, including Black women, will come.

Invisible job descriptions lead to another problem with retention: the invisible job *requirements*. What are these? Let me give an example from my time at Facebook. One morning I received a vague meeting invite from a sourcing manager I worked with often, named "Jody." I'd seen enough vague emails to know that I was going to be chastised for something. The day before I'd had a terse conversation with Matt, who she managed, so I knew this meeting was going to be about that exchange. I was curious about how this conversation was going to go. Matt was an affable white guy who I typically liked working with. He also worked with some of my teammates for different deals, so I knew that while he'd been in sourcing for a time, there were elements of this particular role that were unique and difficult. We had discussed this in team meetings. Supporting a department that is building novel technology is rife with unique issues that can impede getting a deal over the finish line. Matt was always eager to please, but lately he'd been swerving into lanes that weren't his on deals that involved heavy negotiations with the other side. I clicked Accept on the invite and mentally steeled myself for what we'd discuss.

I met Jody on the benches outside the large cafeteria at the complex known as the main campus. We weren't eating, and it was clear this was going to be just a conversation, which was cool with me. Jody's a straight shooter, and I loved working with her because she was so direct. There was no pretense or bullshit. If she thought something about your work, she'd tell you. It was refreshing. Working at a company where every conversation was prefaced with "assume good intent," even when it was clear there wasn't, had grown stale. With Jody, I didn't have to assume anything. So, working with another woman who was comfortable in her own skin, was always prepared, and was direct with praise and critique was refreshing.

"What's up?" I asked her.

"It's about your meeting with Matt yesterday," she said.

"I figured." I sighed.

The conversation with Matt had quickly gone left. We met to discuss a deal we were working on in which custom intellectual property (IP) would be developed. Prior to the meeting, I had provided redlines that he was going to give to the opposing side. Imagine my surprise when we met and I asked him if the company had any response or if they had accepted our changes. He pulled out his laptop and said he had a document to forward to me.

I looked at the document he sent, took a deep breath, and said, "This isn't what I sent. Is this a different deal you're working on with the vendor that is separate from what we're working on together?"

"No, this is it," Matt said. I took another deep breath and lowered my head. *This is completely asinine*, I thought. *We've done this four times already, and I don't understand why he wants to play lawyer at my expense and prolong the close of this deal.* It was now the fifth time I would have to tell him that it wasn't in his purview to make redlines for legal. Considering I'd already done this four times before, my patience was gone. Effectively, Matt was tap-dancing on my last good nerve.

"Matt," I calmly said, "your lane is negotiating and redlining deal terms around price, percentages, supply terms, and quantity. That's more than enough to work with. My lane is the legal terms, especially when it comes to IP. We've done this four times already. We've had this discussion four times. I'm getting frustrated telling you that you're swerving into my lane after I've repeatedly told you not to."

"My thought is this would get us to the finish line faster," he countered.

"This is actually doing the opposite, Matt. Each time you do this, I have to go back to what it is I've already suggested, re-redline this, and then hope that you don't play with the document before sending it off again. Then, when I get it back, I have to run a comparison to see if anything has changed from both you and the vendor. You're actually doubling my work and taking more time. It would be easier if you just didn't swerve into my lane. You're sourcing. I'm legal. They aren't the same. We do different things but work together to create the whole. Are we good?" While I said my piece calmly and directly, just as I'd seen my teammates speak to him when handling deals and he'd stepped out of bounds, I immediately worried that he would take this in a different direction or feel some type of way about it. I walked away from that meeting thinking I'd finally gotten my point across when I saw the document sent off to the vendor and there were no additional changes later that day. What didn't happen spoke volumes, though. The usually very communicative Matt hadn't contacted me to say he was sending the email or asked if there was anything else I thought he should tell the vendor. So, that was out of the ordinary.

"Bärí," Jody started, "you made Matt cry."

"Excuse me?"

"Matt came back from meeting with you and asked to speak

to me. We went into a room, and while he was telling me about the meeting, he cried. He said you yelled at him and belittled him." My mind was racing, and I could feel that familiar heat in my ears. *This is the shit I'm talking about. I saw Ben get at him in a way worse fashion last week and was actually yelling, but I'm the person who gets talked to by his manager?* I could feel the elasticity in my face working overtime while I tried not to grimace.

"He cried because I told him to stop practicing law without a license?" I asked.

"Basically," Jody said.

"Jody, it's literally a legal ethics issue to help someone practice law without a valid license. If I accepted these edits or didn't say anything, I'm breaking my professional ethics obligation."

"Well, it wasn't so much what you said, but how you said it to him. That was his issue," she explained.

"I was just as direct as you normally are with him. I didn't raise my voice. I didn't disparage him. I simply told him to stop doing my job because he was actually prolonging this process."

Jody heard me, and she agreed that perhaps he was overreacting but asked if I would apologize to him because I hurt his feelings. Apologize to a white guy who had cried because I had just told him to stop doing my job and instead do his own. That was the request. It only got worse when I went back to my desk and my manager told me he'd received an email from Matt detailing our meeting and how I'd offended him and made him contemplate quitting. So, now the same man who asked me if I'd gone to college on either a sports scholarship or due to affirmative action was telling me I needed to apologize to an overly sensitive white man who was offended by someone reminding him of the responsibilities of his role. Never mind that Ben had done the same thing the week before and hadn't been asked to do anything. This was peak white fragility, except this time, the weaponized tears were coming from a man and not a woman. Coddling this man was not my job, and if that's what he needed, he should've called his wife or his mama.

The last wrench in this ordeal was how I was silenced and devalued, another knock in retention problems. It's what went wrong with Matt. Hand-holding Matt wasn't on my work bingo card. I merely told him the same thing a (white male) colleague told him, and instead of being praised for setting boundaries, I was not only punished for it but also made to apologize. The kicker? It came up in my annual review. The performance review cycle was a six-month cadence, and my interaction with Matt was outside the review dates. That didn't stop my (white male) manager from bringing it up and docking me for it. Maybe he felt attacked through osmosis. That was the first time I ever wrote a response to a review, but while it made it into my file, no one cared.

Unfortunately, things like this are expected of us because companies are accustomed to allocating invisible job requirements with little to no pushback. Just as I had no clue that coddling grown white men was part of my job, it seems I somehow should have surmised and lived up to that expectation with no warning. There are lots of things that people expect from us but don't articulate. Exhibit A is pedigree. Why this matters, no one can definitively say. Companies' reliance on candidates' academic backgrounds from schools Black people often don't attend is another way the scales are tipped against us. College choice alone is a poor predictor of work performance.

Part of having the requisite "pedigree" is that I should know my place. This translates to sacrificing my well-being to make others comfortable at work and generally demonstrating a disposition of just being happy to be there. I had to be vocal about it. After the fifth time Matt came and gave me more work by trying his hand at law without a license, I was over it. And in doing so, I crossed the invisible requirement line that goes hand in hand with stereotypes of Black women. We're one extreme or the other, the mammy or the angry woman. We're either going to cuddle you, hold your hand, and fix it for you or we're going to tell you all the ways you fucked up. With Matt, I was right in the middle. I was allowed to mammy him, and I did the first four times, but was I allowed to point out the absurdity that he was making my job harder? Of course not, because calling out behavior that actively hurts me is not "knowing my place." That is me going *against* the stereotypes about women in the workplace, reminding men of their moms or wives and never challenging authority.

Invisible job requirements apply doubly to Black women; we are expected to be the den mothers, and we're never supposed to speak up about unfair treatment—like when my manager refused to celebrate my Faceversary each year, so my coworker invited me to hop in on his just so I could get that acknowledgment. We are not allowed to be introverted, have a bad day, or treat a job simply as a means to an end. To do so is to render yourself "cold," "attitudinal," and "unapproachable," which is quite possibly the worst, even though Black women, or any women, really, don't owe you likability. But because I should simply be happy to be there, I should also be willing to be as extroverted as possible in order to fit in and assuage any fears people have about making the right hire. This is what I learned dealing with Matt. He is the standard, not the outlier. Even more relevant, instead of having my back, my manager doubled down on the notion that I should have been gentler with Matt's feelings—to hell with the fact that no one had been gentle with mine when I had been offended or dismissed.

Black women aren't allowed the room to be direct, to be strictly professional without divulging personal information, or to say no to anything. To do so is to hear the kiss-of-death comment: "Bärí doesn't like me." Replace Bärí with any Black woman's name, and there you have it. This is a common refrain my girlfriends and I have heard on loop since we entered the workforce. What's interesting is how much more often we hear it in tech, which is supposed to be a bastion of "Come as you are" and casualness. With that casualness is the expectation that we're there not just to work but entertain. When I fail to live up to being the company or department jester—a "funny, entertaining, sassy, Black woman stereotype," in the words of Sequoia Holmes[158]—I'm quick to be labeled as unapproachable or told I don't like them. Funny how that works. Some stereotypes are embraced, wanted, and expected to dispel others, and perception being reality confirms others.

Holmes continues, "This isn't a huge problem until it's time for reviews, promotions, or layoffs. Then, it quickly becomes an insidious dehumanization tool that can result in job termination because Black women are not afforded the luxury of introversion, especially not in the workplace. I'm used to feeling discriminated against because of my race and gender, but I'm only starting to understand that being an introverted Black woman has also a source of discrimination throughout my life."[159]

For me, I've found that I've been discriminated against for being strictly professional. This ranges from being asked to explain some viral dance challenge or pop culture moment or slang, because that's what I'm expected to do, to being criticized for not smiling enough. I like to joke with colleagues, but I fear I'm running the risk of not being taken seriously when doing my job or being undermined or disrespected. Holmes reminds us that "Black women are not allowed to exist in peace without providing entertainment to others," or being hyperaware and accommodating to others' feelings, "particularly not in the workplace where our livelihoods are at stake."[160] That's a dangerous game.

Yes, the workplace needs to be professional, and employees must be able to work with others. But as Holmes says, it's more than this: "White men are given the freedom to act however they'd like as long as they're good at their job (and sometimes even if they aren't) because they're seen as individuals and not as a stereotype. I've experienced white men who speak over me every time I talk, but they aren't perceived as rude. I've experienced white men who have bad attitudes, but they hit their numbers, so it's all good. Being good at your job and keeping things professional should be all that's required to avoid negative criticism, but that only seems to hold true for white men."[161]

How do we fix this? It comes back to a previous point: transparency about company culture. If someone had let me know that part of Facebook's culture was to coddle fragile white men, that would have saved both me and Matt from so much. If someone had let me know that Retirement 101 wanted me to sit in one spot for forty hours a week and not move to the couches (why were they there if we weren't allowed to sit on them?) just so the boss could see I was working (because *obviously*, I wasn't if he couldn't see me), it would have saved me a year of working there. Why hide the ball at all? Having invisible requirements doesn't help a company other than to give them an excuse to fire people for not living up to conditions they weren't even privy to in the first place. I can't live up to expectations that I don't know exist. They're just playing games, and people's livelihoods and mental well-being are not to be played with, so just get to the point and lay it out there. And if you do set a false expectation, you have no right to be upset when people don't meet it. You also shouldn't be surprised when retention numbers fall, especially for women of color.

On our end, we need to be proactive about calling out this bullshit when it comes to us, meaning we need to circumvent the expectation. I started doing this after I left Facebook. In every interview I had going forward, if there was someone on the panel who I would have to interact with a lot (there usually was), I asked them how they like to work with others. How do they like to communicate? How do they like to receive information? What's their preferred method of communication—in person? Call? Email? Video chat? It is crucial for me to know; that way we can work best together. Alongside companies being more transparent about what their culture is really like and what their expectations and requirements are, there is some onus on us to seek out that information whenever an opportunity presents itself. That is how we're going to make these companies care about what's happening. If we bring the indignities up not just when they happen but in places like interviews, we are sending a message to big tech that we are not willing to play their games and that if they want to retain us, they will have to do better.

Being transparent about job descriptions and requirements extends to the flexibility of working schedules, which, for Black women, is a paramount concern. If tech companies valued productivity instead of face time and emotional vulnerability, remote work would be an excellent way of both recruiting and retaining us. When I started working as in-house counsel in tech, the jobs were all in the Valley. I want to move to a place with a greater sense of Black community and Black excellence—something I've pined after for years. Remote and flexible work arrangements are the key. My 2020–2021 pandemic story isn't special, but staying at home and homeschooling kindergarten, as hard as it was until my mother (God bless her!) put her retired teacher hat back on and stepped in, alleviated a lot of the issues I had at work. Prior to the office shutdown, I was going into the office every day with a commute that took about an hour each way. Making sure I got my kids out of the house and off to school in the morning was the easy part; being able to pick them up after school was hard. Everyone was still sitting at their desks at five every day, and one of my kids was waiting for me to pick them up from school aftercare and another from preschool aftercare, both by six unless I wanted to accrue late fees. In fact, I recall a time I was on the Facebook shuttle and it broke down midtransit to the park-and-ride where all our cars were. We were told a new shuttle would come and rescue us, but those of us with kids decided to break into groups and hop into Ubers so we could get back in time to pick up our kids from childcare. It was the same at Retirement 101, where they said, "Hey, it's a flexible work schedule. You can leave at this time." All that sounds good until you're hiding in a stairwell at 4:30 p.m., trying to catch an elevator on a different floor without letting people see you—even though the company said leaving early for pickup was perfectly okay before you signed your offer letter. If the company culture is being there until 6:30 p.m., say that. Don't lie to kick it.

Black women were hit hard by the pandemic. Dealing with a lack of childcare, being caregivers for older relatives, and trying to hold down a job were all concerns. Add to that the fact that COVID-19 had a disparate impact on the Black community, and Black women were proverbially treading water while not knowing how to swim. A National Women's Law Center report found that job losses hit Black women the hardest during the pandemic. During 2020 Black women lost a net of 562,000 jobs, and their labor force participation rate fell from 62.5 percent to 58.3 percent. The report concludes Black women are overrepresented in low-wage jobs that do not provide paid sick leave or flexible schedules, making it harder for them to balance work and caregiving responsibilities.[162] For Black women, those second-class citizen jobs in tech are often linked to HR, diversity, and marketing—exactly where we congregate the most.

Flexible work schedules and remote work would be excellent retention mechanisms because they allow Black women to build work around their lives instead of the opposite. With caregiving responsibilities being paramount and a lack of disposable income to supplement personal obligations, allowing for flexible and remote work would give Black women autonomy over their work lives. I know I wasn't afforded that measure of grace. I was expected to maintain my same work schedule while simultaneously being a teacher, lunch lady, and full-time head of legal. It was impossible to do all three jobs at complete capacity. That said, I was luckier than most. My mother lives about a ten-minute drive away. Being able to call on her was a luxury many Black women, even in tech, don't have, and I never took it for granted. On the virtual brunches I had to commiserate with friends, most bemoaned living in the Bay Area for their jobs, so far from a family safety net that they had to balance teaching or childcare with working five days a week. Many tech companies with a "work from anywhere or at any time" policy are attractive because performance is judged on results, not responsiveness. Asynchronous work means companies can judge an employee's work on output and productivity, not through an inherent bias for who is, literally, in your face. It is the most objective way to work and judge the output of that labor.

So why aren't there more flexible working schedules in tech? Because these companies have spent exorbitant amounts of money and sunken costs on real estate and contracts for services they can't get out of—they *need* bodies to fill up the buildings and use those services. Is it necessary? For many positions, no. If something does not require in-office work, those people should not have to physically be there. And in tech, that encompasses so many departments, such as HR, marketing, sales, legal, finance, and procurement, to name a few. You could even make the case for engineers and coders. For design teams and user experience and user interface teams, it can be more efficient to work together physically, but does it really require forty hours a week in the office? I don't think so. The pandemic and subsequent lockdown blew a lot of fallacies out of the water regarding remote work, and it's only because these companies are desperate to justify their massive spending sprees that they are asking their employees to return.

Additionally, remote work allows for more diversity in hiring and retention. If companies don't require in-person work for positions that don't need it, they can cast a wider net in terms of where they can recruit people. Recall from chapter 11: many workers, especially Black women, don't want to live in the Bay Area. The Bay is incredibly spread out, so it's harder to figure out where to go for every little service. The questions my ERG had for me from the start (Where do I get my hair cut? Where do people hang out? Where are the good restaurants? Where do I go to church?) have no easy answers when you live in the Bay. Maybe you love the restaurants in Santana Row in San Jose. But the good barber you like is in San Leandro, and you live in Oakland. You work in Menlo Park. So, you're trotting all around the Bay Area just to get stuff done, and who wants to do that several times a week when they've also got caregiving responsibilities either for elderly parents or their children? No one.

The answer is to allow people to stay in the communities they've already built their lives in, where they're comfortable, and have a company that supports them, will include them, and makes them want to stay. If Black women are allowed to work where they have community, as opposed to living and working in a place where the onus is on them to build or find community, it will be easier to recruit and retain them. People do their best work when they're happy, let's not forget. If I'm working where I'm just waiting for the weekend, you can bet all your money that I'm not doing my best work because all I'm asking myself is, *Is it Friday yet?* No company wants their employees to have that mentality, so don't give us any reasons to have it running on a loop.

Uprooting one's life is a demanding task, especially if caregiving or supplemental income duties are involved. Eliminating the burden of building an entirely new life in a new, possibly unwelcoming or isolating environment sets the groundwork for success. Black women will be able to give more at work because they are whole in their personal lives, which leaves room for greater professional satisfaction and initiative.

The four bedrock reasons companies can't retain Black women have unique solutions, but they are all underscored by one underlying action: listen to us. It sounds simple, but it isn't easy to do. Don't discount our experiences or waive our grievances. Directly address problems as we raise them. Treating us as if we are the problem is, well . . . a problem. When the head of legal for HR asked why I was crying in the bathroom, I was honest with them, and what transpired after that admission just made things worse. As an attorney, I know HR is there to protect the company. That is their sole purpose. It is not to protect individual employees, despite what they may tell you. "We're here for you!" Sure. That also means you're here to manage me out via constructive termination if I speak too loudly and too long about what is wrong with my manager. In my experience, I made my troubles known, and people who had the ability to fix the issues bent themselves out of shape and did every manner of mental gymnastics to drum up reasons as to why I should do something differently instead of their addressing the problem. That is where your retention problem comes from: these companies are not actively dealing with the source of the problem. Instead, they suggest, "Well, why don't you move to a different department?" Or, "Why don't you try a different role on a different team?" No. Why don't *you* just deal with the actual root of the problem? That is, the institutional investment in coddling the offended white man.

When we talk about the retention of Black talent, we have to dismiss the attitude of "You should just be happy to be here."[163] That attitude gives rise to the problematic invisible job descriptions and requirements; it makes Black women the issue. It sequesters us alone on an island, devoting all our time and energy to getting back into everyone's good graces. That, along with noninclusive recruitment strategies and a commitment to inflexible working schedules, is why companies cannot retain us. We cannot perform to the best of our ability when we are not set up for success. So, if you *really* want to see what we can do, get rid of the markers that automatically put us at a disadvantage. Meet Black women where we are, and we never disappoint. Get out of the way and watch us work.

Conclusion

From the moment we entered the Information Age, we knew technology would create unimaginable benefits. We also weren't obtuse to the fact that it would come with devastating pitfalls. But the tricky thing about the tech industry, and writing about it, is the difficulty in combating its ever-changing nature. Speed dominates tech; after all, time is money. So, why bother to write about the issues or protest them if everything is always changing and you can assume issues will be taken care of in the latest new product that's due in a matter of months? My answer is simple: those issues *aren't* getting addressed because they're the same ones we've been calling out for years. And with growing consequences amid the painfully slow process of policy and regulation, we can't keep going like this. We have to change. Tech has to change.

We've known for decades that the future of society lies in this industry. From printers to cell phones to the internet and AI, technology has and will continue to lead our lives and shape our futures. Only that future doesn't include *all* of us, does it? Certainly not me, those who look like me, or members of any marginalized community if we continue to disregard the urgency for diversity.

How can we be included when our voices are continually squashed, our ideas stolen and left uncredited, and our experiences trivialized? It's easy to get swept up in the exciting prospect of new technology, but it is imperative that we understand our future is being conceived, designed, and disrupted so menacingly that it's difficult to grasp the severity of the consequences.

Tech has always packaged itself as something convenient and helpful. Take streaming services, for example. How many do you have? Do you use the recommendation feature? Of course; it's so convenient. No more analysis paralysis. Then you go to social media, where you're bombarded with ads for what you just googled five minutes ago, and huh, that's a little weird but still helpful. But we don't realize that the algorithm is curating content based on how it's already profiled you, which hearkens back to the idea that if you aren't paying for the product, you *are* the product. They're aggregating everything you liked and viewed or bought and creating an avatar of who you are, then showing you things that fit that narrative. The point is we're always giving away information unless we're completely unplugged, which most of us aren't. Still, it seems pretty innocent to most of us—which is a problem.

As tech advances, so does its disparate impact. Recall airport hand sensors. Whenever I travel with my kids, the pattern is always the same. My daughter, who is light-skinned, has no problem activating the sensor to get soap or paper towels. I have a difficult time, and my son, who is the darkest of the three of us, has the hardest time. One time, when we were struggling underneath one sensor, this nice white lady, who had just gotten her towels from the one next to us, said, "Oh, this one works." She didn't know ours wasn't broken or why it wasn't picking up our hands, and I didn't expect her to. But not understanding the inputs that made the dispenser not work for us just plays into the growing invisibility of disparate impact and the knowledge that tech can also be not just convenient but actively harmful. These machines, which were designed to make traveling easier, are suddenly making things tougher, but only for a certain segment of people. And just like streaming service recommendations or social media ads, bathroom dispensers are the smallest of those concerns.

When you understand that tech is something innocent until it's indicative of everything else you're not able to do, it begs the question, *What are all the other "dispensers" that we don't know aren't working?* That could be figuring out which schools accept you, whether or not you make the cut for an interview or layoffs, creditworthiness, how much you get in a home loan, how many police patrol your neighborhood, prosecutorial options, sentencing variability, parole eligibility—all things you have no control over, didn't consent to, or have anything to do with but that still have enormous impact on your life. How much of what happens to us is determined by something none of us understand?

We think just because we aren't using tech to create killer robots means the devastating consequences are yet to come, but that isn't true. The ways we use AI *now*, from policing to housing to school admissions, are stoking a slow-burning fire. All those adding up in the aggregate can change the direction of somebody's life, and they would be none the wiser. We don't know when these systems are being used, who's using them, how they're being used, or what data they're based on. We're deliberately being kept in the dark with no way to opt out and no grounds on which to sue. And the way this is going is the same way it's always gone—it will strike certain groups of people first and harder than others.

Black people, in particular Black women, have historically borne the brunt of disparate impact when something has gone unregulated for an extended period of time. With redlining and restrictive covenants for housing, we couldn't get home loans. And if we did, we couldn't live in certain areas because it was written in the mortgage documents that houses couldn't be sold to a Black person. We have often lifelong hurdles based on creditworthiness, state and local voting laws, and lack of affordable childcare, and there is always another hurdle to jump over. Tech and AI are just the latest leading causes to exacerbate all of it. These unintended, discriminatory consequences are the effects of not having diverse voices in tech. They are the ramifications of Black women being both unseen and *too* seen when we are scrutinized and questioned yet still discounted, expected to be mediocre yet perfect, when in reality we have to be exceptional just to hang on while everyone else can coast. If we don't retain more diversity, we will fall into the awful pattern of repeating the past and exploiting labor and culture. We've all seen that movie before. So, let's make a choice to *be* different. To *do* different.

Hiring and retaining more diverse workers is a start, along with being transparent about information inputs since, as with AI, we don't necessarily sign away our data so much as we're defaulted into something we can't always opt out of. But tech companies and employees aren't the only ones with work to do—regular consumers also hold responsibility. The power of consumers is unparalleled, but it's also given up far too easily because we don't realize that we *have* such power. That's how the 2016 presidential election happened; instead of mobilizing back in 2010, we waited for something horrible and drastic to occur, and then we took charge. It's the same as people getting lulled into a false sense of convenience that they're giving away personal information and forsaking their individual rights to get free Candy Crush points—until it becomes clear how those systems are affecting them. Well, news flash: you're not alone. This is happening to all of us, and the easiest way to pinpoint your participation is to count how many streaming services you have. Sure, it may be benign compared to creditworthiness, but they are still curating through an algorithm and telling you what to watch and, more importantly, what to *like*. They're not giving it to you arbitrarily. So, the answer is simple: act before it's too late.

Our attention often focuses on issues at the federal level, but many of these decisions are also being made at the municipal and state levels, and those laws are the ones that affect us day to day. Recently in Oakland there's been a big debate about the use of license plate readers. Is it a privacy issue? Yes, completely, and that's coming from a privacy attorney. But also, as a victim of being caught in the crossfire of a rolling gun battle on I-580W, I see the value in these readers—a few seconds and boom, you've got their name if you've got their license plate number. That is something that likely won't be discussed on a federal level, but at least in my city it will, and that's the type of critical thinking and attitude of awareness of how these technological advances can make us safer, but at what cost to privacy? These are the questions we need to keep asking. Understand what's going on directly around you. Go to those city council meetings and pressure the people who represent you in your districts. Write letters to your senators and your congresspeople because this disparate impact through tech is already happening locally. Extra hurdles are appearing as you read this, inducing an imbalance for marginalized communities, for Black folks, and particularly for Black women.

Ensuring we are given a fair chance to participate in that future as it is being built is urgent and essential. If Black women can be a part of creating the future, we can normalize our presence and experiences in it rather than become the targets of scrutiny and suspicion. We can ensure the world considers and addresses our needs—and those of everyone else—rather than exploiting them. We can make sure that everyone is seen fully as an asset and not a threat, that everyone is heard. Finally. We'll all be better for it. So, what are you waiting for?

Acknowledgments

My writing life would not be possible without the support of many people whom I'd like to acknowledge and thank.

First, I'd like to thank my mom, Linda; my two kids, Gabriel and Adrienne; and my husband, Jaime; for their unwavering belief in me: "*Ugh.* You're still writing?! These better be great stories!"—Thank you, Gabriel. I think they are.

My Strong Women Village: San Francisco Chapter of The Links, Inc. and Alpha Nu Omega Chapter of Alpha Kappa Alpha Sorority, Inc.

My Usher Crew: Shanyn, Cydney, Jamie, Tamika, Haili, Andrea; and my Drake folks: Leah, Katuri, and Jana.

Family who rooted me to the finish line: my brother, Scott, Janet, Big Barry, Hilton, and Dottie.

Mentors: Colin Stretch, Melissa Murray-Hill, and Ed Goines. Legal heroes for me!

Last, to fellow writers in the trenches: Genoveva; Dr. Jason Johnson, who introduced me to the wonderful woman Felice, who changed it all for me; Lisa, who Felice introduced me to; and Luvvie. All of you told me to keep going when I didn't want to or didn't want to tell the whole story or give too much. Thank you. Immensely.

Notes

1. Natasha Singer, "Amazon's Facial Recognition Wrongly Identifies 28 Lawmakers, A.C.L.U. Says," *New York Times*, July 26, 2018, https://www.nytimes.com/2018/07/26/technology/amazon-aclu-facial-recognition-congress.html.

2. "How It Started vs. How It's Going: Layoffs Edition," Layoffs.fyi, December 29, 2020, https://layoffs.fyi/2020/12/29/how-it-started-vs-how-its-going-layoffs-edition/.

3. Bärí A. Williams, "Did Tech Companies Keep Their Promises One Year after George Floyd's Death?" *Fast Company*, May 25, 2021, https://www.fastcompany.com/90640015/did-tech-companies-keep-their-promises-one-year-after-george-floyds-death?partner=rss&utm_campaign=rss+fastcompany&utm_content=rss%3Fcid%3Dsearch&utm_medium=feed&utm_source=rss.

4. Amanda K. Sesko and Monica Biernat, "Prototypes of Race and Gender: The Invisibility of Black Women," *Journal of Experimental Social Psychology* 46, no. 2 (March 2010): 356–360, https://www.sciencedirect.com/science/article/abs/pii/S0022103109002698.

5. Stephanie A. Fryberg and Sarah S. M. Townsend, "The Psychology of Invisibility," in *Commemorating Brown: The Social Psychology of Racism and Discrimination*, ed. Glenn Adams et al. (Washington, DC: American Psychological Association, 2007), 173–193.

6. Valerie Purdie-Vaughns and Richard P. Eibach, "Intersectional Invisibility: The Distinctive Advantages and Disadvantages of Multiple Subordinate-Group Identities," *Sex Roles* 59, no. 5 (September 2008): 377–391.

7. Jess Huang et al., *Women in the Workplace 2019*, McKinsey & Company, October 2019, https://www.mckinsey.com/~/media/McKinsey/Featured%20Insights/Gender%20Equality/Women%20in%20the%20Workplace%202019/Women-in-the-workplace-2019.ashx.

8. Michele Goodwin, "The Death of Affirmative Action, Part 1," *Chronicle of Higher Education*, March 15, 2012, https://www.chronicle.com/blogs/brainstorm/the-death-of-affirmative-action-part-i.

9. Tim Wise, "Is Sisterhood Conditional? White Women and the Rollback of Affirmative Action," *NWSA Journal* 10, no. 3 (Autumn 1998): 1–26, http://www.jstor.org/stable/4316599.

10. Sarah Javaid and Marie S. Cole, *Resilient but Not Recovered: Black Women in the COVID-19 Pandemic*, National Women's Law Center, https://nwlc.org/wp-content/uploads/2022/08/nwlc_BlackWomen_RESILIENT_FS.pdf.

11. Lean In, *Women in the Workplace 2020*, https://leanin.org/women-in-the-workplace/2020; Lean In, "Working at the Intersection: What Black Women Are Up Against," https://leanin.org/black-women-racism-discrimination-at-work.

12. Rebecca Betterton, "The Rising Purchasing Power of Women: Facts and Statistics," Bankrate, January 4, 2023, https://www.bankrate.com/loans/personal-loans/purchasing-power-of-women-statistics/.

13. Tyler Sonnemaker, "Facebook Says It Will Spend $100 Million Per Year with Black-Owned Business," *Business Insider*, June 18, 2020, https://www.businessinsider.com/facebook-underrepresented-groups-30-percent-new-hires-executives-by-2023-2020-6?IR=T&r=US.

14. Mathilde Roux, "5 Facts about Black Women in the Labor Force," U.S. Department of Labor Blog, August 3, 2021, https://blog.dol.gov/2021/08/03/5-facts-about-black-women-in-the-labor-force.

15. Hired, *2020 State of Wage Inequality in the Workplace*, 2020, https://hired.com/wage-inequality-report/2020/#intro.

16. Samantha Delouya, "I Got Fired from my $190,000 Job at Meta for Posting on TikTok, but There Wasn't Much Real Work for Recruiters like Me to Do," *Business Insider*, March 31, 2023, https://www.businessinsider.com/fired-from-my-job-at-meta-for-posting-on-tiktok-2023-3.

17. *Merriam-Webster.com Dictionary*, s.v. "tokenism," accessed November 1, 2023, https://www.merriam-webster.com/dictionary/tokenism.

18. Built In, "The State of DEI in Tech," 2021, https://employers.builtin.com/report-state-of-dei-in-tech/?utm_medium=article&utm_source=builtinwebsite&utm_campaign=dei2021.

19. Richard V. Reeves and Sarah Nzau, "Black Americans Are Much More Likely to Serve the Nation, in Military and Civilian Roles," Brookings Institution, August 27, 2020, https://www.brookings.edu/articles/black-americans-are-much-more-likely-to-serve-the-nation-in-military-and-civilian-roles/.

20. Uwa Ede-Osifo, "A Debate Brews among Black Ivy League Students over Representation on Campus," NBC News, November 4, 2023, https://www.nbcnews.com/news/nbcblk/debate-brews-black-ivy-league-students-representation-campus-rcna117726.

21. Robert Cherry, "Affirmative Action Helps Black Immigrants, but Not Black Americans," American Enterprise Institute, October 7, 2022, https://www.aei.org/op-eds/affirmative-action-helps-black-immigrants-but-not-black-americans/.

22. Jeffrey Cord, "As Black Immigrants Collect Degrees, Is Affirmative Action Losing Direction?" *Baltimore Sun*, March 20, 2007, https://www.baltimoresun.com/news/bs-xpm-2007-03-20-0703200125-story.html.

23. Christine Tamir and Monica Anderson, "*One-in-Ten Black People Living in the U.S. Are Immigrants,*" Pew Research Center, January 20, 2022, https://www.pewresearch.org/race-ethnicity/wp-content/uploads/sites/18/2022/01/RE_2022.01.20_Black-Immigrants_FINAL.pdf; Jason Lalljee, "Black Immigrants Earn about $6,000 Less Than Other Immigrant Groups, Even Though They Have the Same Share of College Graduates," *Business Insider*, January 28, 2022, https://www.businessinsider.com/black-immigrants-bachelors-degrees-earn-less-income-than-peers-caribbean-2022-1#.

24. Eileen Patten, "Racial, Gender Wage Gaps Persist in U.S. Despite Some Progress," Pew Research Center, July 1, 2016, https://www.pewresearch.org/short-reads/2016/07/01/racial-gender-wage-gaps-persist-in-u-s-despite-some-progress/; Jason Lalljee, "Black Immigrants Earn about $6,000 Less Than Other Immigrant Groups, Even Though They Have the Same Share of College Graduates," *Business Insider*, January 28, 2022, https://www.businessinsider.com/black-immigrants-bachelors-degrees-earn-less-income-than-peers-caribbean-2022-1#.

25. US Equal Employment Opportunity Commission, *Diversity in High Tech*, May 18, 2016, https://www.eeoc.gov/eeoc/statistics/reports/hightech/index.cfm.

26. AnitaB.org, *2021 Impact Report*, October 2021, https://anitab.org/wp-content/uploads/2023/03/AnitaB_org-21-IMPACT-REPORT.pdf.

27. Jess Huang et al., *Women in the Workplace 2019*, McKinsey & Company, October 2019, https://www.mckinsey.com/~/media/McKinsey/Featured%20Insights/Gender%20Equality/Women%20in%20the%20Workplace%202019/Women-in-the-workplace-2019.ashx.

28. W. E. B. Du Bois, "Strivings of the Negro People," *Atlantic*, August 1897, https://www.theatlantic.com/magazine/archive/1897/08/strivings-of-the-negro-people/305446/.

29. Camille Lloyd, "Black Women in the Workplace," Gallup, March 5, 2021, https://www.gallup.com/workplace/333194/black-women-workplace.aspx.

30. Michael Kinsley, "The Myth of Meritocracy," *Washington Post*, January 18, 1990, https://www.washingtonpost.com/archive/opinions/1990/01/18/the-myth-of-meritocracy/ff68b614-f5bd-44e3-9c66-f1f0957a3a49/.

31. Ed Grover, "The Myth of Meritocracy Is Increasing Inequality, Book Argues," PHYS.org, October 25, 2017, https://phys.org/news/2017-10-myth-meritocracy-inequality.html.

32. Bill Gates, "Bill Gates, I'm Lucky That My Parents Were Rich," Theoxa, December 25, 2021, YouTube video, https://www.youtube.com/watch?v=i0HhhT2OMXs.

33. Jose Antonio Vargas, "The Face of Facebook," *New Yorker*, September 20, 2010, https://www.newyorker.com/magazine/2010/09/20/the-face-of-facebook.

34. Zameena Mejia, "Jeff Bezos Got His Parents to Invest Nearly $250,000 in Amazon in 1995—They Might Be Worth $30 Billion Today," CNBC, August 2, 2018, https://www.cnbc.com/2018/08/02/how-jeff-bezos-got-his-parents-to-invest-in-amazon--turning-them-into.html.

35. Daniel Golden, "The Story behind Jared Kushner's Curious Acceptance into Harvard," ProPublica, November 18, 2016, https://www.propublica.org/article/the-story-behind-jared-kushners-curious-acceptance-into-harvard.

36. Daniel Golden, *The Price of Admission*, updated ed. (New York: Crown, 2007).

37. Table 302.60, "Percentage of 18- to 24-Year-Olds Enrolled in College, by Level of Institution and Sex and Race/Ethnicity of Student: 1970 through 2018," National Center for Education Statistics, August 2019, https://nces.ed.gov/programs/digest/d19/tables/dt19_302.60.asp.

38. Jess Huang et al., *Women in the Workplace 2019*, McKinsey & Company, October 2019, https://www.mckinsey.com/~/media/McKinsey/Featured%20Insights/Gender%20Equality/Women%20in%20the%20Workplace%202019/Women-in-the-workplace-2019.ashx.

39. Huang et al., *Women in the Workplace 2019*.

40. Alex Butler, "Roger Goodell on Low Minority Hiring in NFL:

'We Need to Change,'" United Press International, January 29, 2020, https://www.upi.com/Sports_News/NFL/2020/01/29/Roger-Goodell-on-low-minority-hiring-in-NFL-We-need-to-change/4281580329659/.

41. Jessica Guynn, "Facebook Turns to NFL Playbook to Fix Diversity Problem," *USA Today*, June 18, 2015, https://www.usatoday.com/story/tech/2015/06/18/facebook-rooney-rule-nfl-diversity-silicon-valley-technology/28919649/.

42. Guynn, "Facebook Turns."

43. Ian Cook, "The Rooney Rule: Using It to Kick Off Your Diversity Recruitment Strategy," Visier, accessed March 6, 2024, https://www.visier.com/blog/how-hr-can-tackle-diversity-using-the-rooney-rule/.

44. Cook, "The Rooney Rule."

45. Jeremy Engle, "Does the N.F.L. Have a Race Problem?" *New York Times*, February 9, 2022, https://www.nytimes.com/2022/02/09/learning/does-the-nfl-have-a-race-problem.html.

46. Jeff Green, "Corporate America Loves the Rooney Rule. But Does It Work?" Bloomberg News, https://ampvideo.bnnbloomberg.ca/corporate-america-loves-the-rooney-rule-but-does-it-work-1.1740585.

47. George W. Bush, "Speech to the NAACP," *Washington Post*, July 10, 2000, https://www.washingtonpost.com/wp-srv/onpolitics/elections/bushtext071000.htm.

48. Tsedale M. Melaku, "Why Women and People of Color in Law Still Hear 'You Don't Look Like a Lawyer,'" *Harvard Business Review*, August 7, 2019, https://hbr.org/2019/08/why-women-and-people-of-color-in-law-still-hear-you-dont-look-like-a-lawyer.

49. Vikram Ahuja, "Why Employee Referrals Are Crucial for Hiring in Tech, and How to Get Them," Talent 500, June 23, 2022, https://talent500.co/blog/employee-referrals-crucial-for-hiring/.

50. Katie Canales, "Tech Employees Are Selling Referrals Online to Job Candidates for under $50 to Help Them Get Hired at Google, Facebook, and Other Industry Giants," *Business Insider*, June 29, 2020, https://www.businessinsider.com/rooftop-slushie-tech-workers-buying-job-referrals-2020-6.

51. See Mark Murphy, "If You Think Your Job Is Hard, Imagine Being Apple's Head of Diversity This Week," *Forbes*, October 15, 2017, https://www.forbes.com/sites/markmurphy/2017/10/15/if-you-think-your-job-is-hard-imagine-being-apples-head-of-diversity-this-week/?sh=384f417b71fe.

52. Bärí A. Williams, "Tech's Troubling New Trend: Diversity Is in

Your Head," *New York Times*, October 16, 2017, www.nytimes.com/2017/10/16/opinion/diversity-tech-women-silicon-valley.html.

53. John Shinal, "Fired Google Engineer James Damore Says Company Is 'Like a Cult,'" CNBC, August 11, 2017, https://www.cnbc.com/2017/08/11/fired-google-engineer-damore-says-company-is-like-a-cult.html.

54. Billy Perrigo, "Why Timnit Gebru Isn't Waiting for Big Tech to Fix AI's Problems," *TIME*, January 18, 2022, https://time.com/6132399/timnit-gebru-ai-google/.

55. David Needle, "Women in Tech Statistics: The Latest Research and Trends," TechTarget, December 14, 2022, https://www.techtarget.com/whatis/feature/Women-in-tech-statistics-The-latest-research-and-trends.

56. Janice Gassam Asare, "Facebook's 2019 Diversity Report Reveals There's Still a Long Way to Go," *Forbes*, July 11, 2019, https://www.forbes.com/sites/janicegassam/2019/07/11/facebooks-2019-diversity-report-reveals-theres-still-a-long-way-to-go/?sh=45b1c7973d1f.

57. Sophia Kunthara, "A Closer Look at Theranos' Big-Name Investors, Partners and Board as Elizabeth Holmes' Criminal Trial Begins," Crunchbase News, September 14, 2021, https://news.crunchbase.com/health-wellness-biotech/theranos-elizabeth-holmes-trial-investors-board.

58. John Carreyrou, "Hot Startup Theranos Has Struggled with Its Blood-Test Technology," *Wall Street Journal*, October 16, 2015, https://www.wsj.com/articles/theranos-has-struggled-with-blood-tests-1444881901.

59. Jessica Guynn, "White Women Benefit Most from Affirmative Action. So Why Do They Oppose It?" *USA Today*, updated June 30, 2023, https://www.usatoday.com/story/money/2023/06/29/affirmative-action-who-benefits-white-women/70371219007/.

60. Jessica Hubbert, "70+ Women in Technology Statistics (2023)," Exploding Topics, November 14, 2023, https://explodingtopics.com/blog/women-in-tech.

61. Jenny Chang, "52 Women in Technology Statistics: 2023 Data on Female Tech Employees," *Finances Online*, https://financesonline.com/women-in-technology-statistics/.

62. Susanne Hupfer et al., "Women in the Tech Industry: Gaining Ground, but Facing New Headwinds," Deloitte Insights, December 1, 2021, https://www2.deloitte.com/us/en/insights/industry/technology/technology-media-and-telecom-predictions/2022/statistics-show-women-in-technology-are-facing-new-headwinds.html.

63. Brian Armstrong, "Coinbase Is a Mission Focused Company," Coinbase, September 27, 2020, www.coinbase.com/blog/coinbase-is-a-mission-focused-company.

64. Armstrong, "Coinbase Is a Mission Focused Company."

65. Emily Sullivan, "Laura Ingraham Told LeBron James to Shut Up and Dribble; He Went to the Hoop," NPR, February 19, 2018, https://www.npr.org/sections/thetwo-way/2018/02/19/587097707/laura-ingraham-told-lebron-james-to-shutup-and-dribble-he-went-to-the-hoop.

66. Joy Buolamwini, "Artificial Intelligence Has a Problem with Gender and Racial Bias. Here's How to Solve It," *TIME*, February 7, 2019, https://time.com/5520558/artificial-intelligence-racial-gender-bias.

67. Jessica Guynn, "Ex-Google Employee Alleges Unequal Pay," *USA Today*, July 21, 2015, https://www.usatoday.com/story/tech/2015/07/21/former-google-employee-alleges-unequal-pay/30481175/.

68. Bärí A. Williams, "8 Ways to Measure Diversity That Have Nothing to Do with Hiring," *Fortune*, April 20, 2017, https://fortune.com/2017/04/20/workplace-diversity/.

69. Alison Cook and Christy Glass, "Above the Glass Ceiling: When Are Women and Racial/Ethnic Minorities Promoted to CEO?" *Strategic Management Journal* 35, no. 7 (July 2014): 1080–1089, https://doi.org/10.1002/smj.2161.

70. Shonda Rhimes, *Year of Yes: How to Dance It Out, Stand in the Sun and Be Your Own Person* (New York: Simon and Schuster, 2015).

71. Quoted in L'Oreal Thompson Payton, "Black Women and the Glass Cliff: 'I Was Supposed to Bring Some Kind of Black Girl Magic,'" *Fortune*, November 6, 2022, https://finance.yahoo.com/news/black-women-glass-cliff-supposed-130000665.html.

72. Quoted in Payton, "Black Women and the Glass Cliff."

73. Quoted in Payton, "Black Women and the Glass Cliff."

74. Quoted in Payton, "Black Women and the Glass Cliff."

75. Minda Harts, *The Memo: What Women of Color Need to Know to Secure a Seat at the Table* (New York: Seal Press, 2019).

76. L'Oreal Thompson Payton, "Black Women and the Glass Cliff: 'I Was Supposed to Bring Some Kind of Black Girl Magic,'" *Fortune*, November 6, 2022, https://finance.yahoo.com/news/black-women-glass-cliff-supposed-130000665.html.

77. Payton, "Black Women and the Glass Cliff."

78. Payton, "Black Women and the Glass Cliff."

79. Roxanne A. Donovan and Lindsey M. West, "Stress and Mental Health: Moderating Role of the Strong Black Woman Stereotype," *Journal of Black Psychology* 41, no. 4 (November 12, 2014): 384–396, https://journals.sagepub.com/doi/10.1177/0095798414543014.

80. Payton, "Black Women and the Glass Cliff."

81. Quoted in Payton, "Black Women and the Glass Cliff."

82. Lean In, *Women in the Workplace 2021*, September 27, 2021, https://leanin.org/women-in-the-workplace/2021/introduction.

83. *Fast Company*, "1 Year, $3.8 Billion Later: How 2020's Race Reckoning Shook Up Big Tech," June 16, 2021, https://www.fastcompany.com/90644593/1-year-3-8-billion-later-how-2020s-race-reckoning-shook-up-big-tech.

84. bell hooks, *Teaching to Transgress: Education as the Practice of Freedom* (New York: Routledge, 1994), 207.

85. Allison Scott, "What Causes Voluntary Turnover in Tech? Unfairness," Kapor Center, May 4, 2017, https://www.kaporcenter.org/what-causes-voluntary-turnover-in-tech-unfairness/.

86. Breanna Edwards, "TSA Body Scanners More Likely to Give False Alarms for Black Hairstyles," *Essence*, updated October 23, 2020, https://www.essence.com/news/tsa-body-scanners-more-likely-to-give-false-alarms-for-black-hairstyles/.

87. Brenda Medina and Thomas Frank, "TSA Agents Say They're Not Discriminating Against Black Women, but Their Body Scanners Might Be," *Business Insider*, April 18, 2019, https://www.businessinsider.com/tsa-body-scanners-might-be-discriminating-against-black-women-2019-4; Kimberly Atkins Stohr, "The Skies, and TSA, Still Aren't Friendly to Those with Black Hairstyles," *Boston Globe*, September 9, 2022, https://www.bostonglobe.com/2022/09/09/opinion/skies-tsa-still-arent-friendly-those-with-black-hairstyles/.

88. Data USA, "Transportation Security Screeners," 2021, https://datausa.io/profile/soc/transportation-security-screeners.

89. Amnesty International, "Troll Patrol Findings: Using Crowdsourcing, Data Science and Machine Learning to Measure Violence and Abuse against Women on Twitter," December 19, 2018, https://decoders.amnesty.org/projects/troll-patrol/findings.

90. Meerah Powell, "Witnesses Describe Arrest of Jeremy Christian after TriMet Attacks," Oregon Public Broadcasting, February 3, 2020, https://www.opb.org/news/article/portland-trimet-stabbing-trial-jeremy-christian-witnesses-arrest-prosecution/.

91. Sydette Harry, "Listening to Black Women: The Innovation Tech Can't Figure Out," *Wired*, January 11, 2021, https://www.wired.com/story/listening-to-black-women-the-innovation-tech-cant-figure-out/.

92. Harry, "Listening to Black Women."

93. Ted Gregory, "'The Original 'Me Too.'': Tarana Burke Discusses the Movement She Made," The University of Chicago Harris School of Public Policy, March 24, 2023, https://harris.uchicago.edu/news-events/news/original-me-too-tarana-burke-discusses-movement-she-made.

94. Sheera Frenkel and Kellen Browning, "The Metaverse's Dark Side: Here Come Harassment and Assaults," *New York Times*, December 30, 2021, www.nytimes.com/2021/12/30/technology/metaverse-harassment-assaults.html.

95. Hannah Murphy, "How Will Facebook Keep Its Metaverse Safe for Users?" *Financial Times*, November 12, 2021, https://www.ft.com/content/d72145b7-5e44-446a-819c-51d67c5471cf.

96. Bärí A. Williams, "'Intelligent' Policing and My Innocent Children," *New York Times*, December 2, 2017, https://www.nytimes.com/2017/12/02/opinion/sunday/intelligent-policing-and-my-innocent-children.html.

97. Aylin Caliskan, Joanna J. Bryson, and Arvind Narayanan, "Semantics Derived Automatically from Language Corpora Contain Human-like Biases," *Science* 356, no. 6334 (April 14, 2017): 183–186, https://www.science.org/doi/10.1126/science.aal4230.

98. Kristian Lum, "Predictive Policing Reinforces Police Bias," Human Rights Data Analysis Group, October 10, 2016, https://hrdag.org/2016/10/10/predictive-policing-reinforces-police-bias/.

99. Elizabeth Nix, "Tuskegee Experiment: The Infamous Syphilis Study," History, updated June 13, 2023, https://www.history.com/news/the-infamous-40-year-tuskegee-study.

100. "Henrietta Lacks: Science Must Right a Historical Wrong," *Nature*, September 1, 2020, https://www.nature.com/articles/d41586-020-02494-z.

101. Christopher Snowbeck, "Regulators Probe Racial Bias with UnitedHealth Algorithm," *Star Tribune*, October 28, 2019, https://www.startribune.com/regulators-probe-racial-bias-with-unitedhealth-algorithm/563997722/.

102. Snowbeck, "Regulators Probe Racial Bias."

103. Snowbeck, "Regulators Probe Racial Bias."

104. Ruha Benjamin, "Assessing Risk, Automating Racism," *Science*

366, no. 6464 (October 25, 2019): 421–422, DOI: 10.1126/science.aaz3873; Christopher Snowbeck, "Regulators Probe Racial Bias with UnitedHealth Algorithm," *Star Tribune*, October 28, 2019, https://www.startribune.com/regulators-probe-racial-bias-with-unitedhealth-algorithm/563997722/.

105. Nicol Turner Lee and Jack Malamud, "Opportunities and Blind Spots in the White House's Blueprint for an AI Bill of Rights," Brookings Institution, December 19, 2022, https://www.brookings.edu/articles/opportunities-and-blind-spots-in-the-white-houses-blueprint-for-an-ai-bill-of-rights/.

106. Eliza Strickland, "6 Reactions to the White House's AI Bill of Rights," *IEEE Spectrum*, October 14, 2022, https://spectrum.ieee.org/white-house-ai.

107. Emily Bender et al., "On the Dangers of Stochastic Parrots: Can Language Models Be Too Big?" *FAccT '21: Proceedings of the 2021 ACM Conference on Fairness, Accountability, and Transparency* (March 2021): 610–623, https://dl.acm.org/doi/10.1145/3442188.3445922.

108. John Harris, "'There Was All Sorts of Toxic Behaviour': Timnit Gebru on Her Sacking by Google, AI's Dangers and Big Tech's Biases," *Guardian*, May 22, 2023, https://www.theguardian.com/lifeandstyle/2023/may/22/there-was-all-sorts-of-toxic-behaviour-timnit-gebru-on-her-sacking-by-google-ais-dangers-and-big-techs-biases.

109. Tony Ho Tran, "How Congress Fell for Sam Altman's AI Magic Tricks," September 29, 2023, *Daily Beast*, https://www.thedailybeast.com/how-congress-fell-for-openai-and-sam-altmans-ai-magic-tricks.

110. Ilana Hamilton, "56% of All Undergraduates Are First-Generation College Students," *Forbes*, updated June 13, 2023, https://www.forbes.com/advisor/education/online-colleges/first-generation-college-students-by-state/.

111. John Bowden, "Ancestry.com Pulls Ad Amid Online Backlash," *The Hill*, April 18, 2019, https://thehill.com/homenews/media/439656-ancenstrycom-pulls-ad-amid-online-backlash/.

112. Alvin Chang, "The Facebook and Cambridge Analytica Scandal, Explained with a Simple Diagram," Vox, updated May 2, 2018, https://www.vox.com/policy-and-politics/2018/3/23/17151916/facebook-cambridge-analytica-trump-diagram.

113. Leah Wright Rigeuer and Bärí A. Williams, "Cambridge Analytica's Abuse Shows Why Diversity in Tech Matters," Huffington Post, updated April 13, 2018, https://www.huffpost.com/entry/opinion-wright-williams-facebook_n_5acf80f1e4b0edca2cb7526f.

114. National Council for Occupational Safety and Health, *The Dirty

Dozen 2019, https://nationalcosh.org/sites/default/files/uploads/2019_Dirty_Dozen.pdf.

115. *U.S. Senate Budget Committee Hearing on the Income Inequality Crisis in America*, 117th Cong. (March 17, 2021) (statement of Jennifer Bates, Learning Ambassador at Amazon BHM1, Bessemer, Alabama), https://www.budget.senate.gov/imo/media/doc/Jennifer%20Bates%20-%20Testimony%20-%20U.S.%20Senate%20Budget%20Committee%20Hearing.pdf.

116. Davi Ottenheimer, "Tesla More Likely to Run Over Black People," *FlyingPenguin* (blog), October 21, 2021, https://www.flyingpenguin.com/?p=36150.

117. Gillian Follett, "Black Creators Drive Higher Media Value for Marketers, Study Finds," AdAge, June 13, 2023, https://adage.com/article/digital-marketing-ad-tech-news/black-creators-drive-higher-media-value-marketers-study-finds/2499446.

118. Kalhan Rosenblatt, "The Renegade Dance Made Jalaiah Harmon a Star. 'I Am: Jalaiah' Explores Her Life Since," NBC News, October 13, 2021, https://www.nbcnews.com/pop-culture/pop-culture-news/renegade-dance-made-jalaiah-harmon-star-i-am-jalaiah-explores-n1281412.

119. Palmer Haasch, "Creators Are Criticizing a 'Tonight Show' Segment with Addison Rae That Didn't Credit Black Choreographers," *Business Insider*, March 30, 2021, https://www.businessinsider.com/jimmy-fallon-addison-rae-tiktok-dance-black-creators-2021-3.

120. Starr Bowenbank, "Jimmy Fallon *Finally* Addressed the Addison Rae TikTok Dance Backlash," *Cosmopolitan*, April 6, 2021, https://www.cosmopolitan.com/entertainment/celebs/a36039881/jimmy-fallon-addison-rae-tiktok-dance-segment-backlash-response/.

121. Taylor Lorenz and Laura Zornosa, "Are Black Creators Really on 'Strike' from TikTok?" *New York Times*, June 25, 2021, https://www.nytimes.com/2021/06/25/style/black-tiktok-strike.html.

122. Beatrice Forman, "Digital Blackface Led to TikTok's First Strike," Vox, June 29, 2921, https://www.vox.com/the-goods/2021/6/29/22554596/digital-blackface-megan-thee-stallion-song-tiktok-first-strike.

123. Murray Stassen, "Capitol Records Just Signed a Virtual Artist, FN Meka. He Has Over 10 Million Followers on TikTok," Music Business Worldwide, August 12, 2022, https://www.musicbusinessworldwide.com/capitol-records-just-signed-a-virtual-artist-fn-meka-he-has-over-10-million-followers-on-tiktok/.

124. Alaina Demopoulos, "Computer-Generated Inclusivity: Fashion

Turns to 'Diverse' AI Models," *Guardian*, April 3, 2023, https://www.theguardian.com/fashion/2023/apr/03/ai-virtual-models-fashion-brands.

125. Amy Adkins, "What Millennials Want from Work and Life," Gallup, May 10, 2016, https://www.gallup.com/workplace/236477/millennials-work-life.aspx.

126. Elizabeth Culliford and Katie Paul, "Twitter Again Slaps Warning on Trump Tweet Threatening Force Against Protesters," Reuters, June 23, 2020, https://www.reuters.com/article/idUSKBN23V0DU/.

127. Megan Rose Dickey and Taylor Hatmaker, "Facebook Employees Stage Virtual Walkout in Protest of Company's Stance on Trump Posts," Tech Crunch, June 1, 2020, https://techcrunch.com/2020/06/01/facebook-employees-stage-virtual-walkout-in-protest-of-companys-stance-on-trump-posts/?guccounter=1.

128. Annie Jean-Baptiste, "Making Product Inclusion." interview with McKinsey & Company, October 11, 2022, https://www.mckinsey.com/industries/technology-media-and-telecommunications/our-insights/making-product-inclusion-and-equity-a-core-part-of-tech.

129. Jean-Baptiste, "Making Product Inclusion."

130. Jean-Baptiste, "Making Product Inclusion."

131. Jean-Baptiste, "Making Product Inclusion."

132. Jean-Baptiste, "Making Product Inclusion."

133. Jean-Baptiste, "Making Product Inclusion."

134. Jean-Baptiste, "Making Product Inclusion."

135. Jean-Baptiste, "Making Product Inclusion."

136. Ruth Glass, *London: Aspects of Change* (London: MacGibbon & Kee, 1964).

137. Andrew Chamings, "Study: San Francisco and Oakland Are the Most Gentrified Cities in the US," SFGATE, July 6, 2020, https://www.sfgate.com/local/article/San-Francisco-Oakland-most-gentrified-cities-in-US-15389147.php.

138. Rachel Swan, "Oakland Threatens to Fine a Church for Loud Music," SFGATE, October 28, 2015, https://www.sfgate.com/bayarea/article/Oakland-threatens-to-fine-a-church-for-loud-music-6573360.php.

139. Quoted in Development Without Displacement Coalition, *Report and Budget Request*, August 26, 2019, 42, https://eqcitieshome.files.wordpress.com/2019/08/dwd_final_082519-2.pdf.

140. Darrell Owens, "Where Did All the Black People in Oakland Go?" *The Discourse Lounge* (newsletter), September 10, 2021, https://darrellowens.substack.com/p/where-did-all-the-black-people-in?s=r.

141. Development Without Displacement Coalition, *Report and Budget Request*, August 26, 2019, 43, https://eqcitieshome.files.wordpress.com/2019/08/dwd_final_082519-2.pdf.

142. US Bureau of Labor Statistics, *Current Employment Statistics Highlights*, October 2023, https://www.bls.gov/web/empsit/ceshighlights.pdf.

143. Kelemwork Cook et al., "The Future of Work in Black America," McKinsey & Company, October 4, 2019, https://www.mckinsey.com/featured-insights/future-of-work/the-future-of-work-in-black-america.

144. Jared Lindzon, "How Recent Tech Layoffs Can Disproportionately Affect Women and People of Color," *Fast Company*, January 25, 2023, https://www.fastcompany.com/90837794/recent-tech-layoffs-affect-women-poc; Jacob Zinkula, "AI Is Helping Your Company Decide Who to Lay Off," *Business Insider*, February 23, 2023, https://www.businessinsider.com/layoffs-today-trends-ai-data-companies-jobs-algorithms-chatgpt-2023-2#:~:text=AI%20might%20not%20take%20your,any%20layoff%20decisions%20in%202023.

145. Elise Gould and Heidi Shierholz, "Not Everybody Can Work from Home: Black and Hispanic Workers Are Much Less Likely to Be Able to Telework," Economic Policy Institute, March 19, 2020, https://www.epi.org/blog/black-and-hispanic-workers-are-much-less-likely-to-be-able-to-work-from-home.

146. Emma Goldberg, "Laid Off in Your Living Room: The Chaos of Remote Job Cuts," *New York Times*, January 25, 2023, https://www.nytimes.com/2023/01/25/business/layoffs-remote-work.html.

147. Trisha Thadani, "Winners, Losers—or Both?" *San Francisco Chronicle*, May 9, 2019, https://projects.sfchronicle.com/2019/mid-market/city/.

148. George Avalos, "Oakland's Uptown Station Is Bought by Singapore-Based Investor," SiliconValley.com, March 4, 2021, https://www.siliconvalley.com/2021/03/04/oakland-uptown-station-singapore-investor-buy-real-estate-tech-office/.

149. Sam Levin, "'There's No Way to Stop This': Oakland Braces for the Arrival of Tech Firm Square," *Guardian*, July 2, 2019, https://www.theguardian.com/cities/2019/jul/02/theres-no-way-to-stop-this-oakland-braces-for-the-arrival-of-tech-firm-square.

150. Lean In, *Women in the Workplace 2022*, https://leanin.org/women-in-the-workplace/2022.

151. American Express, "Woman-Owned Businesses Are Growing 2X Faster on Average Than All Businesses Nationwide," September 23, 2019, https://about.americanexpress.com/newsroom/press-releases/news-details/2019/Woman-Owned-Businesses-Are-Growing-2X-Faster-On-Average-Than-All-Businesses-Nationwide-09-23-2019/default.aspx.

152. Marc Andreessen, "Investing in Flow," Andreessen Horowitz, August 15, 2022, https://a16z.com/2022/08/15/investing-in-flow/.

153. Bärí A. Williams, "This Is How Some Black Women Are Skirting Racism and Sexism to Find Funding," *Fast Company*, July, 11, 2017, https://www.fastcompany.com/40438358/this-is-how-some-black-women-are-skirting-racism-and-sexism-to-find-funding.

154. Linda Brooks, "Representation Matters: DEI and the Underrepresentation of Black Women in the Technology Sector," *Forbes*, January 18, 2023, https://www.forbes.com/sites/forbestechcouncil/2023/01/18/representation-matters-dei-and-the-underrepresentation-of-black-women-in-the-technology-sector/?sh=f20e911721e2.

155. Brooks, "Representation Matters."

156. Quoted in Phoebe Lett and Jeremy Ashkenas, "8 Big Questions about AI," *New York Times*, June 1, 2023, https://www.nytimes.com/interactive/2023/06/01/opinion/ai-technology-future.html.

157. Tara Sophia Mohr, "Why Women Don't Apply for Jobs Unless They're 100% Qualified," *Harvard Business Review*, August 25, 2014, https://hbr.org/2014/08/why-women-dont-apply-for-jobs-unless-theyre-100-qualified.

158. Sequoia Holmes, "Black Women Aren't Allowed to Be Introverted," BESE, August 23, 2019, https://web.archive.org/web/20210119180040/https://www.bese.com/black-women-arent-allowed-to-be-introverted/?utm_content=bufferb7153&utm_medium=social&utm_source=twitter.com&utm_campaign=buffer.

159. Holmes, "Black Women Aren't Allowed."

160. Holmes, "Black Women Aren't Allowed."

161. Holmes, "Black Women Aren't Allowed."

162. Sarah Javaid and Marie S. Cole, *Resilient, but Not Recovered: Black Women in the COVID-19 Pandemic*, National Women's Law Center, March 29, 2022, https://nwlc.org/wp-content/uploads/2022/08/nwlc_BlackWomen_RESILIENT_FS.pdf.

163. Bärí A. Williams, interview by Nillay Patel, "What an NFL Coaching Scandal Can Teach Tech about Diversity," The Verge, February 14, 2022, https://www.theverge.com/22933148/tech-diversity-nfl-coach-scandal-podcast-inclusion-bari-williams-interview-decoder.